About the Book Cover

The main title of the book, "From Darkness into Light", is a metaphor for the life-altering journey of a Jewish boy's escape from oppressive regimes of fascism, Nazism, and communism to a new life in the free world.

The flags are the graphic illustrations of the various regimes and political systems the author lived through during the first twenty-six years of his life.

The subtitle, "My Journey Through Nazism, Fascism, and Communism to Freedom" refers to the author's eyewitness account of events captured in five chronological stories. The journey begins at his birth in 1938 in Budapest, Hungary, and ends in 1964 in the United States, where he is a married man with a child, a graduate of the Massachusetts Institute of Technology ready to embark on living the American dream.

Even though almost all Hungarian Jews had German last names the author officially changed his family name of Reichmann to Rátonyi when he graduated from high school in the spring of 1956. His rationale to Hungarianize his name is described in detail in the book. Little did he suspect that six months later he would end up as a refugee in German-speaking Austria. Since most of his stories take place in Hungary, the author thought it appropriate to include his original name—Reichmann—on the cover of the book.

Robert Ratonyi's book is an amalgamation of a memoir, historic narrative, and lessons on surviving life-threatening events as a child such as the Holocaust, on growing up in poverty and not feeling poor, on taking risks to escape from a brutal dictatorship, and on becoming a self-made, educated, and productive member of society in his mid-twenties in America.

Fulton Books, Inc.
Meadville, PA

Published by Fulton Books 2020

Book cover was designed by Robert Ratonyi

Library of Congress Control Number 2020906914

Subjects: memoir (1938-1964), Holocaust, Fascism, socialism, communism, uprising, immigration.

ISBN 978-1-64654-545-2 (paperback)
ISBN 978-1-64654-546-9 (digital)

Printed in the United States of America

FROM
DARKNESS
INTO
LIGHT

MY JOURNEY THROUGH NAZISM,
FASCISM, AND COMMUNISM TO
FREEDOM

ROBERT (REICHMANN) RATONYI

To my grandchildren:
Reed and Casey

CONTENTS

Introduction

The urge to record the stories of my turbulent early life had arisen every now and then, but I was never motivated to do so before my grandchildren were born. After my second grandson was born in 2002, I realized that if I did not leave something behind in writing, they would never learn about the details of their grandfather's journey during the first three decades of his life. Each of my five stories in this book is a personal account of important historic events and experiences that occurred in the middle of the twentieth century.

The first story begins in 1938, when I was born a Jewish child in Hungary, the year that also happened to be the start of one of the largest twentieth-century genocides, the Holocaust. My fifth and final story ends in 1964 as a twenty-six-year-old college-educated professional, husband, father, and American immigrant, ready to embark on living the "American dream." By the time my grandchildren are old enough to develop an interest in their ancestral history, I could be long gone. Even our children have only limited knowledge of their parents' background. Therefore, in 2003, I decided to write down my stories. Many years later, after many pauses and interruptions, I finished them.

Each of the stories focuses either on a specific period of my life or on a major life-altering event. My childhood and adolescence coincided with a number of major historical events in which I was an unwitting participant. As a Jewish child, I lived through the tragic events of the Hungarian Holocaust as the Second World War was ending. I grew up under Communism, a repressive political and corrupt economic system that subsequently followed the liberation of Hungary by the Soviet Red Army in 1945.

On October 23, 1956, I was a freshman at the Technical University of Budapest when a student-led uprising shook the foundation of the Stalinist puppet regime in Hungary and provided the opportunity to flee the country. The Soviet Union crushed the Uprising within a few weeks. However, I managed to escape and left behind my mother, my friends, my large extended family, and a promising engineering career. I celebrated my nineteenth birthday in Vienna, Austria, and experienced the "free world" for the first time.

My dream of coming to America was not without its challenges because by December 1956 the quota for Hungarian refugees had been filled. My next best choice was Canada, so I immigrated to Montréal in February 1957. From 1957 through 1961, I learned how to live in a free society and restarted my academic career, studying at night and working during the day. That is where I met my future wife, Éva, who shared many of my experiences because of her Jewish-Hungarian immigrant background. Due to some unanticipated events, I ended up coming to the United States in 1961 to finish my undergraduate engineering education at the Massachusetts Institute of Technology (MIT) instead of going to McGill University in Montréal.

My original plan was to get my engineering degree, return to Canada to obtain my citizenship, and embark on my professional career. Getting married and starting a family was far from my mind at that time. However, fate intervened again, and three years later, in 1964, I was married, had a new baby, and became an American immigrant. Armed with my master's degree from MIT, and a student loan of approximately $6,000 (around $49,000 in 2019), I embarked on living the "American dream."

I must admit that while my original intent was to write my stories only for the benefit of my progeny, and for some close friends who encouraged me, I have also benefited from this experience. As I recollected many painful events of decades ago, I had to come to grips for the first time in my life with deep-seated feelings that I never examined or spoke about. As I wrote these stories, instead of being just a passive reteller of them, I found myself incorporating newly discovered emotions that I never realized I had before. Undoubtedly, some of these new feelings and emotions lay dormant in a subconscious part of my brain, and writing them down became a cathartic release.

I did not intend to write my stories as pure memoirs. I have included extensive historical background to provide the proper context for these accounts.

Because short stories have always been one of my favorite literary genres, each of my stories was originally written to stand on its own. Each one has a different theme, a time and a place, and a beginning and an end. Each of my stories has "lessons to learn from" that I hoped to pass on to the reader.

By 2010, I thought I was finished with my writing career. However, fate interrupted my retirement, and I became a storyteller. A close friend from my corporate days convinced me to give a speech about my Holocaust experience at his church, which led to my being discovered as a child Holocaust survivor by the William Breman Jewish Heritage & Holocaust Memorial Museum and the Georgia Commission on the Holocaust.

Since then, I have spoken to over ten thousand middle and high school students as well as adults in Atlanta and other towns in Georgia on behalf of these organizations. In addition, as word spread around the Atlanta community, I was invited to speak to several civic organizations, such as the YMCA Leadership, Rotary Clubs, World War II Round Table, the Winston Churchill Society, and several academic institutions (Georgia Institute of Technology, College of Georgia, University of Georgia).

The feedback I got from my audiences during the Q&A period made me realize that not only were they interested in hearing my Holocaust story, but they also wanted to know what happened to me after the Holocaust. Typical questions following my presentation ranged from how I grew up under a communist regime and managed to escape Hungary, to when and how I ended up in the United States, got an MIT education, and came to Atlanta. There were also other questions that had no relevance to the Holocaust. I was often asked if my stories were published, and the answer was always no. Therefore, I decided to integrate my stand-alone stories seamlessly into a chronologically ordered book.

There are many Hungarian names in this book because the first three, and most of the fourth story, take place in Hungary. I kept the original Hungarian spelling for the sake of authenticity. The only concession I made to English custom is that I put the first names followed by the last names, in reverse to the Hungarian custom. Most of the first names are nicknames, the way I learned to address family and friends. A complete guide to these nicknames, their formal Hungarian version, and their English equivalent is provided in Appendix C.

Journey 1:
A Holocaust Childhood

There are two objectives in telling the Holocaust story. First, I wanted to write about my own experiences as a seven-year-old child. Second, I wanted to use this opportunity to provide insight into the larger scope and context of the European, specifically the Hungarian, history of the Holocaust in order to put my own family experiences into the proper perspective. In fact, I feel that the "big picture" may be even more important than my own experiences. What happened to our family of Hungarian Jews living in the center of Europe during what was considered an enlightened era of the twentieth century was nothing unusual or exceptional. If anything, the fact that I am alive to write this story is the exception.

My family's situation in 1944 was an inevitable result of the downward spiral that started as far back as January 30, 1933, when Hitler became chancellor of Germany. It culminated in the annihilation of close to six hundred thousand Hungarian Jews, starting in early 1944 and ending with the liberation of Hungary in April 1945.

The Holocaust consists of the vast scale of Nazi eliminationist anti-Semitism in Europe that encompassed more than twenty countries, from the Mediterranean in the north to the Baltic Sea in the south, from France in the west to close to Moscow in the east. It begs the question of how this predominantly Christian region of about 500 million people could stand by and at best ignore and at worst actively collaborate in and support such a murderous empire. Six million men, women, and children, more than half of the European Jewry, perished during the Holocaust.

Even though Germany lost the war before completing its Final Solution,[1] Hitler came close to eliminating Jews from Europe. Following the end of the war, three of every four, around three million, of the surviving Jews left Europe for North America, Palestine (now Israel), South America, the United Kingdom, Australia, and South Africa. Jews used to represent a significant percentage of the population of Europe (Poland, 10 percent; Hungary, 6–8 percent; depending on which borders are used). Today, Jews represent a miniscule percentage (less than 1 percent) of each country's population. The largest population by percentage is in France due to the circumstances of the German occupation of France.[2]

When I think of the flight of the Jewish intelligentsia in the 1920s and the 1930s, followed by the obliteration of six million Jews through 1944, then the mass exodus of the survivors from Europe, I have to believe that Europe will never again be a hospitable place for Jews. Sadly, many of the European impulses that led to the Holocaust still exist today. Anti-Semitism is rampant in Europe, and it shows its ugly side not only in the ordinary street crimes committed by its perpetrators but also in the political and social expressions of some of its popularly elected leaders.

I tried to develop a statistical summary of the Jewish population by country prior to the Holocaust, immediately after it in 1950, as well as in 2017, in order to provide a more succinct and visual view

---

[1]   The official name the German Nazis gave to eliminating 11 million Jews of Europe is *The Final Solution to the Jewish Question*.

[2]   Of the 350,000 Jews in France in 1940, almost half were Jews from Eastern Europe. Almost all the 83,000 who died were "foreign" Jews without French passports. Both the Nazis and the French knew that it would be impossible to deport all the Jews without the collaboration of the French authorities. To save their "own" Jews, the French decided to hand over the "foreign" Jews to placate the Nazi warlords. History will judge whether this was a cynical act or not. On the other hand, France has the third-highest number of Righteous Among the Nations (according to the Yad Vashem museum, 2009). This award is given to "non-Jews who acted according to the most noble principles of humanity by risking their lives to save Jews during the Holocaust."

of the impact of the Holocaust on the Jewish people. The best I was able to do is located in Appendix A.

According to Yad Vashem,[1] the Holocaust started in 1933 when Hitler came to power. The killings did not just happen suddenly, by one single maniac or by any of the governments involved. Instead, the killings were the result of a legalized process of singling out the Jews and denying their civil rights. Laws were passed that gradually denied the Jews their freedom of occupation and education, of movement, of their ownership rights and their participation in any form of labor, and of civic or cultural organizations. The writer Daniel Jonah Goldhagen[2] correctly identified the deliberate effort by the Nazis to dehumanize and demonize Jews (and the Roma people) to make it legally, morally, and emotionally acceptable to murder them.

Jews were fairly well assimilated into Hungarian society in the early 1900s. They were accepted as citizens in all professions, including academia and the Hungarian armed services. This moderate view of accepting Hungarian Jews as ordinary citizens who practiced a different religion from the Christian majority changed drastically in the 1930s. At the end of the decade, the Jews were portrayed as a dangerous "race" whose members committed unpardonable crimes against Christianity, and whose very presence in society had endangered the economic, social, and political well-being as well as the morality of the Christian population.

Discrimination against Hungarian Jews in the twentieth century started with the Numerus Clausus law, Latin for "limited number," enacted on September 20, 1920. It declared that from the 1920–21

---

[1] The National Authority for the Remembrance of the Martyrs and Heroes of the Holocaust, established in 1953 by act of the Israeli parliament to commemorate the six million Jewish men, women, and children murdered by the Nazis and their collaborators. *Yad Vashem* is literal translation of "a monument and a name" from Isaiah 56:5: "I will give them, in my house and in my walls, a *monument and a name*, better than sons and daughters; I will give them an everlasting name that shall never be effaced."

[2] Daniel Jonah Goldhagen, *Worse Than War: Genocide, Eliminationism, and the Ongoing Assault on Humanity* (New York: United States Public Affairs, 2009), 331.

academic year onward, only those would be admitted to universities and colleges "who were trustworthy from the point of view of morals and loyalty to the country, and even those only in limited numbers [*the maximum percentage was fixed at 6 percent*], so that thorough education of each student could be ensured."

The term "Jew" was deliberately omitted, and there is no trace of anti-Semitism in the law, yet it closed the gates of the universities to many Jews. Instead of abilities, it was "loyalty to the country," i.e., birth and background, that determined who may attend university. In today's lingo, this was a "politically correct" way of discriminating against the Jews. Soon after Hitler was named chancellor of Germany on January 30, 1933, discrimination, isolation, deportation, and the eventual liquidation of Jews spread from Germany to the occupied lands and eventually to Germany's allies, including Hungary.

The year 1938 was an important year for me, for my parents, and for the Jews of the Third Reich. I was born in January of that year. Subsequently, two historic events took place. On March 13, 1938, Germany invaded and annexed Austria into the Third Reich in what was called the Anschluss in German. Some 97 percent of Austrians voted for the Anschluss, and Hitler was cheered by hundreds of thousands of Viennese when he entered the city following the annexation.

Furthermore, the second historic event took place in November 1938. The official start of the Holocaust is recognized as the year 1933 when Hitler came to power. However, for me personally, it was Kristallnacht, referred to in English as "The Night of the Broken Glass," that occurred on November 9 and 10. This was a massive coordinated attack on Jews carried out by Nazi storm troopers who were aided by local police and citizens. Gangs of Nazi youth roamed through the Jewish neighborhoods of both Berlin and Vienna, capitals of Germany and Austria, respectively, in addition to hundreds of other cities in the Third Reich. During the two days of riots, about twenty-five thousand Jewish men were sent to concentration camps where they were brutalized by SS guards, and some of them beaten to death. The Nazis recorded 7,500 businesses destroyed, 267 synagogues burned, and 91 Jews murdered. Part of my family and I lived in Budapest, less than 175 miles from Vienna, where the news of Kristallnacht was known within days if not hours.

In September 1939, Germany invaded Poland, which started World War II. Hungary then joined Germany as an ally in June 1940, which most likely delayed the execution of the Final Solution there until 1944.

The conclusive chapter of the European Holocaust commenced on January 20, 1942, when Reinhard Heydrich, Himmler's second in command of the SS,[1] convened the Wannsee Conference in Berlin. As a result, fifteen top Nazi bureaucrats officially approved the coordination of the Final Solution, under which the Nazis aimed to exterminate the entire Jewish population of Europe. The whole meeting took no more than an hour, and the translation of the minutes is no different from that of a board of directors meeting of a large corporation taking care of ordinary business matters.[2] The records and minutes of the meeting were found intact by the Allies at the end of WWII and were used during the Nuremberg Trials. Heydrich personally edited the minutes of the meeting, utilizing the following code words and expressions when describing the actions to be taken against the Jews:

> "...eliminated by natural causes" refers to death due to a combination of hard labor and starvation, the cause of my father's death.

---

[1] Schutz Staffel (one word in German), or SS, means "Protection Squad." Originally, the SS was Adolf Hitler's bodyguard, and then it became the elite guard of the Nazi state and its main tool of terror.

[2] A translation of the minutes of the meeting, edited by Heydrich, can be found on the internet at http://prorev.com/wannsee.htm.

"…transported to the east" refers to mass deportations to the planned gas chamber complexes such
as Belzec, Sobibor, Treblinka, and Auschwitz.[1]

"…treated accordingly" or "special treatment" or
"special action" refers to execution by SS firing
squads or death by gassing.

At the time of the Wannsee Conference, I had just turned
four years old, but my, and my family's fate were sealed according
to those minutes. The potential difficulty the Germans were facing
with the liquidation of the Hungarian Jews (742,800 listed in the
minutes of the Wannsee report) is all mentioned within the minutes. It was agreed that in order to deal with the Hungarians, "it will
be soon necessary to force an advisor for Jewish questions onto the
Hungarian government." The special handling was necessary because
of Hungary's status as an ally.

The process of isolating the Jews and stripping them of most
civic, political, social, and economic rights did not begin in Hungary
until 1938. Under pressure from Germany, as well as from internal anti-Semitic forces, the Hungarian parliament began passing
anti-Jewish laws in the spring of 1938, similar to those passed in
Germany five years earlier. A detailed chronology of the most important events of the Hungarian Holocaust is included in Appendix B.

By April 1942, the Hungarian government promised the "reset-
tlement" of close to eight hundred thousand Jews but not until after
the war. Doubts about the outcome of the war and the consequences
for Hungary began to emerge within Hungarian ruling circles. In my
opinion, Hungary's reluctance to execute Hitler's Final Solution was
not so much due to the moral dilemma of killing its Jewish population but more to the cynical and self-serving concerns about los-

---

[1] The largest of the German concentration camps, Auschwitz, was a network of
concentration camps built and operated in occupied Poland by Nazi Germany.
Soviet troops liberated Auschwitz on January 27, 1945. Up to 1.1 million people died there, around 90 percent of them Jews.

ing a highly educated, creative, and productive segment of society, together with the anticipated postwar retributions.

By 1942, the Hungarian government had doubts about a Nazi victory, and Hungarian Jews were hopeful until 1944 to escape the fate of their European brethren. Indeed, had it not been for Adolf Eichmann's[1] personal intervention in Hungary and the installation of a pro-Nazi, anti-Semitic government on March 22, 1944, Hungarian Jewry might have survived the Holocaust. As it turned out, close to one of every ten Jews killed during the Holocaust was an ethnic Hungarian Jew.

The gross statistics and many dates shown in Appendices A and B can be overwhelming and also overshadow the individual and personal tragedies they depict. Therefore, I compiled six pictures shown on page 9 with the caption "Pictures from Auschwitz" to focus on the individual tragedies. These pictures illustrate the fate of 400,000 of the nearly 440,000 Hungarian Jews, including many in our family, who died in Auschwitz. Reading the statistics and the chronology of events in Appendices A and B and looking at these pictures from Auschwitz may be a shocking and mind-blowing experience for my children, grandchildren, and future generations. However, it is necessary to endure the pain of learning the history of their ancestors in order to keep these memories alive. The lessons of history are clear, and I invoke the warning of George Santayana[2]: "Those who cannot remember the past are condemned to repeat it."

I was born on January 11, 1938, just a few months before the Hungarian parliament ratified the First Anti-Jewish Act. The Soviet

---

[1] Adolf Eichmann was the head of a Gestapo section that was responsible for implementation of Nazi policy toward the Jews in Germany and all occupied territories, eventually totaling sixteen countries.

[2] Jorge Agustin Nicolás de Santayana (1863–1952). Spanish-American philosopher, poet, and humanist, literary and cultural critic, George Santayana is a principal figure in classical American philosophy.

Army liberated the Budapest Ghetto,[1] where I survived the last few weeks of the war, on January 18, 1945, exactly one week after my seventh birthday. Therefore, my first seven years on this earth coincided with the Hungarian Holocaust period. Most adults have childhood memories that extend back before the age of seven. Strangely, my memories of those childhood years with my family and friends are mostly gone, except for memories associated with the Holocaust.

---

[1] The Budapest Ghetto is often referred to as the "Central Ghetto" or the "Big Ghetto" in Holocaust literature. They all refer to the ghetto where most of Budapest's Jews (mostly old people, women, and children) were held until liberation in January 1945.

1. Pictures from Auschwitz.

Hungarian Jews arrive in
early summer of 1944.

On arrival Jews are separated by sex:
women on one side, men to other.

Separation of the sexes has
been completed. Now the
infamous selection begins.

Male Jews being assessed by a Nazi
doctor. In a few moments he will
decide who shall live and who shall die.

A family of Hungarian Jews
who have been selected to die
wait in the grove trees.

The ovens in the crematoria, each
capable of holding several bodies.

The Yellow Star

On January 11, 1944, I turned six years old, and soon after I first felt the profound impact of the Holocaust, even though this term was not in my vocabulary until decades later.

When I was four and five years old, I was not aware that my father's absence was due to the anti-Jewish laws forcing him into spe-

2. I remember practicing my alphabet in this last family picture—circa 1943.

cial Jewish military units first and labor battalions later, where visitation rights to one's family were rare. After Hungary became an ally of Germany in June 1940, a decree was passed in the Hungarian parliament on December 2, 1940, ordering Jewish men to enroll in special Jewish labor battalions. My father was twenty-nine years old. It is not clear when exactly my father joined a labor battalion, but it was probably between 1941 and 1943. I accepted that my father, unlike the fathers of Christian children around me, was absent without ever knowing where he was or why. This explains why even as I

was growing up after the war, I could hardly recollect his face, much less remember a warm embrace, a bedside story, a smile, or a kiss.

I often wondered as I grew up why I didn't have any brothers or sisters. After all, both of my parents came from very large families. My mother was the youngest of ten while my father was the second oldest of nine children. Only decades later when I had children of my own did I learn that my parents decided it was too dangerous to bring another Jewish child into their world.

I was already a father myself when I learned that the reason for my lack of siblings was directly attributable to the general condition of Jews in 1938 Hungary. My mother confessed that she did get pregnant at least once when I was two or three years old. According to my mother, my father told her, "I don't want to bring another child into this world. If you don't get an abortion, I will divorce you." When my mother told me this, she was already an elderly woman, but there was unmistakable resentment and hurt in her voice when she told me that if it had been her choice, she would have had more children.

Subsequent events proved my father right. Based on my personal experiences during the critical period of May 1944 through the spring of 1945, I have little doubt that the chances of survival of a younger sibling would have been negligible at best. However, this is not an excuse or an apology for my father's ultimatum to my mother. It is hard for me to believe that there was not a more delicate or sensitive way of conveying his convictions. On the other hand, it is also possible that my mother was a bit melodramatic in describing these events. Therefore, the first victims of my Holocaust were my unborn brothers or sisters. Consequently, I remained a single child, which has always been a regret of mine. This is why the beginning of the Holocaust was Kristallnacht for me.

Sadly, it seemed that my parents must not have had a warm and loving relationship. Since the disastrous times started just when I was born, it is possible that they didn't have the chance to develop one given their short-lived marriage that began on December 4, 1936. In passing judgment, I have to bear in mind that back in those times marriages between children of very large families were not necessarily based on love but were more of an economic or socially driven necessity. My suspicion is supported by the fact that my mother had never divulged any romantic memories about my father. In fact, she hardly mentioned him as I was growing up other than to say that he was a good dancer, loved me very much, and was a strict father.

Therefore, unbeknownst to me, the Holocaust had a significant impact on my life before the age of six. Had it not been for the terrible times already on the horizon, I probably would have had some sisters and brothers. For the rest of my life, I felt envious of those who had siblings.

My naiveté regarding the consequences of being Jewish was shattered in early 1944, when Germany invaded Hungary in March.

On the thirty-first, Eichmann personally traveled to Hungary to plan the deportation of Hungarian Jews. An order was issued for Jews six years and older to wear a six-pointed bright canary-yellow star that measured ten by ten centimeters (four by four inches) on the top left side of their clothing in public. I had just turned six in January and therefore had to wear a yellow star every time I went outside to play or go on an errand with my mother.

My mother didn't observe any of the daily Jewish rituals, but she made sure that during the Jewish High Holidays of Rosh Hashanah, Yom Kippur, Passover, and Hanukkah, we went to my grandparents' home to celebrate. In other words, it was clear that I was Jewish and different from most of our neighbors who were Christians, but I didn't know exactly what those differences were aside from celebrating different holidays. Other than a few well-to-do Jewish families in our building, most of our neighbors were Christians.

Right next door to us lived the Gyura family, a married couple and their daughter, Juci, who was about my age. We got along well with them, and I recall being invited over to their place to see their Christmas tree with all the decorations. Mr. and Mrs. Gyura made sure that I also had a present. Their tree was decorated with all the colorful bulbs, angel hair, and candy hanging from the branches. Their tiny apartment was a mirror image of ours with their kitchen adjoining our own. The Gyuras were Protestants, not Roman Catholics. Protestants, who represented about 15 percent of Hungary's population, were perceived as being more tolerant of Jews as opposed to their Catholic brethren.

One day, before the anti-Jewish laws concerning the Star of David and other restrictions were pronounced, my mother arranged a meeting through the Gyura family to meet their local pastor and discuss the possibility of converting me into the Protestant faith. Clearly, the news about the Hungarian Jews' fate in other parts of the country had spread to the city. This was my mother's last desperate attempt to provide protection for me. I do remember going into the small Protestant church at the corner of Fűzér and Kápolna Streets and the meeting with the minister, but nothing ever happened afterward. There were strict laws against converting Jews, and the penalties were severe: deportation and almost certain death. In addition, as I later learned, the authorities disregarded all such conversions. Escaping the Nazis was only possible through having money and/or connections to forge the proper papers and to pay off those willing to take the risk of being caught hiding a Jew, for which the penalty was death. My mother had neither money nor connections, so we waited for the inevitable.

Bearing the Jewish star in public raised my awareness of being Jewish to a new level. My mother and I had often recalled the bittersweet story of my Jewish friend Bandi Fleishmann, who was a few months younger than I. When Bandi saw me with my yellow star, he, too, wanted one. He cried bitterly and couldn't be consoled by his mother's explanation that he was too young to wear it. We children didn't know that wearing the yellow star or not could mean the difference between life and death in the months ahead.

The year 1944 turned into an apocalyptic year for the Jews of Hungary. Due to my young age, I was spared the mental and physical agony and deprivation that were yet to come to the Jews of Budapest. Moreover, I had no inkling of the fate of Hungarian Jewry outside the capital of Budapest, where several of my aunts, uncles, and cousins lived. I'm not sure how much my mother knew either.

I learned that there was something unusual and dangerous going on in the world that the grown-ups called war. I had no idea of what this meant exactly except that my mother was visibly shaken and more and more anxious as time went on. Since March of 1944, when the Germans took control, Jews were exposed to arbitrary arrests and deportation.

It was in the late spring and early summer of 1944 when phase 1 of the Hungarian Final Solution was implemented. With lightning speed and great efficiency, approximately five hundred thousand—roughly two-thirds of Hungarian Jewish men, women, and children who lived outside Budapest—were dragged from their homes, jammed into cattle cars, and deported. Members on both sides of my family, which consisted of uncles, aunts, and cousins, were included.

Ninety percent of these Jews from the Hungarian provinces and smaller cities were sent to Auschwitz, and of those only 10 percent survived. It took less than sixty days to accomplish this. The deportations were enthusiastically supported by the local government officials, police officers, soldiers, and local population. Historic evidence revealed that even the Germans were surprised by how enthusiastically and ruthlessly the Hungarians supported and aided in this tragedy. My mother and my family who lived in Budapest, including my grandparents, knew that many in our family were deported. However, my mother kept me in the dark.

There were also nightly and daily air raids on Budapest, starting in the spring of 1944. The bombing of Budapest started on April 2, when the Americans bombed the industrial sites in the city during the day and the British by night. On July 2, the Allies delivered the greatest air raid against the city, this time including the residential areas. I do recall the air raid sirens going off in the middle of the night. My mother hurriedly dressed me to cross our courtyard and go into the cellar that ran underneath the length of the apartments facing ours.

Meeting some of our neighbors in the cellar during air raids was actually fascinating. I rarely, if ever, had the opportunity to socialize with those neighbors who lived in the beautiful and spacious apartments across the courtyard, except with the Lesko family, where I often hung out with Tibi, who was four years older than I. The courtyard separated the well-to-do middle-class families from the poorer, working-class families on our side of the building. A good example of this social divide was an older Jewish couple, Mr. and Mrs. Gergely, who lived right across the courtyard from us with their dog.

I rarely saw Mr. Gergely, who owned a retail store on the main road in our neighborhood. He came home every afternoon to take a nap. I was under strict orders, which I frequently violated, not to play outside and to avoid making any noise that might disturb his sleep. My mother and I were never invited to the Gergelys for a social visit that I can recall. However, Mrs. Gergely occasionally invited me in and showed me to their *spájz*, or "pantry" in English, to offer me a candy or a cookie that she stored in glass jars lined up on one of the shelves.

These social barriers miraculously disappeared in the cellar during the air raids. My mother chitchatted with the Gergelys and others as if they were part of her social circle. In addition, I received attention from people who under normal circumstances would barely acknowledge me. Everyone huddled in the darkness around the flickering candles. The whispers of the grown-ups were occasionally punctuated by the whistling noise of falling bombs followed by large muffled explosions.

In late June 1944, phase 2 of the Hungarian Final Solution was implemented. The Jews of Budapest were forced into approximately two thousand selected Yellow Star buildings in the city, which included ours. All the Christians living in those buildings had to move out unless they had special permission to stay so that Jewish families could move in. All I remember is that some of my Jewish friends and their mothers now lived in our building.

One Christian family who stayed in our building was Mr. and Mrs. Lesko with their son Tibi. Although we were neighbors, we lived a world apart. I loved hanging out at Tibi's place. Mr. Lesko was an architect, whom I had rarely seen at home. Mrs. Lesko, a very tall woman, was always busy in her kitchen with her apron on. She was very nice to me and often invited me to join Tibi for lunch or a snack. Most importantly, I enjoyed spending time with Tibi whenever he would tolerate me. If Tibi was not home when I knocked on their door, I asked if I could look at their leather-bound collection of American comics that contained the original drawings and was translated into Hungarian. Thus, my first exposure to American culture came at a very early age.

It was in the early fall of 1944 that my mother had a chilling encounter with Mr. Lesko, an ardent Nazi. They accidentally met at the entrance of our house one day where Mr. Lesko warned my mother, "The day will soon come, Mrs. Reichmann, when you will be happy to be my servant and to polish my boots." The obvious reference was to the eventual enslaving of all the Jews of Hungary. It must have been due to Mr. Lesko's Nazi connections that his family was allowed to stay in our Yellow Star-designated building. It turned out that many years after the events of 1944, Tibi Lesko had an indirect role in my decision to escape from Hungary in 1956, but that is another story.

The day and night bombings were intense, but I don't recall being particularly frightened. The worst time was when I had to go to bed. I insisted that the door to our kitchen be left open just a crack so I could see a little light and hear the whispering voices of my mother and her friends discussing the day's events around our kitchen table. I listened to their conversation and occasionally picked up some foreign-sounding words like "Schutz-Pass," which means "Protective Passport," a document issued by the embassies of neutral countries, such as Sweden, Switzerland, and Portugal. Hundreds or even thousands of these or similar documents were issued to provide protection for Jews.

3. Swedish SCHUTZ-PASS issued to Éva Balog; August 19, 1944.

The Swedish Schutz-Pass shown above declares that "the abovenamed person is allowed to travel to Sweden," which was quite laughable in the summer of 1944, since the only Jews traveling out of Hungary were in cattle cars going to Auschwitz. The document also states that until the abovenamed person can travel to Sweden, he or she can live in a place protected by the Swedish government. This is how holders of Schutz-Passes were allowed to move into several protected houses in an area of Budapest referred to as the International Ghetto, where they were relatively safe from the Nazis. Access to these passports was not easy and not free. Most

Hungarians, including my mother, were not able to secure one for their families.

Swedish Schutz-Passes were issued by Raoul Wallenberg, the third secretary of the Royal Swedish Embassy, who was sent to Budapest in July 1944 to save as many Jews as he could. He is credited with saving the lives of thousands of Budapest Jews. The Canadian post office issued a stamp in his honor in 2003. The question mark at the end, "1947?" indicates that in 2003 we still didn't know the fate of Raoul Wallenberg after the liberation of Budapest by the Red Army in 1945.

4. Canadian stamp honoring Raoul Wallenberg.

The advantage of being almost seven years old was that I didn't quite understand the seriousness of the situation we faced. I was unable to comprehend that we faced a far more sinister danger than the possibility of a bomb directly hitting our building. However, the immediacy of being hit by a bomb became quite clear one day while in our cellar during a daytime air raid.

A very loud whistling noise was followed by a great thud, which was then followed by silence. When the "clear" siren was sounded, we scrambled up the stairs to see what had happened. A massive unexploded bomb fell right through the roof of the building and lodged in the floor of the second-story apartment. The top half of the bomb was inside the second-floor apartment, and the bottom half, with a pointed conical end, hung from the ceiling of the first floor. Had the bomb exploded, we might not have survived that attack.

In September 1944, I was eager to start first grade, but I was forced to stay mostly indoors, much of the time spent in our cellar. By this time, the world had been at war for years already, and millions of people, adults and children alike, had died in the killing fields of faraway places as well as in the Nazi concentration camps.

Having completed phase 1 of the Final Solution for Hungary at the end of July 1944, phase 2 was implemented for the remaining two hundred thousand or more Jews in Budapest, where my mother, grandparents, and I lived.

In order to accomplish the ultimate deportation of the Budapest Jews, orders were issued to herd all of us into a walled prison referred to as the Big Ghetto, located in the middle of Budapest, which was the destination for my mother and me.

There were very few options available to stay out of the ghetto. One was to pass yourself off as a Christian with false identification papers. Another possibility was to be hidden by a Christian family, and a third option was to obtain a Schutz-Pass.

Then, on October 10, 1944, we were awakened at dawn by someone banging on our door and yelling, "Everybody get out!" I was scared because I knew this was not a typical air raid since no sirens were heard. We quickly got dressed and joined the other Jewish mothers, children, and some of the older couples who lived in our building. There were several soldiers with guns on their back ordering the Jews to line up in the middle of the courtyard.

We stood in one line, my mother on my left holding my hand, when someone shouted, "All grown-ups, two steps forward!" I could feel my mother's hand slipping from mine as she started crying, let my hand go, and stepped forward. As a result of the confusion and seeing my mother cry, I joined the weeping chorus of the other children. Then someone shouted, "Turn left and march!" and the row of women began to move toward our gate.

This all happened so quickly that I couldn't comprehend what was going on. A soldier standing near me put his hand on my head and said, "Don't cry, little boy, your mother will return." However, his words, although prophetic, didn't console me. I continued to cry and tried to hold my mother's image in my mind through tearful, blurry eyes long after the last of the grown-ups had disappeared through our gate. This was the last time I saw my mother until the summer of 1945.

Survival

A friend of my mother's, Julia, an elderly Jewish woman who moved into our Yellow Star house, had not been taken away with the other women. Julia decided to take care of me after my mother was taken away. Perhaps it was prearranged between my mother and her, or she simply took the initiative, but that very same morning Julia told me that she was going to take me to my grandparents' apartment house in the city. I knew my mother's parents well. My mother and I had visited Nagymama and Nagypapa, or "grandmother" and "grandfather" in English, every other week, so the idea of being with them was comforting.

As soon as the curfew was lifted, Julia packed up some of my belongings and took my hand to begin the long walk into the city to my grandparents' house. I made sure that Julia packed my new white long pants, which children didn't usually wear back then, most of us sporting shorts and knee-length pants. For me, my striking long white slacks were a testament to my being a grown boy and not a baby anymore.

Trips to my grandparents' place were something I always looked forward to. My mother and I used to take three different streetcars to Lövölde Square, and then walk a short distance to 106 Király Street, located in a Jewish neighborhood in the central part of the city. Kneeling on the bench in the streetcar, I watched the houses go by along with the retail shops that had fancy colorful signs hung above the shops. I always tried to read the signs, having already known some of the letters of the alphabet that my mother had taught me. The streetcars hurtling in the opposite direction thrilled me as the faces in the windows whizzed by at what seemed an incredibly high speed.

Nevertheless, this trip with Julia on October 10, 1944, was very different. The damage to Budapest was significant. Buildings had disappeared where the bombs fell, only rubble remaining. Walls stood without roofs and buildings without facades, exposing floors with furniture and whatever evidence of previous occupants remained. The streetcars weren't running at that time, and we had to make the long journey on foot, by far the longest I had ever taken in my short life.

I recollect fragments of our trip and remember having been fascinated by what I saw. The two of us, an old lady who could have been my grandmother and I with yellow stars on our coats, walked through rubble, torn pavement, pieces of fallen airplanes, and broken vehicles left on the streets in the aftermath of the heavy bombardment on the city. It must have taken several hours for us to get to my grandparents' place given our respective ages.

Distracted by the excitement generated by the strange sights around me, I forgot to think about my mother's strange disappearance earlier that morning. I felt safe with Julia holding my hand and knowing that soon I would be with my grandparents, who loved me and always welcomed me in their home.

Another reason I looked forward to visiting my grandparents was that their building was several stories high. It was a large contemporary building by the standards of those days. Once we passed through the main gate, we walked up several steps that led directly to the elevator in the middle of the foyer. However, I was disappointed in never having an opportunity to ride it as my grandparents' apartment was on the main floor.

I also enjoyed the spaciousness of their apartment. Unlike our tiny two-room apartment, this place had a foyer, a bathroom, a separate toilet, several large rooms, and a very large kitchen. It even had a maid's room, though I can't recall ever seeing a maid there. They also had a large icebox in the foyer, a rarity in our neighborhood and where I learned that certain food items like butter and milk were kept in.

My grandmother was a sizable woman, taller than my grandfather. She had a round face and sad brown eyes that betrayed her smile, and she would often take me into her broad lap. Born as Ida Glück in 1888, Mamuka, as all her children called her, was fifty-six years old in 1944. She had ten grown children, five boys and five girls, and was grandmother to twelve.

Born as Vilmos Spitzer in 1881, my grandfather turned sixty-three in 1944. In contrast to his wife, he was short and thin, probably not taller than five feet, two inches. As a child, I was fascinated by his

5. The Spitzer family. My mother is the youngest girl next to my grandmother. The picture was probably taken around 1930 when my mother was fifteen years old.

handlebar mustache that was curled upward, ending in a sharp point, giving his face a serious martial look. I still remember playing with his mustache while sitting in his lap. Now I have to pause in telling my story in order to introduce a "story within the story." I had already completed the draft of this story in the fall of 2004 when I called my Cousin Miklós Grossman in Sydney, Australia, to say hello and inquire about how he and his family were doing. Miklós and his younger brother Tomi are my first cousins. Their mother, my Aunt Piri, was one of my mother's older sisters. How my cousins and their mother got to Australia from Hungary is another inspiring tale, but outside the scope of my own.

During my conversation with Miklós, I mentioned that I had written down my experiences of the Holocaust and complained to him that there were many holes in my story. I told Miklós that I could vividly remember many vignettes of my experiences, but I was having difficulty putting all the events together. Here is a brief excerpt of our phone conversation:

> Me: I remember many things, but I am missing
> many details.
> Miklós: I remember everything!
> Me, after a long pause: What do you mean? Were
> you there?

> Miklós: Of course I was there. So were my
> brother Tomi and our mother. We were all
> together with our grandparents.
> Me: Why don't I recall any of this?
> Miklós: You were too young and were probably
> confused.

I have to add that Miklós was seven years older and Tomi was about three years older than I. Therefore, in 1944, Miklós was already fourteen years old and was able to retain all that we had gone through together. On the other hand, Tomi can recall even less than I can, which I will return to later.

I was shocked to discover that exactly on the sixtieth anniversary of the events that took place in October 1944, my Aunt Piri and my two cousins were with me during those horrible times. All these years thinking about Julia taking me to my grandparents' house, I failed to remember them, on which my mind is completely blank to this day.

In my excitement, I started asking random questions, which Miklós dutifully answered with all the necessary details.

6. Aunt Piri after she turned ninety in 1999 in Sydney, Australia. My cousins, Miklós on the left and Tomi on the right.

Finally, we agreed that I would call him back and spend more time on the phone to add many of the missing details. My second phone call to Miklós provided a wealth of information about how our little band of family survived the ensuing months in the belly of the beast.

Unfortunately, Miklós had developed emphysema, the result of a lifelong smoking habit, and his health was declining. That, plus the difficulty of discussing events that took place sixty years ago in English and Hungarian over a satellite connection to Australia, made it difficult for me to accurately capture all the information I wanted to. Therefore, following my second phone call, I decided to travel to Australia in December 2004 to hear Miklós's recollection of events face-to-face. I captured several hours of conversations with Miklós on tape and have incorporated much of it in this story.

I have no recollection of what happened once I arrived at my grandparents' house on the day, or possibly the day after, my mother was taken away. I can only speculate that the usual warm welcome was replaced by sadness once my grandparents found out what happened to their youngest daughter. By this time in mid-October 1944, my grandparents must have known that their other children who were not present, as well as their respective families—husbands, wives, sons, and daughters—had been taken away to various forced labor and concentration camps.

Now there were ten of us living in my grandparents' home. In addition to my grandparents, there was me, Aunt Klári and her paraplegic son Iván, and Aunt Piri and her two sons, Miklós and Tomi. Due to the overcrowding, I shared a bed with one of my aunts. In addition, there was a couple I never met, older than my grandparents, whom I later discovered were my grandfather's older brother Samuel and his wife. Before going to sleep at night, I missed my mother terribly.

Unfortunately, my sense of safety and security with my grandparents and extended family didn't last long. Shortly after my arrival, I learned that we had to pack up and move. Of course, I had no idea why or where we were going, but as long as I was with my family, I wasn't afraid.

The final relocation of the Budapest Jews into designated Yellow Star houses was about to be completed, and the house where my grandparents lived on 106 Király Street was not a Yellow Star house. Therefore, we had to move.

Throughout our dangerous journey from house to house in the ghettos to liberation by the Soviet Army, our fate was in the hands of a man I didn't even know existed, according to my Cousin Miklós.

This man was our guardian angel, my mother's Cousin Laci Spitzer,[1] who single-handedly aided us through the terrifying weeks and months ahead and possibly saved our lives.

László Spitzer, Laci for short, was the oldest of three brothers, the sons of my grandfather's older brother Samuel and his wife, Eszter. I knew all three brothers, Laci, Pali, and Imre, and their families rather well much later in life in Montréal, Canada. However, back in Budapest in 1944, I was unaware of their existence.

Laci was a large man with blue eyes and not a trace of "Jewishness" in his features. He was also what we would call a *tough guy*. He somehow managed to get an Arrow Cross[2] uniform and false identity papers for himself. His sole purpose in life in 1944 and 1945 was to save himself, his brothers, and his parents from death. Because his parents were quite old, he asked his uncle, my grandfather, to allow his parents to join us and to care for them. In return, he promised to help the rest of the Spitzer family, now all living at my grandparents' place.

His plan was to secure (probably forged) Swedish Schutz-Passes for his parents, my grandparents, my two aunts, and their three sons, which added up to nine Schutz-Passes. Of course, he didn't know that I joined the family and now needed ten Schutz-Passes. In the end he was able to produce eight of these documents, leaving us two short. Even though they didn't have one, my grandparents made sure that I did. As it turned out, just a few weeks later, my grandparents' not having the Schutz-Passes almost cost them their lives.

The house Laci picked for us was in an area of Budapest that became known as the International Ghetto on the east side of the

---

[1] He isn't to be confused with my uncle, my mother's older brother, also named Laci Spitzer.

[2] The Arrow Cross, legalized in March 1944, was a brutal, viciously anti-Semitic, national socialist pro-Nazi party, which ruled Hungary from October 15, 1944, to January 1945. During its short rule, ten thousand to fifteen thousand Jews were murdered outright, and eighty thousand Jews, including women, children, and the elderly, were deported to their deaths in the Auschwitz concentration camp. Most of the leaders and the head of the party, Ferenc Szálasi, were executed for war crimes by the Soviet courts following the liberation of Hungary.

Danube, across from Margaret Island. The name International Ghetto came from the fact that it was where all the "protected houses" supported by various foreign embassies were located. The Hungarian government reached an agreement with the embassies of neutral countries, such as Sweden, Switzerland, and the Vatican, that all Jews with protective documents or affidavits issued by these governments would be temporarily protected as long as they lived in specifically designated houses.

These affidavits testified that the holders of these documents were approved to immigrate to the issuing neutral country as soon as it was feasible. There were at least fifty of these designated "protected houses" in the International Ghetto.

7. Locations of the Big Ghetto and the International Ghetto.

This area also happened to be where many of the well-to-do Jewish families lived, and for that reason, many of them were designated Yellow Star buildings.

There were important advantages of moving into a protected house as opposed to into the Big Ghetto. First, these houses were not walled-off prisons. There was freedom of movement in and out of the protected houses to buy or barter for food and medicine, visit family, or go to anywhere when the curfew for Jews was lifted. And most importantly, Jews could keep money, jewelry, and all valuables they could carry.

In order to bring us all together under one roof, Laci arranged to have an apartment available for us in a building where his girlfriend, Erzsi, who later became his wife, lived. The house was on Légrádi Károly Street, known today as Balzac Street, and we all moved into a third-floor apartment. Laci deemed this place safe, and the fact that the building's superintendent, a woman, was not an anti-Semite was definitely favorable.

It was quite the frenzy as my grandparents and aunts tried to decide what to pack, what to take, and what to leave behind. Food, sheets, blankets, pillows, clothing, eating utensils, precious family heirlooms, among many other things, had to be sorted out. Arguments ensued as to what was feasible to carry. A wicker basket normally used for shopping at the market was assigned for me to carry. Additionally, a cast iron meat grinder that looked enormous to me was placed in the basket and was topped off with some of my clothing that Julia had brought with us, including my precious pair of white pants.

To this day I cannot figure out why grandmother insisted on taking the meat grinder. The whole city was starving, and even potatoes and bread, never mind meat, were scarce. But no matter how bitterly I complained about the weight of the meat grinder, Grandmother insisted that I carry it. And that is how our journey to seven different places during the course of the next few months began.

So, one day, all ten of us, including Laci Spitzer's parents, packed up with bundles of property; me with the meat grinder and Cousin Iván in his wheelchair with bundles in his lap, began a journey on foot from one place to the next that I shall never forget.

Our building, 106 Király Street, from where we started, literally bordered the northern perimeter of the Big Ghetto. The distance from there to our new destination was a good mile or mile and a half of walking.

More than sixty years after these events took place, I still have this bittersweet recollection of a feeling of indignation for having to carry the heavy meat grinder in spite of my protestations. What had my grandparents or aunts been thinking? Did they think that they could set up a functioning kitchen or have access to one in some stranger's apartment? Did they think that they could actually obtain meat for cooking?

Looking back, I can only conclude that the grown-ups didn't have a clue to the conditions we were about to experience once we left my grandparents' place. Nevertheless, I had to carry my heavy cargo without it ever being in any proximity of meat to grind in the months ahead.

Life was still dangerous for Jews despite having authentic papers to authorize living in a protected house. Our goal was to stay one step ahead of deportation or being gathered together for summary execution on the banks of the Danube. Our survival depended on obtaining sufficient food to avert starvation, on avoiding any serious illness or the arbitrary roundup of Jews by the Arrow Cross, and on not being bombed by the Allies. It was a race against time as the fighting was already at our doorstep and the Soviet Army was rapidly approaching Budapest from the east.

It was on Légrádi Károly Street that my grandparents were caught without their papers. The Arrow Cross men periodically visited the protected houses and demanded to see everyone's papers. We all had to descend to the courtyard and stand in line as the papers were examined. Since my grandparents didn't have any papers, they were told to take whatever they could carry in one bag, and were taken away to the Budapest brick factory, which was a collection center for future deportees. The sudden departure of my grandparents was disastrous for all of us.

Miraculously, two days later at daybreak, my grandparents were spotted from our window walking back toward our house, pulling their knapsack behind them in the snow. Somehow my grandfather managed to engineer their escape before dawn and we were together again. Following the near-fatal incident with my grandparents, we moved out of the house where the grown-ups had felt relatively safe for the previous couple of weeks.

I recall nothing peculiar about our stay at Légrádi Károly Street, our first stop. We still slept in beds, the apartment had windows to keep the cold out, and I didn't feel hungry. I still missed my mother a lot. I certainly didn't have any idea that by this time my mother, together with several thousand Jewish women, would be marching on foot toward Austria under the most miserable and inhumane conditions.

I learned much later that after our separation on October 10, 1944, my mother was taken to a brickyard in Óbuda, an old section of Budapest on the west bank of the Danube. This was a collection point for all the Jews who were to march to Austria.[1] She never spoke about what happened in her entire life, but others did. Here is an excerpt from a letter written by another Jewish woman, Mrs. Szenes, who was also forced to march:

> As the night fell, it started raining. We continued to march through the mud and the water…and finally we arrived at the brickyard in Óbuda. We were driven to the corridor around the burner, which was so crowded that you could barely stand. The walls of the burner kept us warm so at least the cold did not torture us all night long. It was impossible to sleep, and at dawn, everyone was driven out into the courtyard. We were divided into groups of one hundred, four people in each row. The endless column of human beings started marching towards Austria. Civilian guards were ordered to accompany us, who made no secret out of their unhappiness at having to walk ten or twelve miles a day. They kept an eye on people so that none should escape.

---

[1] Organizing death marches was nothing new to the Nazis. In January 1940, they marched eight hundred Polish Jewish prisoners of war ninety-five kilometers from Lublin to Biala Podlaska. In January 1945, they marched sixty-five thousand "fit" Auschwitz inmates from the camp toward Germany. The biggest march of eighty thousand Jews was the one in Hungary in October and November 1944.

These marches illustrate one of the most inhumane, and frankly absurd, policies of the German authorities. Presumably, they needed the labor to build defensive lines near the border of Austria. However, they didn't provide the transportation, food, or shelter to protect those assigned to do the work. Thousands of people died along the road to Austria, and those who survived were all too weak to do any useful work once they arrived at their destination.

Back in Budapest, I knew nothing about my mother's perils. The most annoying part of moving again was that I had to once again carry my basket with the meat grinder. Fortunately, our next stop was a Swedish protected house on Pozsonyi Road just a few blocks away.

It turned out that our new home was also fraught with risks. Arrow Cross men came, and having broken all the understanding established between the neutral countries and the Hungarian government, they herded everybody into the General Ghetto unless they were bribed with money or jewelry. They didn't care if one had a legitimate or a fake Schutz-Pass—they took everyone. Obviously, we didn't have enough money, and only a few days after we settled in, we were all marched into the General Ghetto. I was again in charge of carrying the meat grinder back near my grandparents' house, where we started from a few weeks earlier. This move must have happened in November 1944, before the ghetto was closed on December 10. The borders comprised the core of the old Jewish neighborhoods.

The following streets formed the borders: Dohány Street, Károly Boulevard, Király Street (where my grandparents lived), and Nagyatádi Szabó Street, now named Kertész Street. One of the most memorable events was our entry into the walled ghetto. Families, mostly consisting of older people and children, were lined up next to the wooden fence, and every able-bodied person was carrying something. For a majority of the time we just stood there and then proceeded to walk a few yards. This was fine for me because I could rest my heavy basket on the ground. We approached the ghetto from the west side, where the Great Synagogue is, on Dohány Street.

Finally, as we got close enough, a small gate appeared in the middle of a very high wooden fence stretching between two walls.

Men with guns surrounded the gate and people were let through the narrow opening one at a time. To the right of the gate were high piles of objects heaped on the ground. As I got closer, I realized that these piles were silver dishes and utensils, jewelry, watches, rings, and other valuables that people had to discard before entering the ghetto. The uniformed men with guns, the loud noise of shouting and crying, and the sight of all the treasures piled up on the sidewalk were so strange yet entrancing that I don't even remember walking through the gate.

Moving into the ghetto was a shock to us all. All I remember is that we ended up uncomfortably crowded into one room. There must have been two or three other families already living in the apartment. We were so crowded that Miklós had no room on the floor and he slept on top of a dresser, the only piece of furniture left in the room. The place was dreadfully bug infested, and we all knew that our future prospects were very dim in this place.

Fortunately, Laci Spitzer found out what happened when he came to visit us at our old address and took immediate steps to rescue us. Two days after we were shepherded into the ghetto, Laci showed up fully dressed in his Arrow Cross uniform, followed by a horse and wagon pulled by a man he hired to move us. All our belongings were put into the wagon, along with Laci's parents, and we left the ghetto and headed to our new destination. The good news, in addition to leaving the ghetto, was that I didn't have to carry the meat grinder.

In November, it was still safer to be outside the ghetto in a protected house than to be inside. First, obtaining food was easier. Jews could leave the protected houses for a few hours every day to get food. Second, even though the ghetto was completely walled in, soldiers, who guarded its gates, often allowed Arrow Cross units to enter to commit atrocities inside. However, we soon learned that being outside the ghetto had its own perils. There were no physical barriers to keep the increasingly aggressive Arrow Cross thugs from invading the protected houses and dragging the Jews away for summary execution and then dumping them into the Danube.

The food situation had become critical for everybody in Budapest by now. Access to traditional transportation routes into and out of the city was blocked or significantly hampered by the war conditions. Most staples could only be bought on the black market at inflated prices. It was even more challenging for Jews because many shopkeepers refused to sell food to them.

Once again, under Laci Spitzer's protection, we moved back into the International Ghetto and ended up in another Swedish protected house on 3 Kárpát Street, not too far from the places we stayed before. We were lucky and actually found some food and watches stashed away in a drawer that had been left there by the Jews who were taken away and herded into the ghetto as we were just a few days earlier.

Finding food continued to be the most difficult challenge for us. Whenever Laci came by, he always brought some food for us, but it was never enough. Laci's parents were too old, my grandparents still didn't have any papers, and my aunts had to care for the children. The risky job of finding or stealing food fell onto Miklós's fourteen-year-old shoulders. To quote him, "I was not a child anymore, but I was not quite a grown-up yet."

Why we didn't stay at 3 Kárpát Street for more than a few days is still unknown to me. As the end of the war was getting closer, the daily risk of being exposed to the Arrow Cross thugs was obviously increasing. For whatever reason, we were on the road again and subsequently moved back to an apartment on Pozsonyi Road, where we had first stayed.

There were dozens of other people also crammed into the apartment, and there was barely enough space for people to sleep on the floor. It was in this house that one day Miklós found an Arrow Cross armband on the staircase in our building. He picked it up, making sure nobody saw him, and pocketed it, not really knowing what he might do with it one day. It soon turned out that the armband would be a lifesaver for all of us.

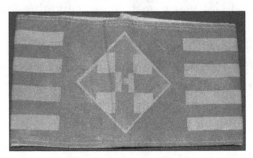

8. Arrow Cross armband.

We were living on Pozsonyi Street when Cousin Miklós witnessed a scene that terribly upset him. It was still difficult for him to tell me at the age of seventy-three.

One day as he went about scavenging for food, he saw about a hundred Jews being marched on the street. Guarding them were three or four teenagers with guns and the Arrow Cross armband on their arms. Miklós recalled:

> They were like sheep going to the slaughterhouse. Why did a hundred people allow a few teenagers to treat them like sheep? If they attacked their guards, and even if only ten Jews would have escaped and survived, it would have been better than submitting so willingly to a few teenage thugs. To this very day I feel ashamed when I recall this scene.

Miklós was visibly shaken in recalling the incident that took place almost exactly sixty years earlier. As I listened to him, I could feel my throat tighten and my anger rising to the surface. Who was I angry at? The Arrow Cross thugs? At the Jews who allowed themselves to be treated like "sheep"? Or at all those countless people, the Hungarians, the Germans, and all the people around the world who by ignorance, indifference, prejudice, or active collaboration allowed such a scene to take place in Budapest?

I really felt my cousin's pain as I looked in his tearful blue eyes, searching for an answer to an unanswerable dilemma. By the time Miklós was sixteen, he was fighting another war in Palestine, and I am sure the experiences in Budapest had built up a great deal of resolve in him.

Miklós had gumption, even at the early age of fourteen. As mentioned previously, it was his job to go out of our building day and night, usually without his yellow star, and scavenge and barter for food for the family. Unfortunately, by November 1944, many of the shops were bombed and destroyed, and many of those that were still open for business refused to sell food to Jews.

Miklós would go into a bombed-out building or store and look for anything that had value—a piece of jewelry, a watch, silverware, or a pack of cigarettes—and then barter that for food for the family. As he was returning one day, he saw that all the Jews of our house, including our family, were herded together in courtyard. Here is how Miklós described the scene:

> There were a couple of sniveling brats and an old man in Arrow Cross uniforms selecting people from the crowd to take to the Danube. The kids were not much older than I was. The guns on their shoulders touched the ground. Everyone was just standing there scared to death and tolerating it. Suddenly, I remembered that I had an Arrow Cross band in my pocket. I put it on and walked up to the old man and said, "These are my Jews, I will take them." The old man looked at me, saw my armband, and said, "All right, but be careful that they don't cheat you."

The "cheating" was in reference to the allowing of Jews to bribe their way out of certain death by giving the thugs money, jewelry, or other valuables.

Once more, we were on the move. This time we moved into one of the protected houses surrounding Szent István Park. By now, I was barely able to walk, much less carry anything as heavy as the meat grinder. I don't remember being hungry anymore or even thinking about my mother. Perhaps I had reached the stage of malnutrition when a certain calmness and indifference take over.

From time to time, we heard bombs falling around us. I didn't know it then, but Miklós told me that the Germans had placed eight guns along the bank of the Danube, right next to the park. One morning the guns were gone, but several Russian airplanes showed up and started bombing the riverbank where they had been. So much for timing!

While we were living at Szent István Park, my grandparents seriously questioned my cousin's sanity. Following one of his missions to secure some bread, Miklós came home exhilarated and claimed that he saw two of our cousins. He witnessed a squadron of labor camp inmates being marched toward the Big Ghetto in the middle of the street guarded by Arrow Cross men. Marching side by side in the front row were Pisti and Gyuri, the two teenage sons of my mother's older sister Aunt Bözske,[1] and each was carrying a loaf of bread.

Upon hearing of this sighting of family members together in broad daylight with bread under their arms, my grandmother declared, "There is something wrong with this child. He must have been affected by a bomb blast and now he is hallucinating. It is not possible that what he describes is true." Despite his protestations, Miklós was summarily ignored. However, Miklós proved her wrong after we moved back into the ghetto for the second time.

The situation in Budapest was becoming more and more critical. The Red Army was moving closer and closer to the outskirts of the city. The Germans were withdrawing but didn't surrender Budapest without a fight.

Knowing that their glorious time of terrorizing defenseless Jews was coming to an end, the Arrow Cross thugs were even more brazen in their attacks. They captured Jews during the hours they were allowed on the streets or dragged them out of their protected houses, taking them to the Danube, murdering them, and dumping their bodies into the river.

One day we were told to pack up and be prepared to move again. All the Jews in the houses on Szent István Park were gathered on the street, and we were marched off, Miklós carrying me on his back. Laci Spitzer was nearby and kept an eye on us, but we still didn't know where we were going. Were we heading to the embankment of the Danube or into the Big Ghetto?

As we turned left on the main road, we knew we were heading toward the ghetto. Suddenly, we heard the roar of airplanes flying over, and we soon saw and heard the bombs exploding near us. Aunt

---

[1] Aunt Bözske ended up in Auschwitz but survived.

Klári panicked, decided to bolt from the row, pushing her son Iván in the wheelchair, and ducked inside a house along the road. Normally, this would have been suicide due to the Arrow Cross shooting all deserters on the spot. This time, Aunt Klári got lucky. Because of the chaos of the bombing, and before anything tragic could happen, my grandfather swiftly dragged her back into the line.

We moved back into the ghetto around the end of December 1944, and this was the last place we stayed until the Red Army liberated the ghetto in January 1945. This second and last entry into the ghetto was through the same gate we used the first time. Unlike our first entry into the ghetto, I cannot recall going through the same gate. Laci came into the ghetto, wearing his black Arrow Cross uniform, armband, and shiny boots, and managed to put us in a single room in an apartment building at 34 Kazinczy Street, right across from a small synagogue.

Somewhere along the way, moving from one place to the next, my new white long pants that I was so proud of and had barely an opportunity to wear had disappeared. I was inconsolable over their loss, no matter how much the grown-ups tried to convince me that I would get another pair.

As soon as we moved into the ghetto, Miklós took off to look for the cousins he had seen a couple of days earlier. He was determined to prove to our grandmother that he wasn't hallucinating. Sure enough, after going from house to house, he found them all and was hoping they still had some of the bread they were carrying on the street. This is when he learned that the bread they had carried was allotted for the whole squadron and was long gone.

Miklós brought our two cousins, Pisti and Gyuri, to visit us in our tiny room, where there was a bittersweet rejoicing at having reunited. Everybody was indifferent by now. Having seen and suffered so much, we all sensed that the outlook was grim. It was difficult to celebrate a reunion when everyone was starving and when so many of our family were missing and presumed already dead.

The food situation in the ghetto was desperate because there wasn't any. A potato skin found on the floor was a treasure. Kitchens were set up at several places within the ghetto that were supposed to dispense about seventy thousand portions a day. Unfortunately, the raw materials the government was expected to provide for the ghetto were rarely delivered. It fell to the International Red Cross to provide the staples, which often fell short. After all, we were on the front line of a war zone.

The food shortage created a despondent situation for everyone in the ghetto, and only those with money or outside connections could secure additional food for their families. Documents found among the papers of the ghetto administrator, Captain Miksa Domonkos of the Hungarian Army, indicate the caloric content of the daily portions distributed:

Child's portion:	931 calories
General portion:	781 calories
Sick portion:	1,355 calories

According to the "Dietary Guidelines for Americans 2005" released on January 12, 2005, by the US government, daily calorie intake recommended for "moderately active" people between the ages of thirty-one and fifty was 2,000 calories for women and 2,400 to 2,600 calories for men. Therefore, nobody could survive on the portions in the ghetto for long.

These documents also showed the weekly menu in December 1944:

Monday:	bean soup with pasta (14 ounces)[1]
Tuesday:	dish of cabbage (10.5 ounces)
Wednesday:	potato soup (14 ounces)
Thursday:	dish of dried peas (10.5 ounces)
Friday:	caraway seed soup (14 ounces)

---

[1]   A can of Campbell's condensed soup is 10 and ¾ ounces.

| Saturday: | sholet[1] (10.5 ounces) |
| Sunday: | vegetable soup and pasta (14 ounces) |

At that time, the only physical discomfort I felt was the cold. Heating materials weren't available as winter arrived in the city; most modern city apartment houses were heated with built-in stoves that used wood and coal. The mean temperatures in Budapest in November and December are 41°F and 34°F, respectively, with the temperature often dropping below freezing at night. The windows were all broken, and the walls of our room provided the only protection against the elements.

I kept getting weaker and weaker until I was no longer interested in getting up in the morning at all. I didn't miss much fun since we were crowded into a small room, sleeping on blankets on the floor and huddling together to keep ourselves warm, just waiting for something to happen.

We were on the second floor of the building, and to my right there were two windows facing the synagogue across the street. There was not a single piece of furniture save for a wall-mounted grandfather clock that hung over my grandparents' heads across the room. All other furniture that once made this room part of a family home had already been sold or used up as firewood. The image of the grandfather clock with its motionless brass arm is stuck in my mind like an old photograph. I was frightened that it could come crashing down on my grandparents' heads at any time. Miklós stated that the building belonged to the clock makers' union, explaining the presence of the wall clock.

I went to Hungary in 2007 to attend a family wedding, and I decided to find 34 Kazinczy Street. Amazingly, this was the only house on the street whose façade has not been renovated. It stood exactly like it was in 1945 with its bullet holes and scars from bomb shrapnel, a testament to the events of more than sixty years ago. The only difference is that all the windows had been replaced. It is now a

---

[1] Very much of an ethnic Jewish meal mostly made of beans and typically served as a Sabbath dinner on Friday nights.

surreal picture of wartime Budapest since almost all the surrounding buildings on both sides of the street have been rebuilt or renovated.

9. 34 Kazinczy Street in 2007, where we survived the final weeks of the Holocaust.

The small synagogue across the house was no longer in use. I thought maybe this house stayed this way so I could take a picture and show it to my grandchildren.

Raids on Budapest continued, but we didn't seek shelter in the basement as my mother and I used to do in our home. There was a cellar under the building; however, the grown-ups decided that it was unnecessary to trek up and down every time the air raid siren went off. The bombs fell on Budapest day and night, some of which landed in the ghetto. Strangely, I didn't fear the bombs, but as I later discovered—twenty years after these events—I didn't totally escape the psychological impact.

In July of 1964, when I was already married and our son was less than a year old, I had just started working for General Electric in Philadelphia. It was my first job after graduating from college, and we had recently rented an upstairs furnished apartment in Broomall, a suburb of the city.

One night I awoke suddenly to the sound of sirens. I immediately broke out in a cold sweat, jumped out of bed, and ran to the balcony. I stared at the sky, seeking the air-raid searchlights that were used in Budapest in 1944, and listened for the familiar sound of bombers flying over. However, it took me a few minutes, standing there stark naked with sweat pouring down, to realize that I was in Broomall, Pennsylvania, and not back in Budapest. It was only the next day that I learned the siren was the call signal for the volunteer firefighters to rush to their station. Fortunately, this was the only such incident.

Back in Budapest in December 1944, I must have been emotionally numb after everything that had happened during the previous months. Bombings didn't bother me, and I was getting used to being hungry and cold all the time. My Cousin Tomi was in even worse shape, though he was three years older. A month or so earlier, a bomb exploded nearby at Légrádi Károly Street, the first place we moved to after leaving my grandparents' place. Consequently, Tomi had become almost catatonic. He completely shut down and to this day has no recollection of anything that happened then. However, the month of December 1944 proved to be one of fateful and historic events:

> **December 15**: The German government fled the city, and the activities of the Red Cross were banned. Armed bands of Arrow Cross soldiers began a string of systematic murders of Jews. On the same day, rail tracks were laid down up to the wall of the ghetto. It seemed that this was in preparation for deportation of the ghetto inhabitants to Auschwitz.

> **December 20**: Several bombs hit the ghetto during the night, seriously damaging five houses where close to six hundred people lived, many of whom died.

> **December 22:** Eichmann personally visited the ghetto and ordered the Jewish Council[1] members to meet him the next morning at nine o'clock. His plan was to personally supervise the execution of

---

[1] A volunteer organization that included some of the leadership in the Jewish community.

the Jewish Council, followed by the massacre of the entire Jewish population of the ghetto.

December 23: Eichmann decided to leave Budapest at dawn as the news spread of the Soviet Army's push to the outskirts of Budapest, thus averting the massacre of seventy thousand Jews.

December 23: Representatives of the neutral countries[1] who had not yet left the city met and delivered a memorandum to the royal government of Hungary, protesting against transporting Jewish children found hiding elsewhere into the ghetto.

December 24: The Soviet Army surrounded the city, and the siege of Budapest began.

December 31: Corpses of the dead could no longer be taken out of the ghetto for burial. Many were lined up in the small courtyard of the synagogue on Dohány Street, today called the Hero's Cemetery. To this day, two thousand victims rest there.

Life in the ghetto became quite perilous in December 1944. In addition to starvation, the cold, and bombs, there were bands of Arrow Cross soldiers determined to take as many Jews as they could out of the ghetto and murder them. An excerpt from the diary of a survivor, Miksa Fenyő, hiding not far from the ghetto on December 23, 1944, illustrates the dangers we faced every day:

---

[1] Nuncio Angelo Rotta of the Vatican; Ambassador Carl Ivan Danielsson of Sweden; Ambassador Harald Feller of Switzerland; Count Ferenc Pongrácz, the *chargé d'affaires* of the Portuguese Embassy; and Giorgio Perlasca, the self-made *chargé d'affaires* of Spain, signed the joint memorandum.

There seems to be no end to the robbery and murder. No day goes by without a few dozen Jews dragged out of the ghetto on the slightest pretext, or on no pretext at all. At night they are shot to death along the banks of the Danube, to save the trouble of a burial.

A couple of stories my cousin recalled illustrate how pure luck played a crucial role in survival. The fear of Arrow Cross men dragging Jews away from the ghetto was so great that a decision was made to post a "guard" at the gate of our building. All grown-ups had to stand guard for two hours all day and night to alert us in case the Arrow Cross men were near. I'm not sure what we would have done if an alarm sounded, but being on guard kept the grown-ups proactive.

One evening my Aunt Piri was on guard when a man in our building volunteered to take her place and told her to go back upstairs and take care of her family. "I am a single man, but you have a family to take care of. I will take your watch," he told her, and she came upstairs. Ten minutes later a bomb fell into the yard near the gate and instantly killed this Good Samaritan instead of my Aunt Piri.

There was another incident that involved Miklós. It was his responsibility to go to the ghetto kitchen and return with the daily soup portions for the whole family. He collected the soup in a big pot and was on his way back to our building when he heard the Soviet planes flying over with their guns blazing. He took cover on the side of a house until the planes disappeared. Upon hearing a sharp noise, he looked down into the pot and realized that the soup was gone. A bullet hole had penetrated the pot, causing all the soup to leak out.

By now, the Red Army was fighting the Germans and the Arrow Cross men city block by city block. The Soviets weakened the resistance by attacking Germans behind the front line via airplane. As we were surrounded by German troops, it was not easy to see the wooden fence boundaries of the ghetto from an airplane flying at 150 mph with guns blazing. According to Miklós, our situation looked very bleak by January 1945, and apathy and hopelessness were spreading.

Desperation for food had reached a new high when we somehow got hold of some starch. We were not sure what we could do with it until Aunt Piri suggested that we try to mix it with the very fine lubricant oil that the clock makers who used to live in the apartment used. A few books were found in the building, and the potbelly stove was fired up. Aunt Piri mixed the oil with the starch, and the fried mixture soon had the appearance of traditional latkes, a traditional Jewish side dish for Chanukah. We all ate it and thankfully nobody got sick, but I doubt that this new recipe for latkes will ever find its way into a Jewish cookbook.

On January 15, 1945, after the Soviet Army had already captured the outskirts of the city, remaining SS units and armed Arrow Cross men planned to launch an attack on the ghetto to slaughter everyone per Eichmann's original plan. Thankfully, Raoul Wallenberg discovered the plan on January 12 and threatened the SS commander, General Schmidhuber, with severe consequences if it was carried out. The massacre of seventy thousand Jews was averted, and thus we survived.

Liberation

My last memory of the ghetto is the day of liberation. I had no idea when exactly the ghetto was liberated until I did the research for this story. Based on my impression that we lived in the ghetto for a very long time, I always thought that it was in the spring of 1945. I felt surprised, as well as dismayed, to discover that the day the Soviet Army liberated the Budapest ghetto was on January 18. Therefore, we lived in the Big Ghetto just a few weeks, not several months as I had thought. The corollary to the saying that *time flies when you are having fun* should be *time stands still when you are miserable.*

According to my Cousin Miklós, the fighting erupted literally under our windows one morning. Then suddenly there was quiet. While I don't recall the fighting, I do remember one of my aunts taking me to the window to look. I saw uniformed men marching off in the distance, pulling what appeared to be guns on two wheels, and then disappearing at the end of the street. All these years I always thought what I saw then were German soldiers. However, according to my cousin, it is possible that these were Arrow Cross men fighting to the very end. For them, liberation meant the end of their regime and possible death. They had nothing to lose by fighting for every inch of territory.

Gunfire continued to be heard in the distance, but it was silent in front of our building. In what seemed like minutes, soldiers of the Soviet Army appeared at the opposite end of the street. They came into the ghetto through the eastern gate, moving west block by block. I then heard yelling and screaming as the Russians drew closer to our house. The Russian word for "bread," *chleba*, was being shouted from the windows and by people rushing out of the houses toward the soldiers.

My grandfather, having been a prisoner of war in Russia for five years during World War I, spoke some Russian, and he was out of our building in a hurry to get some bread for us. By this time even Miklós was so weak that he could barely drag himself to the window to witness the dramatic events.

Finally, on January 18, 1945, we went from being exposed to imminent death to being free within one day. Any memories of celebration or laughter have escaped me. It is possible that everybody was still in shock and ridden with anxiety about what they had gone through and about the fate of the rest of their families.

Laci Spitzer, our guardian angel, showed up in the ghetto the day we were freed and took his parents with him. I never saw him again until we met in 1957 in Montréal, Canada. Like me, Laci escaped from communist Hungary following the Uprising in October 1956. We met many times in Montréal, and I even remember visiting him and his wife, Erzsi, in their lovely apartment in downtown Montréal. He never mentioned anything about what happened to us back in 1944 and 1945, and I knew nothing about the role he played in my family's survival until I visited my cousins in Sydney, Australia, in December 2004.

The very next day my grandfather and Miklós went to scout out the situation at 106 Király Street to make sure that it was safe and ready for our family to move back in. A peasant family from the country who had occupied our home was asked to leave, and by nightfall the next day we were back home. Fortunately, we didn't have to walk too far because my grandparents' home was just a few blocks from the ghetto. Who carried me back remains a mystery, as does what happened to the meat grinder.

A couple of days after the liberation of Budapest, Raoul Wallenberg was captured by the Red Army, and for decades the Soviet Union refused to provide information about his whereabouts or whether he was dead or alive.

10. Members of the International Red Cross examining a pile of dead bodies in the Big Ghetto following liberation in January 1945.

Once we were liberated, there was chaos on the streets. Whether it was deliberate or not, for about a week the Russians let people break into stores and allowed them to grab anything they could find. A large chocolate factory was broken into, resulting in big chunks of hard chocolate being taken home. It was helpful to eat the hard pieces of chocolate to offset the diarrhea from the molasses that we ate. The food situation in Budapest remained critical for a long time. However, it didn't take too long to get back on my feet within a few days once I got some nourishment into my body.

Shortly after our liberation, Aunt Klári asked me to go with her to gather some wood for our stove at home. She found a bombed-out store that had a few scraps of wood, which were probably the remnants of the store's shelves. She started gathering the wood in her arms when all of a sudden a woman showed up and started screaming at Aunt Klári not to touch anything and that everything in the store belonged to her. However, Aunt Klári was not deterred and proceeded with her mission, at which point the woman attacked her, beating her with both hands.

Within seconds they were wrestling each other amidst the rubble in the store. Suddenly, I heard someone laughing behind me. I turned around and saw a Russian soldier sitting on a pile of rubble with a machine gun in his lap, elbow on his knee, and a cigarette in his hand. He was laughing hard and watching with obvious enjoyment the two women fighting over a few pieces of wood. This soldier, who risked his own life just a few days ago to liberate this part of the city, watching two women fight over pieces of wood was a welcome relief from combat.

This surreal scene frightened me, and I didn't know what to do. I somehow missed the humor, seeing my aunt being beaten by another woman. I have no recollection of how the altercation ended or whether Aunt Klári had escaped with any wood.

Within days after liberation, the Stern cousins,[1] Pisti and Gyuri, together with their father, decided to go home to a small town named Eger, about one hundred kilometers from Budapest, where they used to live. They walked the whole way home since there were no trains available yet. Shortly after, Aunt Piri and her sons, Miklós and Tomi, left for Eger to join them.

There was no word yet from my mother, my father, or any of the other missing relatives. My grandmother was ailing, and the decision was made to send me to Eger as well. Again, Miklós was given the task of taking charge, and he returned to Budapest to take me back to Eger with him. Food was more plentiful in the country than in Budapest, and I needed some fattening up. In addition, Aunt Klári's hands were tied with caring for Iván, and my grandparents were too old to care for me. Miklós and I took off for Eger around March 1945.

This was my first train trip ever, which I will never forget. Cousin Miklós and I went to the railway station early one morning. I had never seen so many people all jammed together on the platforms on both sides of the rail cars. It seemed like everyone in Budapest was trying to leave. Miklós figured out which train was going in the

---

[1] Aunt Bözske's sons.

direction of Eger, and we were soon standing in front of a long train with all the rail cars full.

There were people sitting on the top of the rail cars with their luggage and situated between the cars, standing or sitting on the bumpers that connected them. Others were hanging on the steps by the doors on both sides of the cars with absolutely no room for anyone to enter. The windows were open, and you could see that people inside were jammed together like sardines. These people must have gotten there hours before we did.

Not certain whether I was more scared or amazed, I was hanging on to Miklós as he went to work. He begged people in the windows to take me in and offered them bread in return. Finally, a woman from the inside called out to Miklós, "Come over here, my son. I will take this little boy in here with me." The next thing I knew I was shoved through the window and placed on the overhead luggage rack without my feet ever touching the ground. Miklós disappeared after telling me he would claim me when we get to Füzesabony. All alone I was scared to death, wondering if Miklós would come to get me.

There was no direct train connection to Eger. Even during peacetime, travelers had to change trains at Füzesabony, about seventy miles from Budapest, and take an additional short ride of about ten miles to Eger.

In war-torn Hungary in 1945, we were lucky there was a train at all. Our trip lasted many hours, and I had no idea where we were at what time. Finally, at Füzesabony, a small town along the train tracks, my Cousin Miklós arrived, and from there we walked to Eger.

My memories of staying in Eger with my Aunt Piri and my cousins are vague. I went to stay with my family in Eger many times during my summer vacations in subsequent years, and it is difficult to separate my memory of this first visit from some of the later ones despite the conditions being quite different. Nevertheless, I am sure this first experience could not have been as joyful and happy as my later visits.

It was not until April 4, 1945, that all of Hungary was liberated by the Soviet Army when I had already arrived in Eger. Hungary was liberated, but for the surviving Jews, like my grandparents, my aunts, my cousins, and me, complete liberation was still out of reach. We had to agonizingly wait to see which family members had survived and which had perished in the Nazi killing fields.

One of the first to come home was my mother's brother, Uncle Béla. Unfortunately, his wife, his daughter, and a baby son perished in Auschwitz. His woeful story illustrates the fatefulness of one mere decision. Uncle Béla and his family lived in Újpest, a near suburb of Budapest, literally translated as "New Pest." When word spread that the Nazis were rounding up the Jews in the countryside in the summer of 1944, they were asked to come into the city and live with my grandparents. For some reason, Uncle Béla's wife, Szidóra, didn't want to move, which was a tragic decision that sealed their fate.

Then, two of my mother's sisters returned from the concentration camps. Aunt Bözske returned from Auschwitz with a number tattooed on her arm. Aunt Lili returned from the Bergen-Belsen[1] concentration camp. First, she was also taken to Auschwitz with her two sons, Imre (thirteen years old) and Gyuri (ten years old).

Upon arrival at Auschwitz, the old and the young were separated from those who could work, and her sons, too young for work, were sent to the gas chambers. Aunt Lili was sent to Bergen-Belsen where she worked at a munition factory for the Germans until liberation. My Uncle Laci, the darling son of my grandmother, also ended up in Bergen-Belsen, and miraculously, he and Aunt Lili found each other and he was able to bring the very sick and malnourished sister home after the British liberated the camp in early 1945.

In the middle of the summer we got word that my mother had survived and I would be taken back to Budapest as soon as possible. By now, I was comfortable living with my aunts and cousins in an

---

[1] A Nazi concentration camp located in northwestern Germany. About thirty-eight thousand prisoners died in Bergen-Belsen between May 1943 and April 15, 1945. About sixty thousand prisoners in the camp were found following liberation, most of them seriously ill. More than thirteen thousand of them, too ill to recover, died after liberation.

apartment building located next to the ramp of a medieval castle.[1] I made some new friends, and we spent many delightful days playing on the castle grounds. Within days of the news about my mother, I was on a train, guarded by Miklós, and excited to see her again.

My mother was liberated by the Allies in Lichtenwörth, Austria. However, she was sick with typhus and extremely malnourished, so she couldn't travel immediately. Fortunately, her best friend from our neighborhood was with her during their captivity and she looked after my mother.

Manci néni,[2] as I called her, was clever, tough as nails, and projected a great deal of self-confidence, many of the qualities my mother lacked. She became one of the servants of the camp commandant so had access to food that she stole, which kept my mother alive.

Following the liberation of their camp, she stayed with my mother until she was strong enough to travel. She somewhat miraculously managed to get transportation, usually horse-drawn wagons, for my mother to return to Budapest since walking even a few yards, much less many miles, was out of the question for my mother. My mother was immediately taken to a hospital where they more or less brought her back to life before letting her go.

I was elated to see my mother again. I was anxiously waiting at the door when Uncle Béla arrived, pulling a cart that consisted of just a flat platform attached to the axle between two large wheels, and announced, "Look, Robi, here is your mother." I saw what vaguely resembled a human form lying on top of the cart. She resembled a skeleton, covered with tight skin and a pair of large eyes, staring at me out of a skull with no hair on top. No words came from this strange

---

[1]   The Castle of Eger is well-known to every schoolchild in Hungary. This is where a famous battle against the Turkish Army took place in 1552. A small garrison under the leadership of István Dobó (c. 1500–1572), a wealthy landowner, held out heroically for thirty-eight days against the much larger Turkish Army.

[2]   A child or a younger person would normally address older persons by their first name and adding *néni* (pronounced "neighni") if female, or *bácsi* (the letter *á* is pronounced as the *a* in *art*, and the *cs* is pronounced as the *ch* in *child*) if male, after their first name. This was an explicit recognition of a generational age difference and a show of respect. There are no English equivalents for these words.

creature, and I despondently uttered, "This is not my mother." I turned around and ran inside, crying.

The sight of my mother lying on that cart is forever burned into my memory. Even now, more than seventy-five years later, the image of my mother's emaciated body and the devastating effect that my unrecognition had on her brings out the most intense emotional reaction of all my Holocaust experiences.

This reunion with my mother evokes an indescribably painful memory in me even now. It is one of hurt, frustration, and anger at all those who caused her to be an unrecognizable skeleton near death. At the same time, I feel ashamed that at the moment when she needed me most, I was not there for her. It took my mother a long time to fully recover, and we stayed at my grandparents' place in the meantime.

Meanwhile, word must have reached my grandparents that three of their sons, Uncle Jenő, Uncle Feri, and Uncle Jóska, with his wife and four-year-old son, all perished. My grandmother's looks had worsened from a few months earlier when we left the ghetto, and my grandfather, who was not a talkative man to begin with, rarely spoke.

Finally, the time came for us to go home, and Uncle Béla accompanied us. When we arrived at 7 Fűzér Street, we discovered that a Christian family had moved into our tiny apartment. No matter how low we were on the economic scale, there were always people below us. Our tiny and cheap apartment without indoor plumbing must have seemed luxurious to a poor family. By day's end, the family had vacated the premises without any confrontation that I can remember, and we were once again in our own home. I spent the next eleven years in this two-room apartment.

Liberation was still not over for us as we waited to hear the fate of my father. Months went by and there was still no word from him. Unlike my mother, liberation came too late for my father. He died on January 14, 1945, in Donnerskirchen, Austria, in his brother's arms. My mother finally told me one day that my father would not be coming home. She had known for some time but kept postponing telling me.

The actual sense of loss of my father, whom I barely knew as a child, did not register with me until years later. It wasn't until later as a growing boy and teenager that I was able to comprehend the consequences of being fatherless, of missing the normal father-son relationship. It was then that I began to mourn his loss.

As I grew older, I discovered that the grieving never stops. In fact, as I learned of the circumstances surrounding my father's death decades later from my Uncle Elek, who was with him at the time, I grieved even more. In addition, as I discovered the larger historical context of the Holocaust following my escape from communist Hungary in 1956, my feelings of loss, anger, and resentment further intensified. Sadly, now I understand that "liberation" from the Holocaust and the healing of emotional wounds will always be unattainable.

Liberation effected the survival of approximately 200,000 Hungarian Jews out of 750,000 (including Jews in the annexed territories). Of the 180,000 Jews of Budapest, 130,000 survived—70,000 in the Big Ghetto, 25,000 in the International Ghetto, 25,000 in hiding (most of them with Christian families), and 10,000 returned from deportation and labor camps. There were about 70,000 survivors outside Budapest.

Postscript

The impact of the Holocaust on my mother's family, the Spitzers, was devastating. Eleven members of my grandparents' family perished, including three sons, five grandchildren, two daughters-in-law, and two sons-in-law, including my father. In addition, three of the daughters, including my mother, and two of the brothers were deported but survived.

My grandmother died in 1947, never having fully recovered from this tragedy. My mother declared that she died of a broken heart. I don't know what exactly caused my grandmother's death, but the loss of her three boys must have exacerbated whatever ailed her. The Reichmanns, on my father's side, were more fortunate. Out of the nine children, only one daughter, Lena, one son, my father, and one son-in-law did not survive.

Our family was typical of many of the survivors of the Holocaust. Everyone was traumatized. On average, every surviving Jew lost three members of his or her family. All illusions about being assimilated into the "Magyar"[1] society and being different only due to practicing one of the minor religions in a Christian country had vanished.

Postwar Hungary didn't pay much attention to the six hundred thousand Jewish victims and their surviving families. Hungarians were too busy trying to recover from the disastrous effects of the war, including the ruined economy and infrastructure, the political and socioeconomic impact of once again being on the losing side with their German allies as in World War I, and the looming prospect of Soviet domination that was a clear precursor of establishing state communism in Hungary.

---

[1] Hungarians call themselves Magyars. No accurate source for the origin of the name exists. It is speculated that the name Magyar may have derived from the name of one of the seven tribes (Nyék, Megyer, Kürt-Gyarmat, Tarján, Jenő, Kér, and Keszi) that occupied what is now Hungary in the seventh and eighth centuries. Although Jews have lived in Hungary since the thirteenth century, they have never been accepted as citizens with the same rights as their Christian counterparts.

There were no trauma centers, no psychological assistance, nor counseling for the survivors. Every Jew, young and old, was left to their own devices to deal with the trauma of the Holocaust. In my family this meant total silence. Discussing the experiences of the survivors was taboo; we just did not broach the subject.

I didn't learn about the circumstances of my father's death until Uncle Elek, in whose arms he died, was himself on his deathbed, dying of cancer in Toronto in 1985—forty years after. I gathered enough courage to ask him about my father's death, and he told me a few details in a low whisper, looking exhausted and in pain.

My mother—who lived to be eighty-seven and died on April 17, 2002, in Budapest—never spoke a word about her experiences of marching on foot to Austria and her stay in Lichtenwörth, Austria. Whatever bits of information I gathered came from Manci néni, her best friend, who was with her in the camp and primarily responsible for my mother's survival. I don't recall ever discussing my ghetto experiences with my mother.

One time my curiosity overcame my caution about discussing the Holocaust with my family, which I later regretted. Sometime in the 1980s, I invited my mother's brother, my Uncle Laci, and his second wife, Magda, to visit us in Atlanta. I was quite close to Uncle Laci, who was something of a father figure when I was growing up. I took the two of them to Hilton Head, South Carolina, for a relaxing oceanside vacation.

One afternoon, while sitting under the umbrella and watching the ocean as his wife was sleeping inside the condominium, I asked my uncle to tell me of his experiences while he was in a forced labor camp. Within a minute of talking, he choked up and began to sob uncontrollably. In his poor, tortured mind, he could never get past the first humiliating experience of being slapped in the face by an uneducated peasant soldier.

He was a good-looking, proud, and vain man, and I am convinced that the physical hardships he had to endure in order to survive were nothing compared to the emotional humiliation he suffered. Perhaps for the first time in his life, he realized that regardless of his high school education (a major accomplishment in those days), his good looks, and his previous standing in society, he was just another Jew exposed to humiliation and abuse. I got a very serious scolding from my uncle's wife later that afternoon. She made me promise that I would never bring this subject up with my uncle again, which I kept until he died.

I regret that it is just now sixty years later, almost too late, since hardly any survivors are still alive, that I have tried to research the facts surrounding the deaths of many of my relatives during the Holocaust. I feel ashamed that I hadn't tried to memorialize the names, ages, and places of death of some of my extended family that died in the concentration camps. During all those years when I still had the chance to find out who perished where, I failed to do so because "we just didn't go there." Now that my mother, aunts, and uncles are gone, I have no one to ask.

Hungary's reconciliation with its crimes against its Jewish population in the Holocaust didn't begin until after the collapse of the Iron Curtain, when Hungary became a democratic country following free elections in 1991. Memorials were erected to honor the victims[1] and those who aided the Jews.

In the late 1980s, the well-known American actor Tony Curtis[2] donated $1 million to the Emanuel Foundation to finance the design and erection of a memorial, the Tree of Life, to the Holocaust victims of Hungary. The memorial is appropriately located behind the synagogue where all the dead bodies were piled up in the ghetto. As one of the "founding donors," I donated $250 to have my father's name, "Zoltán Reichmann," etched into one of the thousands of the tree's leaves, each of them representing one victim. Uncle Laci made

---

[1] A beautiful statue was erected to honor Raoul Wallenberg and a street is named after him in Budapest.

[2] Born as Bernard Schwartz on June 3, 1925, in New York. His parents were Hungarians who immigrated to the US. The foundation was named after his grandfather, Emanuel.

sure that his brother's names, Feri, Jenő, and Jóska Spitzer, are also memorialized.[1]

The memories of my father and his sister Lena are also preserved on a beautiful memorial erected to honor all the victims of the families of Kibbutz Maabarot in northern Israel. My Aunt Rutka Reichmann left Hungary in 1933 when she was nineteen years old and ended up in Palestine. She married and settled down in Kibbutz Maabarot, where two of her daughters and their families still live today. I visited this kibbutz for the first time in 2000, where I saw this beautiful memorial that has a list of approximately 150 Holocaust victims.

In Budapest, there are several memorials honoring Raoul Wallenberg, as well as a street named after him. It was only a few years ago that we learned the Russians had put him in the infamous Lubyanka prison in Moscow, where he was probably tortured because they believed him to be a German spy due to his fluency in the German language. My personal theory is that the Russians could not believe that a Swede from a well-to-do family would risk his life and come to Hungary just to save Jewish lives. They executed him in 1947 when he was thirty-seven years old.

There are at least two memorials to honor the Jewish victims who were shot and dumped into the Danube River in late 1944 and early 1945. I was fortunate to have the honor of participating in building one of these monuments in a small park at the end of Pozsonyi Road in 1994, when I was working in Hungary as an American consultant. My office was on the same street, and I often walked north toward the Helia Hotel, where I went swimming most evenings.

One night I suddenly heard Israeli music coming from a park right next to the river and decided to further explore this unusual happenstance. Upon arriving, a long line of what I presumed to be mostly Jews were lined up, silently waiting their turn to pick up a

---

[1] Each branch of the Tree of Life has a Roman numeral. The branches where my father's and my uncles' names can be found on a leaf are Zoltán Reichmann XLII, József Spitzer VII, Jenő Spitzer VII, and Ferenc Spitzer XXXIX. The branches are numbered from left to right as one faces the memorial.

stone from a large pile next to a concrete square base that was set into the grass, since putting a small stone on a grave is a sign of mourning in Judaism.

A stonemason was standing by, and as each person placed a stone on the monument, he cemented the stone in place. Within an hour the monument reached the desired height and a memorial plaque was secured to the side of the monument. I too placed my stone there, shed some tears, and went on my way without waiting to hear any speeches.

I have been back to Hungary many times since I left in 1956. In fact, I was working there in 1994 when the Hungarian parliament held a special session on the fiftieth anniversary of the Holocaust. I listened to the speeches denouncing Hungary's crimes and pleading to eliminate anti-Semitism, in addition to racial, ethnic, and religious bigotry. Touched by the sincerity and compassion shown by democratically elected members of this legislative body, I listened through tears in my eyes. I allowed myself for just a few moments to be deluded with the idea that change is possible and the hope that history will not repeat itself.

However, I soon recovered my emotional ambivalence. In a part of my heart and soul I feel a sense of being Hungarian, no matter what history taught me. I feel proud when I see a Hungarian athlete win a medal at the Olympics, and when I think of the scientific and artistic contributions made by so many from our nation. I love the food and the theater in Budapest, and I tend to get emotional when I listen to sorrowful gypsy music or Brahms' Hungarian dances. Yet at the same time I know I don't belong there. Hungary had forsaken my family, all its Jewry, and me at the time of our greatest need for help, and I cannot forgive and forget that.

There is some hope that Hungary will become a more tolerant place someday. Reuters reported not long ago that a state-sponsored Hungarian museum launched a campaign on October 1, 2004, to identify people who had helped save lives during the Holocaust.

"Sixty years have passed and we have not said thanks to those who have given [good] example to society," Maria Schmidt, managing director of the Terror House Museum,[1] told Reuters. She called on people who knew of those who helped Hungarian Jews escape to contact the museum, which is promising. There were many, probably hundreds or even thousands of Christian families, who risked their own lives and the lives of their families to save Jews from being deported and killed. Unfortunately, these people were the exception and not the norm.

Reuters also reported that the Simon Wiesenthal Center launched its "Operation Last Chance" campaign in Hungary in July 2004, declaring it the last chance to find war criminals responsible for the Holocaust in Hungary.

Having grown up in Hungary, I silently dealt with my personal experiences over the years like everyone else I knew around me, trying not to think about it. Perhaps the loss of my father became more tolerable as I was maturing since not a single Jewish friend of mine in our neighborhood had a father.

As I grew older and began to ponder the impact the Holocaust had on me, I concluded that those early childhood experiences left a festering wound in my heart and on my soul, which has never completely healed. I also realized how emotionally vulnerable I became to anything I heard, saw, or experienced that reminded me of the past.

There are days, weeks, and sometimes even months when I don't think about it, but those feelings of hurt, remorse, and anger are never far below the surface. When provoked, they can erupt with an intensity and force as if I were still a seven-year-old child and the events of more than seventy-five years ago just took place yesterday.

Stifling these feelings when they surface has always been futile. Perhaps it is time to concede that I will never rid myself of this "emotional baggage" and that it will stay with me to the very end of my life.

The Holocaust undoubtedly shaped my views on prejudice, fairness, and discrimination, whether based on religion, ethnicity, or

---

[1] The Terror House is located in a central Budapest building, in which Hungarian Arrow Cross party activists and later the communist secret police tortured and killed thousands.

skin color. I abhor all ideologies and political systems that don't provide equal protection to all, especially to those in the minority.

Clearly, I was lucky to survive. A bomb didn't fall on me. I didn't get sick. I didn't freeze to death. I didn't starve to death, even though I came close. But most importantly, I owe many thanks to all my heroes who helped me survive.

In Memoriam

To my close family members who perished during the Holocaust.

The Reichmann family:

My father, *Zoltán Reichmann, 33*; Donnerskirchen,[1] Austria; January 14, 1945
Aunt *Lena Reichmann, 23*; Bergen-Belsen, Germany; May 17, 1945
Uncle *György Huszár, 29* (husband of Aunt Éva Reichmann); Wels, Austria; December 15, 1945

The Spitzer family:

Uncle *József Spitzer, 30*; Auschwitz, Poland; 1945
Aunt *Lili, 26* (wife of Uncle József); Auschwitz, Poland; 1944
Cousin *Tamás Spitzer, 4* (son of Uncle József); Auschwitz, Poland; 1944
Uncle *Jenő Spitzer, 23;* Don River Bend, Soviet Union; 1942
Uncle *Ferenc Spitzer, 20;* Soviet Union; 1944
Uncle *Artúr Groszman, 37* (husband of Aunt Piri Spitzer); Hungary; 1944
Aunt *Szidóra, 34* (wife of Uncle Béla); Auschwitz, Poland; 1944
Cousin *Jutka Spitzer, 15* (daughter of Uncle Béla); Auschwitz; Poland; 1944
Cousin *László Spitzer, 6 months* (son of Uncle Béla); Auschwitz, Poland; 1944
Cousin *Imre Groszman, 13* (son of Aunt Lili Spitzer); Auschwitz, Poland; 1944
Cousin *György Groszman, 10* (son of Aunt Lili Spitzer); Auschwitz, Poland; 1944

---

[1]   A forced labor camp set up for Hungarian Jews southeast of Vienna, Austria.

The Weisz family (my wife was born as Éva Weisz):

Uncle *György Weisz, 26*; disappeared with labor battalion in Soviet
    Union; 1944
Grandfather *Zsigmond Weisz, 56*; Auschwitz, Poland; 1944
Grandmother *Jolán Weisz, 51*; Auschwitz, Poland; 1944

The Blum family (my wife's grandparents on her mother's side):

Grandfather *Jenő Blum, 57*; disappeared; presumed shot into the
    Danube in Budapest; 1944

Journey 2: Growing Up Under Communism

My "growing up" years span from 1945, the end of World War II, through October 1956, when the Hungarian uprising took place. A devastating war and a bloody uprising are bookends to my childhood and adolescent years. Those eleven years were economically, politically, and emotionally extraordinary times for my family and me. I didn't have what one would call a normal childhood. Therefore, a brief overview of the economic, social, and political circumstances in Hungary during these crucial years provides the proper context to my story.

Hungarian society was in shock after the war ended in early 1945; the country lay in ruins. The relentless allied bombing, together with the subsequent fighting between the Soviet Red Army and the Germans, destroyed 60 percent of Budapest. The economy was at a standstill, and a large percentage of the city population was starving following "liberation" in the spring of 1945. I focus on the word *liberation* because other than the Jews who faced liquidation in 1944 during the last days of the fascist Hungarian regime, a large part of the population despised the Russian liberators and were fearful of the ultimate outcome of their occupation. One must remember that

Hungary was an ally of Germany in World War I and World War II, both times on the losing side.

Unlike in Western Europe where the Marshall Plan[1] infused $13 billion for reconstruction between 1947 and 1952, there was no significant aid from the Soviet Union. In fact, the Treaty of Paris,[2] signed February 10, 1947, required Hungary to pay $200 million in reparations to the Soviet Union, $50 million to Czechoslovakia, and $50 million to Yugoslavia. Next, to exacerbate Hungary's bleak future, the Soviet Union began to impose their own economic priorities on Hungary, along with large-scale nationalization of virtually all businesses and farms starting in 1948.

In other words, life in Hungary became extremely difficult for the majority, especially those in the working class, for decades to come. My mother, who never worked a day in her married life, was forced to earn whatever meager salary she could get by working in a factory. These poor economic conditions didn't improve much while I lived in Hungary.

After the war, while most Hungarians mourned the loss of about three hundred thousand victims, mostly soldiers, and the loss of territories to Czechoslovakia and to Romania, the surviving Jews of Hungary had additional mourning to cope with.

Approximately three out of four Hungarian Jews perished during the Holocaust, leaving no surviving family untouched. The loss of almost six hundred thousand ethnic Hungarian Jews, 10 percent of the total European Holocaust victims, was a massive and unparalleled devastation that to this day the remaining Jews of Hungary have not recovered from. Barred from escaping Hungary due to the Iron

---

[1] The Marshall Plan was the United States' primary plan for rebuilding and creating a strong foundation for the allied countries of Europe and for repelling communism in war-torn Western Europe. The initiative was named for then secretary of state George Marshall.

[2] The Paris Peace Conference (July 20 to October 15, 1946) resulted in the Paris Peace Treaties signed on February 10, 1947. The victorious Allies (United States, United Kingdom, France, and the Soviet Union) negotiated (*dictated*) details of treaties with Italy, Romania, Hungary, Bulgaria, and Finland.

Curtain[1] that descended in 1945, they had to reconcile remaining in a predominantly anti-Semitic Hungary while trying to recover from devastating losses.

The silver lining for the remaining Jews was that all anti-Jewish laws of the previous twenty years were rescinded, and anti-Semitism was driven underground. In addition, the Red Army was fundamental in preventing the elimination of the entire Jewish population. Because of this, the surviving Jews' attitude was more accepting of the new leaders. The fact that most of these leaders of the puppet regime were Jews, led by Mátyás Rákosi[2] and established by Moscow in the postwar period, was not lost on the surviving population.

Considering all the aforementioned negative circumstances that affected my daily life from the age of seven through eighteen, it would be reasonable to assume that I would have suffered some permanent psychological effects, resulting in my growing up to be pessimist and bitter, resenting the cards life dealt me. As the ensuing story reveals, nothing of that nature occurred. In fact, even considering that I was raised without a father, my childhood years were quite happy.

---

[1] The Iron Curtain was the symbolic, ideological boundary dividing Europe into two separate areas from the end of World War II until the end of the Cold War, roughly from 1945 to 1989. The physical boundary separated the West, the democratic countries of Western Europe, from the Central and Eastern European countries under the dominance of the Soviet Union.

[2] Mátyás Rákosi was born as Mátyás Rosenfeld (March 9, 1892–February 5, 1971). He became a committed communist and follower of Stalin and ruled Hungary in a Stalinist-type dictatorship from 1945. Khrushchev, Stalin's successor, removed him in 1956. It is important to note that Rákosi and his fellow Jewish associates were all atheists; they renounced all religions, including their own.

Life in the Working Class

Life was difficult for us even before the war, when my father was alive and working. Undoubtedly, life became much harder after the war. My widowed mother had to find a job, and not having more than eight years of schooling, the best she could aspire for was physical work. She ended up working for a local plant of the Chinoin Pharmaceutical Company,[1] one of Hungary's leading drug companies. The plant was on the same street where we lived, about a fifteen-minute walk away. I have fond memories of the plant, where I was a frequent visitor, and meeting many of my mother's coworkers.

The circumstances surrounding my mother's becoming the party secretary for the Chinoin plant, the person in charge of disseminating the Communist Party propaganda, are still clear in my mind. She didn't want to accept the responsibility of being the "cheerleader" for the Communist Party, organizing meetings and overseeing all the important functions at the plant.

Under the communist system, the party secretary had more power than the plant manager. She correctly surmised that she had neither the leadership skills nor the commitment of a true believer of the system to do the job justice. However, her friend Manci néni strongly advised her to take it. In fact, she might have had something to do with my mother's nomination for the job since she was a well-regarded member of the local district chapter of the Communist Party.

I was impressed when my mother asked for my opinion. I must have been around sixteen years old, and this was the first time I was consulted on a grown-up matter that affected our lives. The material benefits of the job were significant. She could work fewer hours and spend time on official party matters that were not as physically tiring; in addition, it was an increase in salary.

---

[1]   Chinoin Co. Ltd.—now a member of the Sanofi Group of France—has been a leading player of the Hungarian pharmaceutical industry for a century. It was established in 1910.

After having thought about it, I told her that she should take the job and make the best of it, which she did. An additional fringe benefit was that I had the privilege of eating in the plant cafeteria, where the food was a lot better than the state-run public cafeterias.

Chinoin is the only place my mother worked, from what I can remember. She most likely did various kinds of manual work, but I can recall only one. She sat on a stool in front of a long workbench along with a row of women hunched over a methane gas burner, slowly twirling a glass vial in her gloved hands until it melted. The vial, containing some kind of medication or vaccine, was then sealed. I was mesmerized by the bright colors of the flame and the melting glass. The work was piecemeal, and my mother's biweekly salary seldom lasted to the next payday. Thus, we were perpetually short of money.

Following the war, our tiny two-room apartment, which was supposed to be a temporary residence when we moved in there in 1939 when I was a year old, now became a permanent residence. There was no hope in sight of an opportunity to upgrade into a better living quarter.

We lived in District X, known as Kőbánya, literally translated as "quarry." It was, and I believe still is, a working-class district. I don't know where the name originated from because I never saw a quarry as long as I lived there. There were several large factories in Kőbánya in addition to Chinoin. Dating back to the Austro-Hungarian Empire, a famous beer was brewed at the Dreher[1] Beer Factory, whose product I became quite familiar with as a teenager. Indeed, the very first time I got drunk was on Dreher beer when I was nearly eighteen.

My mother allowed me to attend a Communist Party social with a man who worked at the Dreher plant as my chaperone. Naturally, I drank too much and got sick on the streetcar on my way home. After that, all I remember is falling on my bed at home and not waking up

---

[1]   This first modern lager beer is attributed to the Austrian brew master, Anton Dreher. He first brewed this revolutionary light-colored beer at his own brewery in Vienna in 1841. The only Dreher beer-producing company still operating is the one in Kőbánya, but it is now owned by South Africa Brewery.

until the next morning; my mother had to undress me while I was out cold.

Our district was also the home of a large canning plant where I worked in the summer of 1956. This was also a memorable experience, not so much for the miserable working conditions in the steamy, smelly, and extremely hot work environment, but for my very brief but intense encounter with a fellow worker. With blue eyes, black hair, and dark, olive skin, I fell in love with her at first sight. Unfortunately, her shift ended a couple of hours after mine at 10:00 p.m., so we could never arrange how to get together outside the plant.

I usually went home from work and spent all my free time studying in preparation for my final high school oral and written exams required for graduation. One evening, instead of going home from work, I decided to wait for her at the train station where she commuted to her home outside Budapest. This was our only chance to meet, hold hands, and exchange a few kisses.

When I got home after eleven o'clock, my mother was waiting for me, extremely upset. She demanded to know where I was, and when I told her the truth, she called me irresponsible for neglecting my studies for meeting with some "riff-raff stranger," and for good measure, she slapped me across my face. I was shocked. This was the only time my mother ever struck me. However, my mother was right. I felt guilty about the situation; thus, that was the last time I met with my coworker.

The Grünfeld Glass Company, where my father used to work as an assistant to the truck drivers delivering glass products all over Hungary, was also located in our district. We moved to Kőbánya when I was a year old so my father could work close to home. My mother hated to move away from the central part of the city, where her parents and siblings lived, but she had no choice. My father promised my mother that this living arrangement was temporary until he found a better-paying job, a promise that he could never fulfill, since he was killed in a concentration camp during the Holocaust.

The street we lived on, Fűzér[1] Street, began with a soccer field on the left, which was surrounded by a tall fence. Next to the field was a post office and then our building. Along both sides of the street sat two-story houses that stretched for about a mile or so to the railroad tracks. There were wide sidewalks with mature trees situated about every twenty feet. The road was made out of cobblestones that were later paved over. The buildings on our street were probably built around the turn of the nineteenth century for upper- to middle-class families.

Our building was originally L-shaped, two stories high, with the main entrance gate in the short part of the letter L. Wooden stairs led down to the cellar that ran underneath the apartments. There were four luxury apartments on each floor with elegant bathrooms, a maid's room, big kitchens with a pantry, and two or more additional rooms. Then, probably in the 1920s or early 1930s, a row of six two-room apartments was added across the courtyard to alleviate the shortage of housing for working-class people, turning the shape of the building from an L into a square-shaped ∐ with the gate in the middle.

Unlike the original building that had a cellar for the foundation, these apartments were constructed right on top of dirt without any foundation. Each apartment had two rooms: a kitchen and a second room that served as a bedroom, living room, or however one chose to utilize it. The tiny kitchen was about eight feet wide and fifteen feet deep. Our room next to it measured approximately fifteen by fifteen feet. The kitchen's linoleum floor was laid on top of packed dirt, as were the dark-brown stained wooden planks in the second room.

There was no indoor plumbing; access to drinking water for all the apartments on our side of the building was from a single cold-water faucet located at eye level on the outside wall of our apartment. Any tenants that needed water for cooking, bathing, or drinking were required to use this one outlet. The faucet was located right between our two windows that faced the courtyard, a convenience

---

[1]   The word *fűzér* means "string" in English, as in *string of pearls.*

that was offset against the inconvenience of the loud noise resulting from turning the faucet on.

In the wintertime, a wooden box padded with some rags was put over the faucet to prevent it from freezing. This feeble attempt wasn't successful when the temperature dropped significantly below zero degrees Celsius. We had to anticipate the freeze and stock up on water in buckets to make sure we could drink, brush our teeth, and bathe.

Additionally, there was no central heating in these apartments. The kitchen was equipped with a wood- and coke-fired cooking range, and a potbelly stove sat in the corner of the second room. Smoke pipes in both the kitchen and second room thrust through the ceiling and out through the roof. There was no bathroom in any of the apartments, which made taking a bath a complex procedure.

First, wood kindling and coke were brought up from the basement across the courtyard, with the kitchen range being fired up next. Subsequently, water brought in from the outside was heated up in a big pot on top of the stove. When the water was hot enough, the white enameled basin, no more than about three feet wide and normally kept under the kitchen table, was put on the floor right in front of the entrance door, the only place big enough to accommodate it. Only after all these steps was I ready to take a bath.

I was a teenager when I embarrassingly discovered that if one stood at the balcony on the second floor across from our apartment, one could peer through the small window above our front door into the kitchen and see exactly where I usually took a bath. Three sisters about my age lived in that second-floor

11. My mother in our kitchen, with the bath basin under the table.

apartment. It was through one of their boyfriends that I learned I was unwittingly providing great entertainment to them for many years.

Our very narrow kitchen door opened to the courtyard. Fruit preserves prepared by my mother sat in jars on top of the cabinet in the back. On the right was a small dresser where I kept my athletic gear, our kitchen stove, the door to our only other room, and a large wooden box where we stored the firewood. Above the box sat a small medicine cabinet mounted on the wall with a mirror on the door.

Luckily, I didn't have to shave but once every week, even when I was past eighteen years old. When I did, I would heat up some water, place the basin on the wooden box, and proceed to perform the delicate task of shaving, careful not to cut all my pimples off my face. On the left was a table with two stools and the bath basin, about three feet in diameter, placed under it.

I don't know when my mother took a bath because I never saw her do it. Perhaps she did when I was in school, after I went to bed, or where she worked, since almost all plants provided facilities for bathing.

There were three toilets located across the courtyard that were used by all six families living on our side of the building. The toilets were protected from the rain or snow, were not heated, and one had to supply one's own "toilet paper." The truth is that we didn't buy toilet paper because it was a luxury item, if it was available at all, and we couldn't afford it. The poor-quality communist propaganda papers made for the perfect substitute. I spent seventeen years in this apartment, from 1939 until 1956.

As a seven-year-old child, the changes the war brought to our home didn't seem so drastic. I understood that my father was gone, but it was in the context of not having a father for at least two years before 1945 since he was rarely able to visit us while a conscript of the Hungarian Army's Jewish labor force.

The immediate burden of my father's death fell on my mother's shoulders. After barely surviving her deportation and imprisonment in an Austrian concentration camp in 1944, she was now a widow with bleak prospects of escaping the relatively poor living conditions we faced.

The immediate consequence of my mother's widowhood was her need for employment in order to support the two of us. Having a child to support also significantly reduced her chances of remarrying. First, very few eligible, single Jewish men survived the Holocaust. Moreover, those few single or widowed men who survived preferred a childless bride. However, my mother had a few opportunities to wed, but these never materialized until years after I escaped from Hungary.

One of my mother's suitors, the only one I remember well, was a divorced man called Lajos Erőd,[1] whose son, Gabi, became a close friend of mine as we grew up in the same neighborhood and went to the same elementary school. The Erőd family lived in a beautiful apartment on 2 Román Street, only ten minutes in walking distance.

The building they lived in consisted of several luxury apartments and once belonged to Gabi's grandmother, who lived with them. I spent many joyful hours at Gabi's place, playing games and enjoying the spacious living conditions that are vividly etched in my memories. Clearly, this marriage would have been a perfect arrangement for me. Gabi was one year younger than I, so I would have had an instant younger brother and would have loved trading living quarters. I am sure my mother felt the same way.

Unfortunately, the grandmother, apparently having much influence on her son, opposed the marriage, killing any hope of its fruition. I learned about this from my mother many years later after I left Hungary.

Grandma Erenreich told her son that if he married my mother and we moved in to live with them, I would be a bad influence on Gabi because we came from a much lower socioeconomic stratum. Apparently, Grandma felt that our sharing the same roof over our head, sleeping in the same bedroom, and eating at the same table would jeopardize her hopes for a bright future for her grandson.

Frankly, I don't know whether this is a true story. Perhaps Gabi's father used that excuse for not marrying my mother, or my mother

---

[1] The family's original name was Erenreich. As with many Jews after the war, Gabi and his father's name was changed to the Hungarian Erőd.

made up the story to assuage her heartbreak. In any case, the result was the same. Therefore, these marriage plans never materialized, and my mother remained a widow for fifteen years until she married in 1961. This meant that I grew up without a stepfather and under the care of my mother and the extended family on my mother's side.

It was during the turbulent times after the war that I came to realize the importance of my mother's best friend, Manci néni. I believe that she and her husband, who also perished in a forced labor camp like my father, and my parents were friends before the war. She was with my mother when the Hungarian fascist government deported them to Lichtenwörth, Austria, in October 1944. My mother revealed that she would not have survived captivity had it not been for her friend's help.

Since I had gotten to know Manci néni's character and personality as I grew up, this information didn't come as a shock to me. She was smart, resourceful, and tough as nails. After the war, she managed to get a highly regarded job as the manager of the local Household Store,[1] a government-owned chain that sold everything from toothpaste to gasoline by the liter. The fact that she was an open supporter of the communist regime might have had something to do with her position.

When I was older and got to know her better, I concluded that she was a "true believer" in the communist system. Unlike my mother, I couldn't see Manci néni as a pretty woman, even when she was young. She wore her dark hair in a very unattractive fashion, framing her somewhat masculine and pockmarked dark face. She had a low, raspy voice and was quite articulate whenever she expressed an opinion, which she disclosed in abundance on practically any topic. She hobbled slightly as she walked due to an injury she suffered in the concentration camp.

As a child, I had a lot of trouble with my mother's best friend. She constantly advised my mother to keep me on a short leash. She advocated for severe punishments and scolded my mother when she

---

[1] Literary translation from the Hungarian "Háztartási Bolt."

was too lenient or spent money on me. Perhaps the fact that she never had any children explains her attitude.

When I was about ten years old, a friend, which might have been Gabi, and I decided to catch a ride on the mail truck from the post office right next to our house. The plan was to hop on the rear platform of the truck as it left the driveway and ride it to the main intersection of Fűzér Street and Kőrösi Csoma[1] Road, where the truck had to make a stop.

At first, everything went smoothly. However, as the truck gathered speed, we both panicked and decided to jump off. Naturally, we stumbled on the cobblestone road, scraping and bloodying our hands and legs.

Unfortunately, Manci néni just happened to be on her way to visit my mother and witnessed our tumble. She walked me home and told my mother that I deserved severe punishment for what I did. Consequently, I had to spend the next hour facing the wall and kneeling on some hard corn kernels in the corner of our room, all thanks to Manci néni.

The reality was that Manci néni became my mother's financial supporter. My mother constantly borrowed money from her because her paycheck rarely lasted until the next payday. She also arranged for me to have small, part-time jobs in her store, which were likely designed to put some extra money into our household.

I will always remember the job she gave me for several years since I was about eight years old on All Saints Day[2] in November.

One of the largest cemeteries in Budapest was located close to our district. The Household Store set up tables in front of the

---

[1] Sándor Kőrösi Csoma (March 27, 1784–April 11, 1842) was a Hungarian philologist and orientologist, author of the first Tibetan-English dictionary and grammar book. He traveled to the Far East, looking for the ethnic origins of the Magyar ethnic group. He was said to have been able to read in seventeen languages.

[2] All Saints' Day is a Roman Catholic holy day when people remember their deceased loved ones by lighting candles at their graves in the cemeteries. The holiday falls on November 1, but it usually included the nearest weekend when people could take time to visit the cemetery.

cemetery gate and sold candles to the visitors. During the weekend, thousands of people came to pay their respects to their loved ones. I became a free agent, selling candles to people getting off the street-cars before arriving at the cemetery gate.

My hands and pockets were filled with candles as I accosted passengers getting off the streetcar, yelling "Candles!" at the top of my voice. It didn't take long to sell out, compelling me to run back to the gate and refill my pockets.

I don't remember the exact deal I struck with Manci néni, but I think she told me to charge a price higher than the official one so I could pocket the difference. People undoubtedly knew that they were paying a premium, but enough of them couldn't resist the charm of a little blue-eyed, blond boy aggressively pushing his candles. I loved this job and proudly went home and handed over all the money I made to my mother.

The Household Store Manci néni ran was right around the cor-ner from us at the corner of Fűzér Street and Kőrösi Csoma Road, the main commercial street that had streetcars running through our neighborhood. She would often ask me to work a few hours on weekends and in the afternoons at the store. I was fiercely proud of working behind the counter, assisting customers, or running down to the basement to bring up various products from storage. Manci néni would pay me and never forgot to remind me that I had to give all my money I earned to my mother.

Manci néni's full name was Maria Balogh, and she lived with her mother in a nice second-floor apartment in the corner building where her Household Store was located. Her brother Laci, a large man who looked and spoke like a farmer, showed up a few times a year. He was officially residing in his sister's apartment, although he never actually lived there.

Under communism, limitations were imposed on the size of apart-ments families could occupy, depending on the number of people living there. The apartment Manci néni lived in with her mother (large foyer, kitchen, maid room, walk-in pantry, bathroom, and two large living/bedrooms) was deemed excessive and socially unacceptable. Without her brother registered to live there, she would have had to give up her "luxury" apartment, which happened after her mother died.

As a child, I slept many nights in Manci néni's apartment, where we shared her bed. Without any explanation, my mother would just tell me that I was to spend the night there. I actually liked sleeping there, in much greater comfort than was possible in our apartment. As I got older, I realized that those nights were when my mother wanted to have the apartment to herself during her courtship with Lajos Erőd and perhaps others.

Manci néni played a significant role in my life up until the very last days I lived in Hungary. I still have the silver cigarette holder she gave me as a present for my eighteenth birthday. Of course, she couldn't resist inscribing the following admonition on the inside:

Remember and listen to good advice.
From Manci néni
1956, January 11.

While growing up, I always loved working, no matter the job. It wasn't just the money but the knowledge that every little bit I could make helped my mother. I just liked working, especially if it was outdoors.

Before high school, I could only handle odd jobs like the ones Manci néni gave me. I held two different jobs for the Budapest Transit Authority. In the summer, they would hire young people to remove the grass from around the tracks of the streetcars. In the winter, it was to shovel the snow off those same tracks after midnight when the streetcars stopped running. When I got older, in high school, I shoveled coal for the railroad company, dug ditches for an irrigation system, and worked in a canning factory during a summer break.

I didn't have many luxuries in life. I never had a bicycle to ride or a new soccer ball to kick around when I was a child. Even certain food items were scarce. We had meat once a week, typically chicken. However, no matter how poor we were, there were families living in even worse conditions.

I recall my mother telling me that she didn't throw out some of my pants, jackets, or shirts that I outgrew or that were too worn out for me to wear. Instead, she gave them away to another family in need. I was surprised to see one of my classmates sporting my old pants in high school. Of course, I didn't say anything, not wanting to embarrass my classmate, but somehow I could tell that he knew where his pants came from.

He lived in a tenement area on the other side of the elevated railroad tracks that went through Kőbánya in a neighborhood in which I never set foot. When I relayed this coincidence to my mother, she disclosed that she knew the mother of my classmate and promised to help her with some used clothes.

My mother had very strong feelings about our class status, which she articulated often. In her mind, we were middle class, despite all the physical evidence surrounding our daily existence. Part of this was sheer denial. But another part of it was a stubborn clinging to the life she used to have before she got married, living with her parents in much better conditions.

My mother was the only sibling who remained unmarried after the war. Her widowed sisters and one brother who lost his family all remarried and had a relatively comfortable lifestyle. Poor luck was to blame for our situation. My mother spoke with disdain with regard to the "proli,"[1] the lowest or poorest class of people. In her view, only gypsies existed below the proli, thus teaching me about the importance one attaches to his or her perceived class status.

I am not a psychologist or sociologist, but I am willing to speculate that people have an instinctive psychological need, perhaps even a biological one, to find a stratum of people within their society that occupies the level below them. This self-delusional manner of looking down on or even despising a group of people most likely attempts to compensate for a lack of self-worth.

My mother's attitude about our status reflected her opinion about our neighbors, who lived in similar apartments. We had no

---

[1] A slang expression for the *proletariat* or *working class*.

social contact with any of them, except the Gyura family, who lived adjacent to us. A wall separated their kitchen from ours.

Mr. Gyura was a painter and painted our apartment every few years to cover up the inevitable trace of the smoke from our stoves. They had one daughter, Juci, who was my age. We literally grew up together in very close proximity for seventeen years, which explains my early familiarity with the female anatomy. I never forgot the time when we were about eight years old and Mrs. Gyura found us in the yard behind some rubble with our pants down playing "doctor."

I liked the Gyura family a great deal. They were decent people, except for Mr. Gyura's occasional bout with drinking. Through them I was introduced to their pastor at the neighborhood Protestant church in 1944. My mother asked the pastor to convert me in order to escape the pending deportation of Budapest's Jews. This may be speculation, but it is probable that my mother may have made a deal with Mr. and Mrs. Gyura that if I became a Protestant and something happened to her, they would take care of me.

I have many pleasant memories of living next to the Gyuras. I still recall helping Juci decorate their Christmas tree. I was always invited to their apartment on Christmas Day when Juci opened her presents. To my great pleasure, they usually had one for me too.

In 1955, Mr. Gyura decided to install plumbing in order to have a water outlet and a sink on their kitchen wall. This was an opportunity for us to do the same. My mother paid Mr. Gyura to install a faucet and sink on our side, a great improvement in our standard of living. It was revolutionizing to no longer go outside for water every time I wanted to drink or if my mother wanted to cook. Other than that, the only other "upgrade" to our apartment during my seventeen years of residence was the installation of a small wall lamp above my bed.

Because her factory shift started as early as six o'clock in the morning, my mother usually went to bed early. As an avid reader from an early age, I could have sat on one of the two very uncomfortable backless wooden stools at the ends of the kitchen table, reading my books. Instead, I could read in bed with the small wall lamp providing just enough light without disturbing my mother. With some knowledge of electricity, I decided to do the wiring myself. It worked just fine as long as I gently turned the switch on. Due to occasional carelessness, I got shocked quite a few times.

There were other families on our side of the courtyard with children close to my age, but I hardly ever played with them. These people fell into the "proli" class, as my mother referred to them, but never explicitly told me to stay away from them. I could sense that she preferred that I did.

The only other family I became familiar with was the Kovács family, who lived two doors down. I don't recall ever seeing Mr. Kovács, but Mrs. Kovács was known as the "washerwoman." She did the wash for other families in a cellar room located under the apartments across the courtyard. It contained a hot water boiler, a huge washtub, and a mangling machine that squeezed the water out of the washed sheets and clothing. Even my mother hired Mrs. Kovács from time to time to do our wash, though she could barely afford it.

I watched Mrs. Kovács do the wash many times, fascinated by the process. I even spent a few nights at their place, sharing a bed with her older teenage son, when my mother asked me to do so. Looking back, I often wonder why I never questioned why it was necessary for me to sleep at other people's homes.

The last apartment on our side to the right belonged to the superintendent and his wife. They were an elderly couple whose job was to take care of the garbage, lock the building gates at night and open them in the early morning, place the wooden box over the public water outlet for the winter season, take care of the clogged toilets, and maintain the public places in our building.

Interestingly, I never felt resentful about the fact that I was deprived of what other kids had. Even as a child, I fully understood that my mother did the very best she could do for me. Maybe I was "brainwashed" by Manci néni and my mother's older brother, Uncle Laci, that I had some responsibility to shoulder my mother's burden of hard, physical labor. It is now evident that a sense of duty and appreciation for my mother's hard work were instilled in me from early on.

A speech made at my bar mitzvah on January 11, 1951, my thirteenth birthday, illustrated my industrious background. It was given by Dr. Kálmán, the chief rabbi of the great synagogue of District X in Budapest. I found his handwritten speech on the inside of the Hebrew prayer book he gave me as a present, which I translated from Hungarian:

> My son! Let this prayer book be your life's guide and source of strength.
>
> *My first advice:* Try to recover from the wounds inflicted on you. Do not brood over the past: become a man of sound mind, sound heart, of strong will, and action. Your challenge will be how to accomplish that.
>
> *Listen to my second advice for the road you will travel:* Depend on yourself to make up for what the mad devastation of which the evil years deprived you: a father and his advice! Depend on yourself to harden your own character, to develop your own principles, to enjoy work, and to brace against life's inevitable disappointments.
>
> *My third advice:* Trust yourself! You grew up in front of me. I know you to be more responsible than many grown-ups. I have known you for years and we like each other. Look at me! Promise me that you will always be a truly good man, an affectionate son of your self-sacrificing mother, and a devoted student of the ancient Torah— may its blessings follow your life.
>
> January 11, 1951 [5711 in the Hebrew calendar] Dr. Kálmán, Rabbi

My response was a short speech, which I cannot believe now that I was thirteen. The word *responsibility* appears at least three times in my speech of only fourteen lines:

Shema Yisrael: Adonai Eloheinu, Adonai echad!
[Transliteration from Hebrew]

Hear, O Israel: The Lord is our God, the Lord is One!

Almighty Father!

This is my bar mitzvah celebration and I pray to you, amongst the ancestral Torahs, and in front of all who are present.

Lord! Give me a sound mind in a sound body to fulfill all the responsibilities that await me towards myself, my dear and loving mother, and towards all of society.

I wish that on the road I will travel, all my steps be guided at all times by serious and sober-minded considerations. I want to adhere to noble principles at all times with rock-solid steadfastness.

I know that I have more responsibilities than others because only the spirit of my father is here with me. But I feel that I have the confidence not to shirk additional responsibilities and the work that awaits me. Oh God, I hope you can see that, young as I am, in my soul, there is the desire to remain faithful to our past traditions and to follow the biblical parental command, "Love your fellow men because they are like you." I like to work; I want to be productive and to be a useful member of society.

I pray to you, God, please grant these wishes. Amen!

There was no big party and celebration at my bar mitzvah. The whole ceremony lasted no more than twenty minutes. I had to read and chant a portion of the Torah, which I did rather well. Mr. Lőwinger, the cantor of the synagogue (the religious official who leads the musical part of the service), came to our house for about two months to teach me how to chant my assigned Torah reading. I was worried that my neighbors would hear me sing in Hebrew, a strange language, and I didn't want to be embarrassed.

It is possible that a few of my Jewish friends from our neighborhood were there, but I don't recall any of my extended family being present. Looking back now, I realize that in 1951 we were living through the worst of the Stalinist era. People were afraid to go to church or synagogue and openly practice their religion.

The fact that my Uncle Laci didn't attend my bar mitzvah has bestowed a long-lasting feeling of resentment that has been difficult for me to reconcile. I had no male family members present at such an important event in my life. My mother alluded to some kind of excuse for him, but I think she, too, was very upset.

As I got older and entered into high school, I spent my summer months working. I don't recall any vacations, except once when my mother and I went to the famous Lake Balaton, the largest lake in Central Europe, for a few days. During the Communist era, only the privileged class, which consisted of politicians, high-level Communist Party officials, and members of the Interior Ministry (the secret police), could regularly vacation there. In addition, companies (all government owned) would send their best workers and their families there for a week of paid vacation. My mother and I must have gone there when she was the party secretary of the local Chinoin plant.

While vacations were rare, we had frequent weekend outings. Since Saturdays were compulsory workdays, the weekend was only on Sunday. A popular destination for the well-to-do middle-class from Pest was a place called Római, a small village along the western shore of the Danube, just north of the city. In English, the word "Római" means "Roman," derived from the Roman Empire, which occupied most of western Hungary.

Just a mile south of the village are the ruins of the ancient city of Aquincum, where about six thousand Roman soldiers were garrisoned around AD 41–54. Aquincum is now a museum I frequently visited as a child. Designed as weekend or summer getaways, the houses at Római were tiny. For those who could afford it, the idea was to find respite for a few days or weeks from both the air and noise pollution of the city.

We could never afford to have a weekend house at Római, but once again Manci néni came to our rescue. Through her we became friendly with Mr. and Mrs. Ferenci, whom I called Misi bácsi and Sári néni. They had a small house there with a little garden in both the front and back of the house.

Misi bácsi used to own a paint store that was taken over by the government and merged with the chain of Household Stores, which is probably how Manci néni met them. The couple had no children of their own and adopted a baby girl whose name was Kati.

I must have been about thirteen years old when we met the Ferenci family. By then, Kati, who was two or three years older than I, was a fully matured young lady. We became friendly with Kati and her parents and visited them many times in their expansive apartment off Baross Street near the center of the city. Kati took piano lessons for many years, and I still remember their grand piano in the living room.

During the summer months, I always anticipated spending a Sunday at the Római with Kati and her parents, along with some other friends of the Ferenci family. Either my mother or Manci néni prepared lunch before departing early in the morning, taking at least two connecting streetcars to the Buda side of the city where the electric train journeyed toward Római.

After less than an hour, we disembarked the train at Aquincum and walked about a mile or so to the house owned by the Ferencis'. Upon arrival, we immediately donned our swimsuits and enjoyed the fresh air and the breeze emanating from the river. The highlight of the day was the *ebéd*, the midday lunch, which according to European custom was the big meal of the day.

After lunch, all the grown-ups proceeded to take a nap and Kati and I went for a walk or a swim or just hung around in the backyard. It's hard to believe that one could actually swim in the Danube in those days before the river became thoroughly polluted during the ensuing decades.

Misi bácsi belonged to a rowing club, and we occasionally had the opportunity to take a boat out on the river. Being a city boy who grew up on the asphalt of the city, spending a day at Római was a refreshing experience.

I also looked forward to the trip home from Római. As dusk settled in, we packed up all our belongings and everyone, including the Ferenci family, began our walk toward the train station. There were several outdoor beer gardens along the way, and we usually stopped at one to have a small snack and a beer. Since there were no age restrictions or cars to drive, I was permitted to partake in the beer drinking. By this time of the evening, I was tired and sunburned, so it was a welcomed pleasure to listen to the gypsy band while sipping a brew.

I would be remiss if I didn't mention that being with Kati provided another attraction for me. She wasn't particularly beautiful and was a bit on the stocky side, yet was rather promiscuous. Although she had a boyfriend in the building where she lived, she didn't hesitate to make sexual advances toward me and other boys she knew. While we didn't go all the way, there was plenty of kissing, touching, and hanky-panky happening out of sight of the parents.

My other favorite weekend destination during the summer season was the Palatinus open-air swimming complex. It is located in the middle of Margaret Island in the center of the city and has eleven different heated pools that catered to the very young to the very old. I went there many times with my mother when I was a child. As I grew older, I frequented the place with my friends. We sported our small and tight-fitting swimsuits, as was and still is the custom in Europe, wanting to get as deep a tan as we could. The highlight of these visits was always to meet some girls our age and just have fun.

I tried my best to be a good son to my mother and help her out as much as possible. I'll never forget my daily winter routine after coming home from high school or track-and-field practice while my mother was still at work. The apartment was always freezing, and it was my responsibility to get the potbelly stove fired up.

I would first empty the ashes, then take them out to the garbage dump. If necessary, I would go down to the cellar across the courtyard to fetch some wood kindling and coal. Within thirty minutes of starting the fire, the room would be warm enough to be comfortable. Afterward, all that was left was to ensure that the fire stayed lit by feeding the stove with wood or coal.

And so, I lived the life of a young boy in the working class: short of the many physical comforts of those in better neighborhoods, surviving on a restricted diet of meat only once a week, seeking pleasure in my sports activities, finding happiness with friends and family, reading books, and attaining satisfaction in my school activities.

Food is a recurring theme in this story, not because I have some sort of food fetish, but because I never had the good fortune to have a proper diet when I most needed it in my adolescence. My worst memory is the years while I was in high school. School typically ended around one o'clock in the afternoon, and I needed to have a midday meal, the main meal of the day in Europe.

I could never afford to eat in a restaurant, and the only choice left was to eat in our neighborhood government-run eatery, a small place with about ten tables and the kitchen in the back. With white tablecloths and a couple of waiters in white aprons serving the mostly working-class patrons, it was clean enough. They offered a weekly subscription with a slight discount to two types of menus: one with meat and one without. Naturally, I could only afford the one without, the main course consisting of some kind of vegetable and/or pasta dish.

Fortunately, Hungarian cooking is extraordinarily creative when it comes to making a dish out of vegetables. Unlike the typical American style of cooked vegetables, Hungarian vegetable cooking requires the use of roux. During my high school years, I had my daily fill of beans, cabbage, carrots, cauliflower, green beans, kohlrabi, lentils, mushrooms, peas, potatoes, spinach, string beans, and many others. These were made in a variety of ways, only exceeded by the variety of pasta dishes in the Hungarian kitchen. In fact, our Hungarian cookbook describes dozens of varieties of pasta dishes.

Since I preferred noodles over vegetables, it wasn't unusual for me to have a bowl of soup, followed by a hearty serving of pasta. The best part of the meal was the daily fresh-baked bread, with no limit on how much I could eat. On the rare occasion that my mother took pity on me, I would have enough money to pay for the menu with meat.

Fortunately, the lack of sufficient protein in my diet didn't adversely affect my desire to read everything I could put my hands on. From the very first time I went to school, I was captivated by reading. I devoured everything, even if I didn't understand the content.

It was an added bonus when I could decipher every visible sign as my mother and I traveled into the city on a streetcar to visit family members. Kneeling on the wooden seat next to the window, I would try to read the names of the small retail establishments we passed by. Any new word fascinated me. I will never forget the name of the owner of a retail store: *Mrs. Oszwald Postpisil.* I made a sport out of trying to catch that name every time we rode by.

As I got older, I joined the local library, which I often frequented. My mother's friend Mrs. Klein lived in a nice apartment and had a collection of classical books. Mrs. Klein was educated; she spoke English, German, and French. She was a widow and had a son about my age, Róbert. He and I never became friends, but I was invited to visit Mrs. Klein's apartment, and she would select a book for me to read.

Some of the books weren't available in the library because of the regime's strict censorship of any "Western" literature that might have shed some light on the unfavorable differences between our way of life and that of the rest of the free world. It was thanks to Mrs. Klein that I was introduced to some of the writings of Stendhal, Maupassant, and Maugham.

My favorite writer was Alexandre Dumas. I must have read *The Three Musketeers* a dozen times as a teenager. The names of the key characters, d'Artagnan, Athos, Porthos, and Aramis, remained in my mind forever.

Reading at night after my mother had gone to bed, with the aid of my little wall-mounted light, was one of the happiest experiences I had as a child. Through these books, I was able to transplant myself into different worlds, experience different customs and lifestyles that I knew were unattainable for me.

The year of 1956 was an important milestone. Graduating from high school and entering the university would start a new chapter in my life, and I was ready. Well, almost. I knew I had the grades to meet the entrance requirements unless something drastic happened during the final written and oral examinations. The only thing lacking was a suit for my graduation; fortunately, my mother's ingenuity came to my rescue.

I never owned a suit prior to my graduation from high school. Back in the 1950s, there were no department stores to offer reasonably priced suits. In fact, a consumer economy didn't exist in Hungary at that time. If one needed a suit, one had to go to a tailor and have one custom-made, which was quite the expense. Nevertheless, my mother decided her son deserved a new suit for his graduation.

The only well-known tailor in our district at that time was Mr. Fehér, who had a shop in his apartment on the main street in our district on Kőrösi Csoma Road. My mother made a deal with Mr. Fehér

12. High school graduation picture.

85

to pay for my suit in cash and in alcohol. The cash part was paid over time while the alcohol was delivered, as my mother smuggled it out of her chemical factory.

The moral dilemma of my mother's smuggling alcohol out of her factory might have had an impact on my sense of right and wrong. In reality, we lived in a socialistic society where all means of production, factories, businesses, farms, etc., were owned by the state. In fact, the communist propaganda proudly extolled the virtues of a society where the workers and farmers, not the rich and the elite aristocracy, owned everything. A logical extension of this philosophy was incorporated in the sarcastic and popular saying, "Since we owned everything it was okay to take from the state. After all, we took only what was ours anyway." On the other hand, my mother did try to impart that stealing was wrong.

One day, when I was about nine years old, I walked out of our house and discovered half of an envelope sticking out of the wall-mounted mailbox that was next door. Curiosity took over and I pulled the envelope out and opened it to find a short letter, together with a ten-Forint[1] bill. I immediately realized that what I did was wrong but decided to cover up my infraction by telling my mother that I found the money.

My mother was suspicious, so I finally told her the truth. She scolded me and forced me to go next door to the post office, hand over the bill, and tell the post office clerk what I did and apologize. She followed me and watched me at some distance away to ensure I did what I was told. This morality lesson about stealing stayed with me all my life, and created a moral conundrum of how to square that with my mother's smuggling alcohol out of her factory in order for me to have a suit for graduation.

Naturally, I was thrilled to have my first custom-made suit. I could hardly wait to show up at graduation and show it off. First, the material was selected with great care. Mr. Fehér showed us several

---

[1] The exchange rate (as reported by the *Wall Street Journal* on 10/23/2008) ten Forint would translate into slightly less than five cents, but back then it was probably more like twenty dollars.

foreign-made fabrics and suggested a rather heavy navy-blue English cloth. Then he started measuring my shoulders, arms, chest, waist, and legs to cut the fabric to fit me precisely. I had to see him several times for fittings as he proceeded with assembling the various pieces. Finally, linings, shoulder pads, pockets, and all the other necessary pieces were added, and my suit was finished just in time to wear for my graduation.

I graduated from high school in May of 1956 with good grades, and I was accepted at the well-respected Technical University of Budapest. In addition to the prestige and pride of being a university student, it also provided some financial relief for my mother.

Education was free in Hungary, and those with a low-income family background qualified for financial assistance from the government. In other words, I was paid to go to the university. It wasn't much, but it was enough to minimize my mother's perpetual dependence on Manci néni and other family members. I turned all my "earnings" over to my mother except for some small pocket change. This was the least I could do to pay her back for all she had done for me.

My Family

The story of my adolescence would be incomplete without including my mother's and my father's families. Both the Spitzers and the Reichmanns were large families with ten and nine children, respectively. Fortunately, several of my uncles and aunts and their children survived the Holocaust, and I had the opportunity to get to know those who stayed in Hungary while I was growing up.

Many surviving family members on both sides left Hungary after the war. In an illustrative way, the flight of the Spitzers and the Reichmanns represents a microcosm of the European Jewish Diaspora following the Holocaust. Those family members who no longer felt safe living in Hungary, where their parents, brothers, sisters, and children were murdered, sought a new life in Palestine, which became Israel in 1948. The only exception to that was my Aunt Rutka Reichmann, who wisely decided to leave in 1932 and immigrate to Palestine long before I was born.

The Spitzers

For obvious reasons I became better acquainted with my mother's family, the Spitzers. They had a greater influence on me while growing up than my father's family, the Reichmanns.

The Spitzer family was very close. The surviving brothers and sisters all deeply cared about each other and their families. Many fights and arguments were had among my uncles and aunts, but they loved each other and helped each other when needed.

It didn't occur to me at the time, but it is clear that my mother's surviving sisters and brothers took special care of me. I am sure that it was a natural familial obligation for them since that I was the only orphaned nephew in the family in Hungary. All my widowed uncles and aunts who survived the Holocaust remarried soon after the war, save for Aunt Piri, who remarried after she left for Israel in 1948.

My earliest memories of the Spitzer family are from when I was with my grandparents and two aunts, Piri and Klári, and their children while trying to survive the final months of the Holocaust in late

1944 and early 1945. Following the war, my mother and I often visited my grandparents, Nagypapa and Nagymama, in their spacious apartment on 106 Király Street.

I shall never forget their apartment, where the whole family would gather for major family events like the Jewish High Holidays of Rosh Hashanah,[1] Yom Kippur,[2] or Passover.[3] Most if not all Jewish holidays center around meals, and those images are clear in my memory even now.

Vivid flashbacks of the women scurrying around the kitchen, preparing meals, and the large table set up in the living room to accommodate us all still bring me great joy. It was always impressive that nobody would sit down to eat until my grandfather took his place at the head of the table. He was the first to be served the soup, so hot the vapors rose like smoke from his bowl.

For many years after the war, I was the youngest child who could read in Hebrew, and it was my duty to read the "Four Questions" during the Passover Seder.[4] The words of the opening question are as follows:

> In transliteration it says, "Ma nish-ta-nah ha-lailah hazeh mi-kol ha-lay-lot?"

> In English: "Why is this night different from all other nights?"

I admit that I always needed some help by the time I reached the third question. Passover was exciting because I always got a modest present from my grandfather after I found the hidden half of the *aphikomon*, a piece of matzo hidden by the head of the family during the Passover meal.

---

[1] The Jewish New Year, literally translated as the "head of the year."

[2] Known as the *Day of Atonement*, the most solemn and important of the Jewish holidays.

[3] Celebration in memory of the exodus of the Israelites from Egypt some three thousand years ago.

[4] Seder is a ritual meal held on the first night of Passover.

Unfortunately, my grandmother died when I was about eight years old, so I have vague memories of her. She was a heavyset woman, taller than my grandfather, often with a kind smile on her face. All her children admired her. My grandfather remarried after my grandmother died, and I still remember my mother's explanation to me that he "needed to be taken care of"—which I didn't quite understand at the time.

My grandfather lived for another five or six years, and we used to visit him and his new wife, Olga. He didn't speak much but always had a few questions about my well-being or school. On one of these visits when I was still quite young, he asked me to sit on his lap, where I put my arm around him and kissed him. It was on the way home on the streetcar when my mother told me that my Nagypapa had tears in his eyes when I embraced him, to which I was oblivious. Perhaps I was distracted by his huge handlebar mustache that always mesmerized me.

Two separate incidents at my grandparents' apartment remain clear in my mind. Both of these situations were when I was young and probably happened during one of the holiday celebrations when the apartment was full of people.

The first incident occurred when I decided to take a frozen stick of butter from my grandparents' icebox and slipped it into my pocket as we left the apartment. My rationale was simple. We could rarely afford butter, and there seemed to be plenty left in the icebox.

Unfortunately, not yet aware of the laws of physics, the butter started to melt soon after we boarded the streetcar for the forty-five-minute ride home. It was then that I reached into my coat pocket, and to my surprise, I felt the melted butter stick to my fingers. I got scared, and I was compelled to bring this unanticipated situation to my mother's attention.

Needless to say, she panicked; thus, we embarrassingly disembarked at the earliest stop in order to empty my pocket of the remaining butter that had not yet soaked into my coat. She indignantly asked me, "Why did you take the butter?" The only answer I could conceive was, "So that we could have some too."

The second episode happened on a cold day when all the guests had their winter coats hung up in the foyer. At that time, I was into collecting buttons in order to play button football with my friends. This game required a large, flat table and enough larger buttons to assemble two teams of players with a smaller-sized button—like that on a shirt—as the ball. The buttons were moved around the table by pinching our thumb and forefinger together and pressing down on the edge of the button to propel it forward to "kick" the ball. This game kept us entertained, and we were always on the lookout for additional players (the buttons).

That particular evening at my grandparents' house the temptation was so overwhelming that I decided to cut off some appropriately sized buttons from several of the winter coats hanging in the foyer. Since we usually left first, having lived in the outskirts of the city, nobody noticed the missing buttons until we were well on our way home.

Both of these incidents resulted in a lecture on respecting private property and the serious consequences of appropriating things that are not mine. These incidents remained as part of the family folklore, and decades later when I visited Hungary, they brought forth lots of laughter and fond reminiscences.

Perhaps the most influential Spitzer for me was my Uncle Laci, my mother's oldest brother. Following the war, encouraged by my mother, he assumed a certain parental responsibility due to the loss of my father. On numerous occasions he reminded me that I had a special responsibility to help my mother, who worked hard to support us. He was the one who always encouraged me to study hard and make something of myself. His words still ring in my ears: "Don't forget that you are Róbert Reichmann. Your father, poor Zoli,[1] died young, and you have to become an educated man and make something of your life." Alternatively, his other favorite saying was, "You have to get an education because that is the only thing they cannot take away from you."

---

[1] Nickname for Zoltán, my father's first name.

Uncle Laci was an authority figure for me. When I ran into some trouble at school, my mother would take me to Uncle Laci, who gave me a "lelki fröccs," a Hungarian colloquial expression meaning a spiritual exhortation or warning. He preached that I was to behave responsibly and not create any headaches or hardship for my mother; that my responsibilities included not only to study hard and do well in school, but a frequent reminder was also to help my mother in any way I could. I took these speeches seriously and felt appropriately guilty for my mischief.

13. Uncle Laci visiting us in Atlanta in 2008.

It was clear from a young age that my mother and the other surviving siblings of the Spitzer family all looked up to Uncle Laci, who became the de facto family head. At the same time, his siblings, certainly on my mother's and her sisters' side, definitely felt a resentment that Uncle Laci got preferential treatment from their parents. He was clearly a "mama's boy." He was an educated man, having finished high school, which was quite impressive in those days. Uncle Laci was very articulate and had an impressive mastery of the Hungarian language. He also had an excellent sense of humor that I didn't come to fully appreciate until much later in life. He was good-looking, dressed impeccably, and exuded confidence.

Only much later in life did I learn that this man also had many weaknesses. He was an unashamed philanderer, extremely vain, self-centered, and somewhat aloof. His affairs were an open secret to everyone in the family except his wife, Aunt Klári.

Uncle Laci married Aunt Klári (not to be confused with my mother's sister, Klári), a widow with a son, Péter Oszmann, soon after

92

the war. I recall seeing pictures of Aunt Klári as a stunning beauty around the time of her marriage to Uncle Laci. I didn't get to know Aunt Klári and her son Péter well until after 1952 when I was in high school. I learned much later that the reason we didn't visit Aunt Klári during the years 1948 to 1952 was that she was serving time in jail for being peripherally involved in her sister's escape from Hungary in 1948.

14. Péter Oszmann when he was twenty years old.

Unless I was in some trouble, I looked forward to meeting with my uncle and aunt in their upscale high-rise apartment building located in the center of the city at 18 Balzac[1] Street. They lived on the fifth floor, and riding the elevator was a simple pleasure for me. Their building had central heating that, in comparison to our potbelly stove, was a marvel of technology. The foyer was about as large as our living room. Their elegantly furnished living room had a sofa bed, where Uncle Laci and Aunt Klári slept. Their son, Péter, four years older than I, had his own room with an upright piano in it.

Spending time with Péter, whenever he happened to be around, was appealing because of his many talents, and I was enticed by one of his early childhood love stories. More than six decades later, I can still recount the Latin phrase "Odi et Amo"[2] that Péter used as a dedication in his collected poems.

---

[1] Named after Honoré de Balzac (1799–1850), famous French novelist and playwright.
[2] Latin meaning "I hate you; I love you." It is the first line of a poem written by the Roman poet Catullus to his lover in the first century BC.

Péter's talents extended to music, painting, and poetry. One summer afternoon he took me to see Gershwin's *Porgy and Bess*[1] musical production at the outdoor theater on Budapest's Margaret Island. After the show we went back to his apartment, and he sat down in front of his piano and replayed some of the key tunes from memory.

Over the years I became very fond of my step cousin, and I always considered him one of my favorites. I wished that I had only a fraction of his talent. It is conceivable that these early childhood impressions influenced my decision to take up playing the piano at the age of sixty. Several of Péter's sketches hang on the walls of our home, and I still enjoy reading his poems and stories.[2]

Clearly, compared to our standard of living, Uncle Laci, Aunt Klári, and Péter lived a luxurious life to my occasional benefit. For example, I remember that my first real ski boots were Péter's hand-me-downs. They were a little too big but still better than wearing my school boots to go skiing.

I had a pair of old wooden skis without a safety binder, which didn't evolve until the 1950s or '60s, that my mother somehow got for me. Before Péter's boots, using my school boots resulted in them being completely soaked, which necessitated drying them next to the hot potbelly stove to go to school in them the next day.

Skiing in Hungary in the 1950s was quite different from skiing in the Colorado mountains in my later life. On a hill called Normafa, almost 4,500 feet in elevation at the outskirts of Budapest, there wasn't even a rope tow. There was one ungroomed trail. Only the hardiest of skiers could make two or three runs a day since the only way to the top was on foot, carrying your skies on your back.

Of all the first cousins I have had on both sides of my family, I feel closest to Péter. His talents and his superb sense of black humor have intrigued me all my life. But most of all, I have to thank him

---

[1] Opera with music by George Gershwin (1898–1937), libretto by DuBose Heyward (1885–1940), and lyrics by Ira Gershwin (1896–1983).

[2] Sadly, Péter died suddenly due to heart failure in December 2010 in his London apartment. His writings can be found on the following website: http://www.authorsden.com/Peteroszmann.

for being a great older cousin when I needed someone like him while growing up in Hungary, as well as for being a good friend during the decades that followed.

My other Spitzer uncle was Uncle Béla. He lost his entire family during the Holocaust and got remarried after the war to Aunt Piri. (This Piri is not to be confused with my mother's sister Piri.) They soon had a son, Gyuri, one of my youngest cousins. My mother and I visited them frequently, but Gyuri was so much younger that I never really got to know him well until much later in life.

I learned early on that Uncle Béla was the only Spitzer son who didn't finish high school, and perhaps this fact contributed to his undeserved reputation as the "dumb" uncle in the family. From my perspective, he was the kindest uncle I had. All his life, he worked tirelessly and supported his siblings, including my mother, whenever they needed it. I don't think he was dumb at all; just a simple man with a simple desire to raise his new family.

He was an excitable man with a natural disposition for laughing and a good sense of humor. His and his second wife's love for me was obvious. I was welcomed in their home, and they always expressed great interest in my affairs.

They lived in a very nice second-floor apartment in the city at 25 Visegrádi Street. Aunt Piri spoke with a strong accent, something I always associated with her upbringing in a foreign country. In fact, I learned through research for this story that her accent was from a dialect found in a very small town called Dány, only fifty kilometers from Budapest. I could never take my eyes off her tattooed arm, a reminder of her imprisonment at Auschwitz, where her parents and sister perished.

Life has its ironies, and I wish that Uncle Béla, his brothers, and sisters were alive today to witness the academic and business success his only grandson, Tamás, has achieved.[1] Similar to me in the

---

[1] Tamás has an MS in business administration, an MS in computational engineering, and he is now working on his PhD in knowledge management from the University of West-Hungary. He, his Mexican wife, and two daughters now live in Utrecht, a suburb of Amsterdam.

Reichmann family, Tamás Szirtes[1] became the first Spitzer to become a college-educated man.

In order to explain my relationship with my three aunts, Lili, Piri, and Bözske, it is necessary to provide a little more background on the historic Hungarian town of Eger, where my grandparents sent me right after the war. At the risk of sounding like an agent of the Eger Tourist Bureau, I have to describe Eger as I experienced it during my summer vacations there as an adolescent. After all, there was no other place in Hungary, except our tiny apartment in Budapest, where I spent more time than this town. My summers in Eger became an indelible part of my coming-of-age experiences and the source of my fondest memories that I treasure to this day.

Eger is about one hundred kilometers northeast of Budapest. I never lived anywhere other than in a working-class district in a city of two million people characterized by city noise, big apartment buildings, wide paved roads, and congested streetcars and buses. Living in a small town of less than fifty thousand people like Eger was a welcome cultural and environmental change.

Eger is best known for its historic castle, the thermal baths, its Turkish minaret, and its red and white wines. The town has existed since the Stone Age. It had been inhabited by many different nationalities until the Hungarians took over in the tenth century.

Eger and its castle play an important role in Hungary's history, dating back to the sixteenth century. During the Turkish occupation of Hungary, Eger became an important border fortress, successfully defended by Hungarian forces in the 1552 Siege of Eger against overwhelming odds.

The castle's defendants, under the command of Captain István Dobó, numbered fewer than two thousand, including women and children, yet successfully held off the Turkish army of eighty thousand soldiers. Every Hungarian child learns about this heroic battle in

---

[1] My Cousin Tamás changed his last name from Spitzer to Szirtes (*rocky* in English) in 1969, a very Hungarian name, following our Uncle Laci's example (he changed his name to Szirtes soon after WWII).

school, and all were required to read the novel *Eclipse of the Crescent Moon*[1] by nineteenth-century Hungarian author Géza Gárdonyi.

In 1596, Eger was attacked again by a bigger Turkish Army that captured the castle after a short siege. More than ninety years of Ottoman rule followed. The Turks converted the churches to mosques, built minarets and public baths, and rebuilt the castle. The Eger minaret, one of only three minarets left in Hungary, is 120 feet high and still standing.

Luckily for me, my Aunt Piri and Aunt Bözske lived in a two-story building built right along the steep cobblestone ramp leading up to the main entrance of the castle. No sooner would I step out of the gate than I was on the ramp leading to the main entrance. Thus, it was a wonderful opportunity as a child to explore the castle and learn firsthand of its history of famous battles with the Turks.

There was another young boy about my age living in the same building. The two of us spent many days exploring the various hidden tunnels of the castle and, with some trepidation, ogle the hundreds of skulls displayed behind a glass window in the catacombs. Occasionally we found some pieces of ceramic fragments that must have been remnants of a Turkish pipe. My friend and I would go for long walks, surveying the surrounding neighborhoods.

There were many fascinating contrasts between Eger and Budapest. The houses were more colorful and had steep roofs. People were dressed differently, and some even had a strange accent when they spoke. In general, there was a more leisurely and peaceful ambiance in Eger than in Budapest.

It was in the castle that I tried my first cigarette. Hiding in one of the gun placements in the castle wall with my friend, we struck up a match and inhaled the first breath of cigarette smoke. We both choked and coughed violently, and it was a few minutes before we could breathe normally again.

Another favorite place to frequent was the public swim park. It had several pools, including one with only a few feet of water for children to play in, where I taught myself how to swim. I watched

---

[1] "Egri Csillagok" in Hungarian, literally translated "Stars of Eger."

how the older children swam in the regular pool and imitated them. First, I mastered the breaststroke underwater, followed by freestyle swimming.

I spent my first summer vacation living with my Aunt Piri and Aunt Bözske when I was around nine or ten years old. They lived either together or next to each other. Both aunts were widowed after the war, but Aunt Bözske remarried Andor Susinski almost immediately after. Frankly, I don't recall much of my physical living arrangement with them. I was well fed and had all the freedom to do whatever I wanted to do with my time.

Back then,[1] Eger was safe enough for children to wander around, the only danger being that I would get lost and not find my way home, which I came dangerously close to once or twice.

One day on my way home, I came across a park with tall shrubs and several trails winding in different directions. I was contemplating which way to turn when a boy perhaps a few years older than I jumped from behind a bush, screaming and yelling some obscenities. I was scared to death that he was going to kill me right on the spot. There was nobody around us, and the only thing that came to mind was to run like hell.

After this experience I was more careful about finding my way around the city. Perhaps this childhood incident explains my recurring nightmare of being lost and looking for the right street to find my way home.

My older cousins, Aunt Piri's sons, Miklós and Tomi, and Aunt Bözske's sons, Pisti and Gyuri, escaped Hungary in 1946, so I never had a chance to get to know them. I learned much later that Pisti and Gyuri left because they were upset about their mother's marrying less than a year after their father died. Aunt Piri also left Hungary in 1948 and immigrated to Israel to join her sons.

While I very much enjoyed my vacation with my Aunt Piri and Aunt Bözske, I didn't quite feel at home. Both were tall and beautiful

---

[1] I visited Eger with my family in 1998 and found a thriving tourist attraction where the restaurant menus were in five languages: Hungarian, Russian, English, German, and Italian.

women, especially Aunt Piri. They had a certain manner that exuded class and self-confidence that I wasn't used to with my mother in our modest apartment. In other words, they had certain "airs" about them. There were no warm and fuzzy feelings or being treated as if I were one of their sons.

They took care of me in every physical respect, but there was an emotional distance between us. I missed the affection, the hugs, and the kisses I was used to at home and with my other family members. I noticed that there was no visible emotional relationship between my Aunt Bözske and her second husband, Andor.

The Hungarian language, as many others, has different ways of addressing someone close, such as a relative or a friend, versus others such as a stranger or a distant acquaintance, and both my aunts addressed Uncle Andor, and vice versa, in the formal way. This was unusual, as I had never experienced such formality with any other relatives within the Spitzer or the Reichmann families. This conventionalism created an impression that they were more sophisticated than the rest of us. Of course, there was no basis for this since all the Spitzer girls had the same level of education—eight years of public schooling.

Both my aunts were heavy smokers. I can still see them holding their cigarettes in their long, ivory cigarette holders, modeling their usual elegant pose, and blowing out the smoke through their noses. Only nonfilter cigarettes existed in those days, and the butts were disposed in an ashtray.

When the ashtray was full and nobody was looking, I would pick out some butts, collect the tobacco, and roll some cigarettes with my friend for a smoke at our hiding place in the castle. We were obviously oblivious to the fact that smoking was bad for you, possibly leading to cancer.

When I was about twelve or thirteen, I spent one or two summers with my third aunt, Aunt Lili; her husband, Artúr[1]; and their young daughter, Zsuzsi, in Eger. Tragically, Aunt Lili lost both her sons, Imre, aged thirteen, and Gyuri, aged ten, in the Holocaust in Auschwitz. Zsuzsi was born after the war in 1948 and was almost ten years younger than I, too young to be a playmate.

Living with Aunt Lili and her husband Artúr was totally different from living with my other aunts. Aunt Lili was a very kind, soft-spoken, and warm-hearted woman. I could tell that she loved me as if I were her son. She would lovingly bring me lunch when I spent a whole day at the Eger public swim park.

Tickets to the swim park were good for a single entry. I used to go to the park in the morning and be able to stay all day because she made the effort to bring me my meal. At the designated time, I would meet her at the entrance, where she handed me a home-cooked meal in a special carrying dish.

My Aunt Lili differed from her two sisters, Piri and Bözske, even in stature. She was significantly shorter, like my mother, and I never heard her raise her voice. I felt very comfortable in their home. I liked her husband, Uncle Artúr, a great deal. No matter how early I woke up in the morning, Uncle Artúr was already up, reading one of his books. His favorite topics were history, geography, and nature. Sometimes he would explain what he read to me, and I was amazed by the variety of subject matters that interested him.

Since I was an avid reader myself, my uncle's love of reading helped establish a connection between us. Before heading to work, he made his favorite breakfast, a dish called "lecsó," which was made up of onions, green peppers, tomatoes, sausage, and occasionally eggs. Because of this, I prepare lecsó as a weekend brunch to this very day.

Uncle Artúr managed a toy store on the main square of Eger, Dobó Square, named after Captain Dobó, who fought off the Turks

---

[1] Uncle Artúr survived the Holocaust in Miskolc, where his family lived, by hiding with Christian identification papers. How he managed to get hold of these documents and managed to stay alive is another story of Jewish survival outside the scope of my book.

in 1552. The shelves of the small store were overflowing with toys, stuffed animals, and games. The highlight of my stay with Aunt Lili and Uncle Artúr was when he took me to the annual country fair, where he set up his table and displayed the toys. This was another unusual experience for me that I thoroughly enjoyed. When lunchtime came, Uncle Artúr gave me some money for a grilled sausage fresh off the grill at a nearby stand. No frankfurter or hot dog has ever tasted as good as these sausages. Just thinking about it makes my mouth water.

Aunt Lili lived on the opposite side of town from her sisters. As a result, I became familiar with the part of town that was near the cathedral of Eger, the largest in Hungary, built between 1831 and 1836. Aunt Lili was in charge of a home for orphaned children close to my age. My aunt and her family lived in a separate house from the one where the children lived.

Once I became friends with some of the boys my age, I was allowed to sleep in their dormitory. Otherwise, I slept in the same large bed with Zsuzsi on one side, Aunt Lili and Uncle Artúr in the middle, and I on the other side. The home had a few girls too.

One of them, a girl about my age or even younger, was so strong that none of the boys, including myself, could ever wrestle her to the ground. It was surprising that a skinny little girl, physically smaller than us boys, could fight us off just by being feisty and strong spirited.

It was at Aunt Lili's place where I found a sizable tree limb in the yard that must have weighed about thirty or forty pounds. I tried to lift it and hold it above my head like a professional weight lifter, despite not being able to do even a couple of push-ups.

The next day I played with that piece of wood and continued to lift it every day that summer. In two months, I could do several repetitions of consecutive push-ups without any problem. Additionally, my pectoral muscles had visibly grown. It was then that I first realized the possibility of changing the shape of my body with physical exercise.

This propensity for physical fitness stayed with me throughout my whole life, having always been a "jock" and taking great care to stay in shape up until to this very ripe old age of eighty-two.

Today there are no more Spitzers left in Eger. My cousins left in 1946. Aunt Piri left in 1948, and the rest—Aunt Bözske and her husband Andor, Aunt Lili and her husband Artúr, and their daughter Zsuzsi—all left in early 1956. All of them ended up in Israel, and Eger has since turned into one of Hungary's most successful tourist attractions.

My fourth Spitzer aunt, Aunt Klári, never left Budapest, which is where I got to know her as I grew up. She, her husband, Sándor, and their paralyzed son, Iván, lived with my grandparents. Iván passed away very soon after the war, so I never got to know him well. The only image I have of Cousin Iván is when his mother was helping him to urinate.

Since Iván was paralyzed from the waist down, Aunt Klári had to hold a pot for him to relieve himself into while he was sitting in his wheelchair. I had a direct view of Iván peeing into his mother's face instead of aiming it into the pot, all the while laughing hysterically. This blatant insult to my aunt was quite shocking, and this, together with my aunt's subsequent anger and verbal scolding, is vivid in my memory.

Even though I was never close to Aunt Klári as a child, I could tell she was different just by listening to the conversations and arguments among the brothers and sisters. My mother often complained to Manci néni about her unwillingness to get a job and support herself and her lifestyle. It was baffling at the time, because Aunt Klári had a husband, Sándor Schwartz (who later changed his name to Fekete);[1] who looked and acted quite healthy and able to work.

Uncle Sándor was very good-looking, tall, and debonair, with a very friendly disposition, and was always impeccably dressed. Only much later, I learned that he was a cardplayer with other similar vices, leaving him perpetually broke. Aunt Klári frequently got all done up, sporting her high-heeled shoes with stockinged feet and makeup on her face. I was told that she never worked a day in her life.

---

[1] *Schwartz* is the German word for "black"—which translates into *Fekete* in Hungarian.

According to my mother, she announced that having already lost two children (both died of polio, but I only knew Iván, the older one) was enough tragedy for her to bear. She expected her husband to keep her in style, and when he couldn't, it was the rest of the family's responsibility to finance her extravagant taste.

This was the source of my mother's anger at her sister for expecting everyone to contribute to her frivolous lifestyle while she worked tirelessly to provide for her family. Nevertheless, support her they did, so Aunt Klári always had enough to live the life she wanted.

When I would visit Aunt Klári in high school, she never missed an opportunity to ask me if I had a girlfriend and was curious about my "love affairs." Unfortunately, those conversations were rather brief. I liked Aunt Klári and was rather fascinated by her and her husband's seemingly unconventional lifestyle. It became clear to me much later that they had what today would be called an "open marriage." Aunt Klári had her love affairs and her husband had his. Yet they stayed together and maintained an amiable relationship to each other.

All my Spitzer uncles and aunts are dead now. The last of the Spitzers, the self-described "Last Mohican," Aunt Piri, died in January of 2005 in Sydney, Australia, at the age of ninety-six. My living cousins, some of whom I got to know only after I left Hungary, are spread all over the world.

Uncle Béla's son Gyuri Szirtes still lives in Budapest. Cousin Zsuzsi Antebi, Aunt Lili's daughter, lives in Toronto, Canada, and Aunt Piri's younger son, Tomi Grossman, lives in Sydney, Australia. I had the good fortune to visit almost all my cousins and to establish a connection as adults. While a few of my cousins have passed away, I still maintain good relations with those who are still alive.

As I mentioned earlier, my mother's family, consisting of my grandparents, aunts, uncles, and cousins, were very important to me in my adolescence. They gave me a sense of belonging and a strong feeling of being loved. Perhaps the reason was because I was the only nephew in the family without a father. All my cousins had fathers since everybody remarried after the war except my mother.

The strong sense of familial duty to protect everyone in the family extended beyond taking care of Aunt Klári to helping my mother with raising me on her own. I regret that I didn't express my appreciation to my family of all the support they provided to my mother and me while they were still alive. I am forever grateful for their kindness and genuine love for me.

Finally, the last ethic the Spitzer family instilled in me was the importance of education as a means of making my life meaningful. From early childhood on, getting a college education was given, not an option, and I never questioned it.

The Reichmanns

Understandably, my interaction with my father's side of my family was much less frequent than with my mother's. My mother ensured that I also got to know the Reichmanns as I grew up. It would have been easier and probably more convenient for my mother to forget about them, but had she done that, I would have missed out on a lot of wonderful relationships in both my early and later years.

Supposedly, I met my grandfather on the Reichmann side many times when I was very young and my father was still alive, but I have no recollection of him. Therefore, all my knowledge about him comes from hearsay through my uncles, aunts, and cousins. He was a warm-hearted, generous man with a passion for cards and a difficult time sup-

15. Reichmann Nagypapa, in his forties, and Nagymama, probably in her seventies.

porting his large family. Apparently, education was not a high priority for the Reichmanns since none of the boys finished high school like the Spitzers. Instead, the older ones, like my father, had to work and help support the family from the time they were teenagers.

On the other hand, I have very fond memories of my grandmother. A recently discovered picture of my Reichmann grandfather, posted on a genealogical website by one of my cousins in Israel, shattered the family folklore of the "Reichmann look."

All my life I have heard references made about the Reichmann look that were attributed to some of my uncles, aunts, and cousins, which primarily characterized the shape of their lips. Indeed, I found this single feature present on the Reichmann uncles. Now I am convinced that the Reichmann look doesn't come from my grandfather at all, but is most definitely inherited from my grandmother. At the risk of antagonizing some of my family, I characterize this look more so as the "Rosenberg look," my grandmother's family.

Unfortunately, the only picture I have of my Reichmann uncles and aunts is from about 1933, five years before I was born. Guessing that my Uncle Bandi, in the front, is about two years old in the picture and seven years older than I am, I would have been minus five years old when this picture was taken. Ergo, the date of the picture is 1933.

16. The Reichmann children, circa 1933.

In the back row from left to right are Uncle Sanyi, my father Zoli, and Uncle Elek. In the middle stand Aunt Lena, Aunt Elza, and Aunt Vica,[1] and in the front are Uncle Bandi and Aunt Magda. The only Reichmann sibling missing from this picture is Aunt Rutka, who

---

[1] Vica is a nickname for Éva, but I never knew her real name until many years later after I left Hungary.

was already in Palestine. In fact, this picture was taken to be sent to her.

By the time I was old enough to have any memories of the Reichmann family, Uncle Sanyi, the oldest one, and Uncle Bandi, the youngest one, had left Hungary in 1946. Aunt Lena perished in the Bergen-Belsen concentration camp in early 1945 when she was twenty-three years old. Growing up, I only had the chance to get to know Uncle Elek and my aunts: Vica, Magda, Elza, and their families.

The most extensive memories I have are with Aunt Vica. She and my mother had a very good relationship. As a result, I probably visited her more frequently than any of the other Reichmann family members. I can recall her very large and spacious second-floor apartment at 13 Baross[1] Square, with

17. Reichmann Nagymama visiting my mother in our kitchen in 1958.

a narrow balcony facing the Eastern Railroad station of Budapest. Their living room was approximately eighteen feet by twenty feet, but in square footage it was twice the size of our "living room." My grandmother lived with Aunt Vica, where I recall meeting her several times. She was one of the few relatives who came to visit us at our home in Kőbánya.

Aunt Vica survived the Holocaust as I did in the Budapest Ghetto. In fact, that is where she gave birth to my Cousin Jutka on December 10, 1944. Unfortunately, Aunt Vica's husband was murdered in Austria in early 1945. He was forced to march on foot with

---

[1] Gábor Barros (1848–1892), minister of Public Works and Transport. He is credited with the founding of the Hungarian State Railway. The station was built in 1884 and was Central Europe's most modern railroad station for decades.

fellow Hungarian Jews to a concentration camp in Austria. Because of a leg injury, he couldn't keep up with the others, and a German guard shot him in the head. Jutka never got to know her father.

Aunt Vica's generosity toward me was illustrated by her willingness to let me stay with her while I was working for the railroad one summer. I had to catch the train around six in the morning, leaving the Eastern Railway station near where Aunt Vica lived.

I would leave the house around five in the morning to arrive at the station on time. I would get off someplace outside Budapest and shovel coal from a railroad car onto a siding for the next six hours before taking the train back to Budapest. I looked like a coal miner by the end of the day from all the dirt, but I didn't mind. It was hard, physical work. I considered it good exercise; and they paid me well.

Due to living in an outlying district of the city, it took me an additional hour to get back and forth to the railroad station. Aunt Vica was kind enough to allow me to stay with her many nights that summer, saving me hours of travel.

In 1948 Aunt Vica remarried Miklós Schwartz, whom she knew from her youth when they were both active in a Hashomer Hatzair (*Youth Guard*), the Zionist youth movement in the early 1930s. I got to know Uncle Miklós when I was a teenager, and he started to indoctrinate me on his political philosophy, economics, finance, and other "grown-up" topics that I never quite comprehended. He probably should have been a teacher because he enjoyed lecturing.

He actually completed his higher education under the Communist era in the 1950s, earning a degree in architecture, which led him to a job as an asset appraiser in a bank. He transferred some of his enthusiasm from Zionism to Communism but was eventually disillusioned by the ruthless realities of the system. I respected Uncle Miklós because he treated me as an adult, even though he didn't give me much opportunity to contribute to our discussions.

My mother was always happy to take me along when she wanted to visit Aunt Vica. My presence assured that Uncle Miklós's attention was directed at me and that she didn't have to listen to what she characterized as his "süket duma"—a slang Hungarian expression loosely translated as "claptrap," of which she understood even less than I did. In a testament to his dedication to the Zionist cause, he "Hungarianized" his name in 1950 to Somrai, a derivative of Hasomer. Their son, my Cousin Pisti, was born in May 1956, the year I left Hungary, and I got to know him years later when we met in Israel.

As mentioned before, the oldest Reichmann son, Uncle Sanyi, left Hungary with his wife, Ella, and only daughter, Éva, in 1946 and headed for Palestine. I had very little chance to get to know my Cousin Éva while she lived in Hungary, although she claims that we spent a lot of time together. We remained in close contact through letters and pictures throughout our youth. In fact, she became one of my closest Reichmann cousins, as we got to know each other and our families some decades later in Canada and in Israel.

18. Cousin Eva Reichmann in her IDF (Israeli Defense Forces) uniform.

She sent me a picture in her Israeli Defense Force uniform when I was nineteen years old, and I remember how proud I was to have such a beautiful cousin. She wrote on the back of the picture, "To Robi from your older cousin with love, Éva." In one glance at the picture, I immediately fell in love with my cousin, whose beauty I remember bragging to my friends about.

My only recollection of her family in Hungary is limited to an incident with her mother, Aunt Ella. Aunt Ella had a tendency to faint at any place, at any time, without any warning, which is exactly what happened while we were on a streetcar. She had to be taken off the car and laid out on a bench at the stop until she came to. My mother was so upset that Aunt Ella couldn't control herself and had the audacity to faint in public, causing a nuisance for everybody.

I always felt a somewhat strange relationship with Uncle Elek because of the circumstances surrounding my father's death. As a child I wanted to know about what happened to my father in Austria, but I knew not to ask him, and he never said anything. In retrospect, as I look back and try to analyze this situation, I conclude that our shared tragedy of my father's death and my uncle's silence about it had created a barrier between us instead of bringing us closer.

Uncle Elek got married after the war, and his two boys, Tomi and Gabi, were much younger than I. My mother made sure that we visited Uncle Elek occasionally, which is how I got to know his wife, Magda, and her side of the family.

We also paid visits to Aunt Elza, her husband, Norbert, and their two small children—Gyuri and Ági—in their third-floor apartment in the city at 18 Dessefy Street. They lived in a four- or five-storied apartment building shaped like a square with a large courtyard in the middle. Entrance to each apartment was from a walkway that ran around each floor and was protected by a cast-iron railing. Visiting them gave me an anxious feeling, wondering how it would feel plummeting to the courtyard from that height.

Unfortunately, my cousins were too young for me to play with; Gyuri was six and Ági was seven years younger. I was never excited about these visits; I would have preferred to stay home and play with my friends instead. However, thanks to my mother's insistence, these brief encounters helped to establish a relationship with my cousins later on in my life.

Nobody was left out on my mother's list of Reichmanns to visit, and I also got to know my youngest aunt, Magda. Her husband, Tibi, had a book collection that was kept in a large book cabinet behind glass doors. Aware that I was a prodigious reader, Tibi would lend me books to read. Considering the tight censorship of books available under the communist regime, Tibi's books provided rare opportunities to pore over some classics of Western literature.

They had two daughters, Erzsi and Zsuzsi, who were ten and seven years younger than I was respectively. Because of this age difference, I never got to know them well while I lived in Hungary.

My mother's insistence on knowing the Reichmann family proved to be wise. Because of my early exposure to the family, I was able to establish a much closer relationship with them decades later. Had I not met the Reichmanns while growing up in Budapest, I might have missed out on important relationships that evolved during the ensuing years.

Since many of my extended family lived in Budapest, they were conveniently within an hour of travel. The six-day workweek was standard in Hungary for decades after the war, and Sunday was the only day for my mother to rest, cook, and take care of her other affairs. Yet, at least once or twice a month, we still managed to find time to visit some family members.

I looked forward to our family visits, particularly when I was younger. I would dress up in my finest outfit, and we would take what I considered to be a thrilling streetcar ride. A fringe benefit of these visits was the lunch or dinner we were typically offered.

The fact that nobody ever came to visit us from either side of the family didn't surprise me. It was always my mother and me venturing to their homes. This was because we lived far away from everybody and our tiny apartment wasn't suitable for having visitors. Having only two armchairs in our bedroom / living room and not enough space to entertain a family with kids, my mother couldn't really afford to entertain and feed multiple people.

Just like my Spitzer cousins, my surviving Reichmann cousins live all over the world today. Uncle Elek's sons, Tomi and Gabi Révész, live in Toronto, Canada. Aunt Magda (her husband, Tibi, died a couple of years ago) and their married daughters, Erzsi Ladányi and Zsuzsi Köves, and their children live in Budapest, Hungary. Aunt Vica's children, Pisti Shomrai[1] and Jutka Kutzi, live in Kfar Saba, a suburb of Tel Aviv, Israel.

Aunt Elza's children, Gyuri Eldar and Ági Kasanski, live in Raanana, another suburb of Tel Aviv, Israel. Uncle Sanyi's daughter, Éva Sachar, lives in Kibbutz Magen in Israel. Uncle Bandi, his second wife, Dália, and his children from his first marriage, David Reichmann and Judy Black, live in the suburbs of London, England.

---

[1] Pisti added the letter *h* to Somrai to make the English pronunciation similar to the Hungarian one after he immigrated to Israel.

Aunt Rutka's two daughters, Era and Ziva, live in Kibbutz Maabaret, Israel. I regret the fact that I never met my Aunt Rutka before she died. I met Cousin Era for the first time in London in June 2010, when I visited my Uncle Bandi on his eightieth birthday.

Before ending this story about my family, there is one family member I cannot neglect to include: my father.

One would think that with seven surviving siblings there would be a trove of information about my father, in addition to many in my mother's family who knew my father as well. However, for some unknown reason, virtually no depictions of my father were present while growing up.

Nobody explained to me who he was, what his personality was like, or his likes and dislikes. Did he have a sense of humor, and what were his favorite dishes? What were his goals and aspirations in his short life? Did he have any hobbies, such as sports, music, or books?

I would have liked to know what his general view of politics was, in particular toward the system in which he lived. From my mother I learned precious little, other than that he loved me, which isn't sufficient in creating a mental picture of a father.

On my father's side there were several sisters and brothers close to his age who could have shared information about him. Here is the list of his siblings by their Hungarian nicknames and their birthdates in ascending order: Elza, 1909; Sanyi, 1911; Zoli (my father), 1912; Rutka, 1914; Elek, 1915; Vica, 1920; Lena, 1922; Magda, 1929; Bandi, 1930.

Uncle Sanyi, the older brother of my father, left Hungary with his family in 1946 when I was eight years old, which may be why I didn't learn much about my father from him. Aunt Rutka left Hungary in 1932, long before I was born, and I never met her. Aunt Lena perished in the Holocaust; and the youngest siblings, Aunt Magda and Uncle Bandi, were too young to know my father well.

My father was eighteen years old by the time Uncle Bandi was born. That left Aunt Elza, Aunt Vica and Uncle Elek in Hungary at the same time I was living there. One would think that during those eleven years in Hungary there would have been ample opportunity for me to learn about my father, but it didn't happen. Perhaps it was my fault for not asking, but because my mother rarely spoke about my father, I didn't consider taking the initiative.

I tried to fill this void in my father's background in 2004 when I traveled to Israel to spend a week with my Aunt Vica, the only living sibling of my father old enough to remember him. Even after three hours of a taped conversation with my aunt, she could recall very little of my father. Most of her story focused on her own life, no matter how hard I tried to turn the conversation back to him. Granted, she was eight years younger than he and too young to socialize.

Back in those days, this age difference meant even more than it would today. My father was a working man since he was fourteen years old, and by the time he turned eighteen, he had his own life and circle of friends.

The best I can piece together from Aunt Vica's comments is that my father was responsible toward his family and supported his parents and siblings throughout his single working life. At the same time, he developed his own circle of friends and acquaintances through a membership to a lower/middle-class social club.[1]

My father would come home from work, clean himself from head to toe, and head out to his club. He paid Aunt Vica twenty pengő[2] to have his clean shirt, underwear, socks, and shoes ready for him to go out. He loved reading, and he would often fall asleep with a book in his hands at bedtime.

Through repeated questioning, my aunt described my father with the following adjectives: somewhat self-centered, honest, decent, responsible, hardworking, regular, very clean, and calm. That's all I have of him.

How can you miss a father you never had? I don't know, but I know I missed a father very much throughout my adolescence. In retrospect, it might have been quite comforting during the critical years of my youth if my family were more forthcoming and instilled in me some sense of who my father was.

---

[1] The actual name of the club was Kispolgári Klub, but the exact translation to Petit Bourgeois Club doesn't accurately describe it.

[2] Hungarian currency in the 1927–1946 period that completely lost its value due to inflation following the war.

School and Friends

Naturally, much of my time growing up was spent in school. I spent the first five grades of elementary school on Kápolna Square, where it still stands today in our former neighborhood. A quick walk past the post office and the soccer field, then a left turn onto Kápolna Street, took me straight to the school at the end of the street, a twenty-minute journey. Busing children to elementary school didn't exist at that time. Everybody went to a neighborhood school that was within reasonable walking distance with hardly any concerns about safety.

I loved going to school from the beginning. I still remember how excited I was about my first homework assignment in the first grade in the fall of 1945,[1] which involved circling the first few letters of the alphabet in a newspaper article. By the time I started first grade, I knew the letters and was able to read pretty well.

I remember the schoolyard where we used to play during recess and where the choir I sang in used to assemble, which I always enjoyed. Even though I vaguely remember my music teacher's face that beheld a neat mustache, I distinctly remember his suit, with pants that were impeccably ironed and had a razor-sharp edge running down the center of the leg.

I used to meet and walk to school with Gabi Erőd, whom I have mentioned previously. I don't remember who instigated it, but occasionally Gabi and I managed to do some mischief.

Right at the corner where we met on Kápolna Street and Fűzér Street was a small outdoor farmers' market with daily fresh produce on display. One farmer usually had a sizable barrel full of pickled cucumbers stationed right near the sidewalk. We occasionally dared each other to sneak one cucumber out of the barrel while the farmer was busy with a customer or wasn't looking. Nothing was more delicious than savoring a pickled cucumber on our way to school. I now

---

[1] Because of the war, I couldn't start school in the fall of 1944. This loss of one year was made up in the 1950–51 academic years when I completed both sixth and seventh grades in one year.

wonder if the farmer knew what we were up to but pretended not to notice.

Streetcar 36 ran along Kápolna Street and stopped at the corner of Fűzér Street, the first stop from our elementary school. The streetcars were and still are designed to be identical at both ends in order for the conductor to operate them in either direction without needing to turn the streetcar around.

It was fascinating to watch the conductor get out of the cab and remove a very long pole with insulated handles attached to the outside of the streetcar. He then used the hook at the end of the pole to gently pull away the spring-loaded electric connector mounted on top from one of the live wires and move it over to the other live wires located above the tracks going back the other direction. After this switchover operation, the conductor would take his bag and walk over to the other end of the streetcar to take his seat. After waiting for the proper amount of time, he started his journey back to the other end of his destination many miles away.

On board were the conductor and the ticket inspector. Once the car was in motion, the ticket inspector started at the front, asking all passengers to show their tickets or to buy one. Gabi and I realized that, depending on how many people got on at our school, the ticket inspector often didn't reach the end before its first stop at the corner of Fűzér Street. Our plan was simple.

After school let out, we waited at the streetcar stop, and as the car started moving, we would jump on the rear steps and hold on to the handles. We typically arrived at our corner before the ticket inspector showed up, asking for our ticket.

Sometimes we jumped off before getting to our destination in order to avoid paying for the ticket. The thrill of a free ride was exhilarating, despite the fact that our parents would have been terribly upset if they knew about our jumping off a moving streetcar.

In the sixth, seventh, and eighth grades I attended a different school, but still within walking distance from home. Unfortunately, I didn't get into our neighborhood high school that was within walking distance. They had no room, and I was forced to go to a new high school that was at least a thirty-minute ride on two streetcars.

The official name of our high school was Szécsényi István Gimnázium,[1] located on the corner of Kendeffy Street in Budapest in District VIII. Our high school building was coed, while all the classes were segregated. Only during breaks could we mingle with girls, giving us little opportunity to establish social relationships.

Only one of my friends, Pisti Papp, was lucky enough to establish a good enough relationship with one of the girls to qualify as his "girlfriend." She was blond and beautiful, and Pisti was a good-looking guy. The whole school, boys and girls alike, were envious of them. The two of them looked so mature holding each other and kissing. I would have traded my track shoes for the opportunity to have a girlfriend like that so I could demonstrate my manliness to all my friends.

There was an excellent opportunity to meet high schoo-aged girls at the dance club I joined. It wasn't a social organization, but a school where formal dancing lessons were given by professional teachers. Lessons were free (or almost) because they were probably state sponsored, and I learned how to dance the classics like the tango, the foxtrot, and the waltz. I loved dancing and became relatively good at it, but most importantly, I was able to meet some girls and enjoy the brief but exciting physical proximity of a female companion.

It was at the dance club that a chance meeting with a girl from my school led to the only romantic relationship I had while in high school. I can't remember her name or her face, only the stylish pair of black-framed glasses she wore. What I do remember is that I was totally smitten by her—never having felt such emotions about a girl before.

---

[1] István Szécsényi was born into one of the richest noble families in 1791. He was an excellent writer and politician and the founder of the Hungarian Academy of Sciences. He was also minister of transportation in the first independent Hungarian government (1848) and the creator of the first permanent bridge between Pest and Buda over the river Danube, called the Chain Bridge. Teaching at this school commenced in 1911.

I was impressed that she played the cello and often saw her lugging her cello case, which was almost as tall as she was. I was also captivated by her sophistication and interest in a wide variety of topics.

One day at school, after she had been absent, I found out from one of her friends that she was sick. I decided to visit her after school and stopped by a flower shop to buy her some flowers as a gesture of my affection and love. I was met at the door by her mother, who ushered me into her bedroom. Unfortunately, she neglected to warn me that her daughter already had another visitor.

I was shocked to see another young boy having an animated discussion with my first true love. I tried to join the conversation but quickly discovered that I wasn't in their league. After a few minutes of emotional torment, I excused myself and left, very heartbroken.

I loved high school. There were twenty-three of us in the class, and we got to know each other well during the four years we spent together. Unfortunately, because I left Hungary in December 1956, I lost touch with my schoolmates for decades.

In mid-October 2010, I got an unexpected phone call from Sándor Méry (Kis-Méry, or "Little Méry," as we called him by his nickname), one of my schoolmates of my graduating class of 1956. He informed me that it took almost two years to locate me. Through him I learned that eighteen of us, out of twenty-three, are still alive, and ever since 2000 there has been a yearly reunion held in Budapest.

I always thought that following the 1956 Hungarian uprising, our graduating class scattered all over the world and I would never have the chance to reunite with my old friends. Since Kis-Méry's phone call, I have exchanged emails with several of my old friends and rediscovered the names of all my classmates and our teachers. I promised to attend our next reunion in the fall of 2011, which I kept.

I enjoyed learning most of my high school subjects, save for chemistry, history, and Russian. Our chemistry teacher, Dr. Rózsa Szabó, was a large, unattractive middle-aged woman with a lisp and a slight limp. We bequeathed her the nickname Shaky because of the way she walked. She wasn't an attractive-looking lady. In addition, spittle formed at the corners of her mouth when she spoke. I regret to admit that this provided sufficient distraction and an excuse for not paying too much attention during her classes.

History was terribly boring because our teacher, Dr. Zoltán Vécsey, a slender gentleman in his sixties, did nothing but read from the officially approved history book that was carefully edited to provide the kind of slant on contemporary history the communist authorities had approved. I was never sure who was more bored, our teacher monotonously reading day after day, or we students trying to stay awake.

Most of us hated learning the Russian language because it was compulsory. There was no option to learn English, French, German, or any other languages. Speaking and reading Russian was a necessary step for the future generation of Hungarians to fulfill their destiny in the larger orbit of the Communist empire. I managed to learn enough by my senior year to read the requisite Russian literature in its original version.

My favorite teacher, Dr. László Faragó, taught math and physics—two of my preferred subjects. Only an excellent teacher could make math and physics exciting subjects for adolescent boys. I never had the guts to ask him, but I always suspected that he probably taught at a university before the communists took over.

He was a tall man with a rather round face, thin lips, and frameless spectacles. He spoke with a careful, deliberate cadence that was easy to follow. He always stood in front of the blackboard to explain the subject matter at hand. He frequently asked volunteers to answer his questions, and I was always the first to raise my hand.

I also remember my gym teacher quite well but couldn't recall his real name, or his nickname, until Kis-Méry reminded me in one of his emails. I had an excellent relationship with Miklós Bánki, aka Tipő,[1] since I was a good athlete and represented our high school in

---

[1] He had difficulty pronouncing the word *cipő* (means "shoe" in Hungarian), hence the nickname Tipő to approximate his slight lisp.

many track and field events. I was very much involved in a variety of organized sports in high school. I liked swimming, but I had to travel almost an hour to practice on Margaret Island.

One winter I got such a terrible cold going home on the streetcars that I had to quit. I also tried gymnastics, but I fell off the parallel bar doing a handstand and literally landed on my head against the metal post footing. I abandoned gymnastics then and there and became a middle-distance runner, specializing in the 400-, 800-, and 1,000-meter distances. There were eight of us in my class in track and field, and we trained at a neighborhood sport club with a professional trainer.

I was a good runner, but my anxiety level before each meet was so high I often had the runs just before the start of the meet. However, this didn't stop me. It was no big deal; I just ran to the toilet, emptied my bowels, and felt perfectly fine.

I was delighted when I finally got my first pair of professional track shoes with metal spikes. The trainer, a short guy who used to run marathons, got them for me. They were a size too big, but I stuck pieces of an old sock into the toe to make them fit. Nothing made me feel more satisfied than going home on the streetcar in my warm-up suit with my tied-up track shoes dangling from my shoulder. I was showing the world that I was an athlete.

19. My high school track and field teammates. I'm second from the right in the back.

I don't remember the circumstances, but I joined a Hungarian handball club in my junior year in high school. The Locomotive Association of Hungary sponsored it, and they accepted junior members to be trained as part of the senior team.

European handball is like soccer with two teams with a goalie, except the ball, slightly smaller than a soccer ball, can be thrown and handled by hand only. This game was fast and physical, and I loved playing it. I still have a box of medals I won in handball matches and running races somewhere in our home.

In general, I was a very good student and my mother didn't have to worry about my grades. My problem was that I talked too much and interrupted my teachers with too many questions. In subjects that I liked, such as math or geometry, if the teacher asked a question, my hand went up first, not worrying whether my answer was right or wrong.

A few times my mother was called in to discuss my behavior. Following such meetings, I had to visit Uncle Laci, where he gave me one of his famous lectures that left me with a feeling of genuine remorse and a promise to do better in the future.

I was quick to learn, and I always looked forward to going to school, where I made lots of friends. From a young age, the importance of education and working hard in school was instilled in me.

Of all the years I spent in middle school and high school, I was involved in two regretful fighting incidents. One day in eighth grade I was bored in class and decided to pester one of my classmates, who sat in front of me. I tore a piece of paper from my notebook, chewed it to make some tiny, wet pellets, which I then proceeded to shoot at my classmate's head through a straw. Strangely he acted as if nothing happened.

On our way out the door after class was over, a heavy blow came down from behind on the left side of my head. I watched my classmate's grin as I fell to my knees. This attack was witnessed by several of my classmates. One of them openly challenged my attacker to a fight for being so cowardly for striking me from behind. Of course, he knew nothing of what had provoked the assault.

My head was still buzzing from the blow when we proceeded to go to the boys' bathroom. According to an unspoken principle, all issues to be physically resolved were conducted out of earshot of the teachers. It was there that my defender, as well as my assaulter, held the proper boxing stances and proceeded to brawl.

Within a few minutes, it was over, after my guardian angel landed a few blows on my assaulter's chin and he gave up. We all went back to class, and the whole affair was forgotten. However, I felt ashamed for pestering my classmate and then letting someone else do my fighting for me.

The second incident took place in high school during a physical education class when we were playing basketball. Feri Makk was one of the tallest guys in our class, and he and I played on opposite teams. During a game I jumped to grab a high ball when a sharp elbow to my throat literally gagged me. After having recovered, I flew into a rage and started to punch him in the face. My surprise attack didn't faze him; he recovered and in short order started to outbox me with his long arm reach that I couldn't penetrate.

Our gym teacher, Tipő, was standing by and spectating all this time, and finally stepped in when it was obvious who was going to win this fight. By then I had a nice bruise on my lower lip from one of Feri's well-directed punches. I was upset because I lost my temper and ended up losing the fight in front of all my friends on top of it.

As far back as I can remember I wanted to be an engineer, which was the result of my mother's and my Uncle Laci's influence on me. My response to the inevitable question of what I wanted to be when I grew up was always, "I want to be an engineer." After all, I was gifted in math, geometry, and physics—all prerequisites for engineering.

This goal fit nicely with the emphasis the communist regime placed on strengthening the engineering profession to build up Hungary's industrial production capacity in response to the priorities set in Moscow. My mother was proud to assert that her son would be an engineer, one of the two highly prized professions, the other being a doctor.

In the early spring of 1956, I was informed that if I decided to go to Moscow to study engineering, I would be accepted. I had all the qualifications: excellent grades and a worker's background. Many Hungarian students traveled to Moscow to pursue their university education. Clearly, these Hungarians would be indoctrinated in Moscow to become the future leaders of the country.

While I understood that graduating from a Moscow university would have guaranteed a successful professional and political career, I considered leaving Hungary for only a fleeting moment. Interestingly, those Hungarian students who ended up in Moscow in the fall of 1956 were stranded when the October uprising took place and couldn't return to Hungary and escape to the West as I did.

Looking back at my school years in Hungary, I must admit that the one thing I didn't learn was how to study. I never developed the discipline of carefully listening to my teachers, taking notes during class, completing my reading assignments until I understood everything, or completing my problem-solving exercises—unless we had to turn them in.

Later on, in the fall of 1956, while attending university, I paid dearly for this neglect. The subject matters were too difficult to grasp, forcing me to buckle down and learn the hard way.

I had many friends in high school but didn't socialize with them outside school and sport activities. Perhaps this was because of a new high school that was set up in 1952 to compensate for the overflow of students from a number of different districts. Therefore, everybody came from a different neighborhood, and it wasn't practical to hang out together after school or during the weekend.

In high school there were two other Jewish kids in class besides me, Tamás Jokel and Péter Boschán. Both of their fathers were killed during the Holocaust. Tamás was the least intelligent student in our class, by far. I actually tutored him in math one year and helped him to prepare for his graduation finals.

Tamás had an aunt in New York who would send him records of American hit songs, and he invited me once or twice to his apartment to listen to them. That is when I first heard of Doris Day.[1] In fact, the first time I tasted a banana was at his place.

Tamás told me they received a package that included bananas from a family member in Austria. He then showed me this stark black object that looked nothing like the bananas I saw in pictures. He peeled off the skin to reveal an unappetizing mushy black and brown substance. However, I couldn't refuse to taste it despite its appearance, so I had a piece. It was sickeningly sweet and gooey, and

---

[1] Doris Mary Anne Kappelhoff (April 3, 1922–May 13, 2019) was known as Doris Day. She achieved huge success as a singer, film actress, recording artist, and radio and TV performer.

I decided if that was what bananas tasted like, I would never have another bite of a banana again.

Tamás managed to graduate with me and immigrated to New York after escaping Hungary in 1956. Some years later I heard that he became wealthy in real estate, making one question the predictive value of high school grades. Péter Boschán stayed in Hungary, got a doctorate degree in economics, and taught at one of the universities. I met him once when I returned to Hungary while it was still a communist country.

Despite having lost touch with my schoolmates, from time to time while visiting Hungary I met one or two of them who lived in our neighborhood and who kept in touch with my mother. However, that was the extent of my contact with my high school class until the fall of 2010. Kis-Méry found me on Facebook through my Cousin Éva Reichmann and invited me to our fifty-fifth reunion in 2011 in Budapest, which I attended.

I did make a few friends outside school with boys in my neighborhood. Bandi Klopfer, who changed his name to Kárpáti about the same time I changed my name to Rátonyi, lived at the other end of Fűzér Street near the railroads in a nice apartment. He, too, was without a father. Their foyer was large enough to have a Ping-Pong table in it, which we played there many times.

He also escaped in 1956, and my mother told me he settled down in Amsterdam. I once tried to look him up when I was in Amsterdam on business, but I forgot that he changed his name from Klopfer to Kárpáti. I must have called all twenty Klopfers in the Amsterdam telephone book, but sadly, none turned out to be my friend.

Gabi Erőd, my almost stepbrother, and I became good friends, a friendship that survived decades of separation and long distances. We saw each other recently in mid-2019 when he stopped by in Atlanta on his way home from Florida to Ottawa, Canada, where he lives with his British wife.

Moreover, Vili Fodor became a lifelong close friend. We probably met in elementary school, but our friendship evolved more during high school, despite going to different schools. Whereas I attended a general high school, Vili attended a technical school that qualified him to be an electrical technician. Vili lived with his parents and younger sister, Mari.

Vili's home was no more than a twenty-minute walk from our house to 18 Vaspálya Street, which ran along the elevated railroad line. They lived in a small apartment very much like ours, with a kitchen and a bedroom / living room combination. They had a double-wide bed against the wall with a single bed across its foot. Vili slept in the single bed, while his parents and sister were in the double bed. I think I even slept there once or twice when Vili's father was out of town.

I liked visiting Vili. His father was a big, strong man with a good sense of humor. Whenever he was home, we always ended up playing Ulti, a Hungarian card game. While Ulti is the most popular card game in Hungary, it is practically unknown outside the country. It is a risk-taking game for three people. In each hand one player, the winner of the bidding, chooses trumps or no trumps, playing alone against the other two players in partnership. Vili, his father, and I played for a "fillér" a game, equivalent to a penny. Invariably, Vili's father would win.

My mother would ask if I played cards with Vili, and I usually denied it. My mother was forever concerned that I inherited my Reichmann grandfather's addiction to playing cards, which thankfully I did not.

Vili's sister, Maria, was eight years younger than we were, but she liked hanging around when I was visiting them. She was a cute girl with big black eyes and a ponytail that almost reached to her waist. She liked to pick a fight, and I wrestled with her a few times. I must admit that she was much stronger than she looked.

I did have a weak stomach when I was growing up, and many times I didn't feel like eating the food my mother prepared for me. However, my appetite would miraculously return as soon as I entered the Fodors' apartment. For some inexplicable reason, food always tasted better at the Fodors' house. Vili's mother, Fodor néni, was an excellent cook, and she often invited me to share a meal with them.

I remember her as a very kind, soft-spoken, and gentle lady with a sweet smile on her face.

Vili and I played handball together and used to go to school parties when we were about seventeen and eighteen. We escaped Hungary together in December 1956, and we stayed in close touch with each other and our families for more than six decades now. When I lived in Sarasota, Florida, our home was about an hour and a half from his near Orlando, and we visited each other from time to time to play golf and socialize.

I can't truthfully say that Tibi Lesko was a friend, but he and I lived together in the same house for seventeen years. He was four years older than I and came from a well-to-do family. They lived in one of the nicer corner apartments on the other side of our building, and I took advantage of every opportunity to hang out with him whenever he would tolerate me. As we got older, Tibi used to tell me about his adventures with girls, which naturally fascinated me.

He was in the border guards when the October Revolution broke out, and I met him at home as he was preparing to run for the Austrian border to escape. In fact, his decision to leave was a strong motivator for me to consider doing the same. Within a couple of weeks after he left, Vili Fodor and I were on our way out of the country too.

To illustrate that our life paths wind in unpredictable ways, I did connect with Tibi Lesko after about fifty years of separation. When I last spoke with him in 2005, he was living in Palm Springs, California, where he played the bass in a jazz band. To play jazz music was his life ambition. I vividly recall him demonstrating his skill with the string bass in his home in 1956.

Having friends has always been important to me. Good friends with whom I stayed in touch or reconnected with after decades was important to me and remained just as important later on in my life. Obviously, I cherish the company of others, particularly those with whom I can share my life experiences.

I graduated from high school in the spring of 1956 and became the very first in my family to pursue a college education in September of the same year.

Isms

Zionism

I don't know how my mother would have been able to work full-time were it not for the Jewish day care center that belonged and was adjacent to our neighborhood synagogue in Kőbánya. This facility provided tremendous help to the surviving Jewish children, many of us without fathers. I spent many happy hours there after school. The center had a yard large enough for a friendly soccer game, and the facility was well equipped with games, educational materials, and various sporting equipment to keep us busy and happy.

Food was plentiful at the center, and we often had cans of fruits, condensed milk, chocolates, and other foods from America. The center was financially supported by the American Jewish Joint Distribution Committee,[1] also known as the JOINT. We all knew the name JOINT but had no idea what it was, who was behind it, or what its mission was. Dr. Kálmán, the chief rabbi of the synagogue, provided local support to our day care. Weekly Jewish education classes were held for the children, and we participated in all the Jewish holidays.

An unmarried young couple, Moshe and Eszter, ran the day care. I now know that they were ardent Zionists, and both of them ultimately ended up in Israel, where they got married. In addition to running the day care center, they were in charge of indoctrinating Zionist ideals as well. Their mission included preparing the older

---

[1]   The American Jewish Joint Distribution Committee, known colloquially as the JOINT, is a United States Jewish charitable organization whose mission is to "serve the needs of Jews throughout the world." Late in 1944, JOINT entered Europe's liberated areas and organized massive relief efforts. By the end of 1947, some 700,000 Jews received aid. After May 1948, when Israel proclaimed its independence, JOINT helped some 440,000 Jews to reach Israel from Europe, mostly through clandestine means.

boys and girls to make Aliyah,[1] which led to the illegal immigration of surviving Jews around the world to Palestine.

The effort was organized in 1939 by various Jewish organizations to save Jews after the British restricted immigration to Palestine. Aliyah continued after the war, and in countries like Hungary, it meant the evasion of the authorities to smuggle Jewish youth out of the country. Indeed, many of my older cousins ended up in what is now Israel through the Aliyah movement.

My Aunt Vica and her second husband, Miklós, were active in Hasomer Hatzair (The Youth Guard), a Socialist-Zionist youth movement founded in 1913 in Galicia, Austria-Hungary. Many of the Reichmanns were born in

20. Synagogue in Kőbánya.
The building is now owned and operated by an Evangelical church.

Galicia, including my father, whose birth certificate is in Slavic.[2]

Hasomer Hatzair believed that the liberation of Jewish youth, before and after the Second World War, could be accomplished by Aliyah. I suspect that my Aunt Rutka, who left for Palestine in 1932,

---

[1] A Hebrew word that means "ascent" or "going up"; colloquially a return to Palestine or Israel after 1948.

[2] Galicia changed hands several times and is now part of Slovakia, bordering Hungary on the northeast.

was active in Hasomer Hatzair. It is quite possible that Moshe and Eszter were also members.

I did not realize at that time that we were being trained to leave our home and families to make Aliyah to Israel. We learned many songs in Hebrew and went on hiking trips to areas close to the Yugoslav border. We slept in tents and learned useful skills about how to survive outdoors. It was fun, but I was clueless as to what the ultimate goal was.

Moshe and Eszter did their job well, and one day I discovered that several of the older boys I used to play with all the time had disappeared. I still remember the names and faces of two of the boys who disappeared, Gyuri Ádler and Pali Snitzer. I learned much later that they left for Palestine.

I still recall one rather painful experience I had with Gyuri Ádler. He must have been at least four years older than I and had a glass eye. I never learned what accident or illness caused him to lose one eye.

One winter afternoon we were playing in the courtyard, throwing snowballs at each other, when Gyuri Ádler showed up. I took aim at him, and I hurled a hard-packed snowball that hit him directly over his glass eye. I immediately knew that I was in trouble as he wiped the snow off and started to charge at me with a murderous look on his face.

I sprinted toward the gate and down the street to evade him, thinking I could outrun him. However, I was quickly proven wrong, and he steadily closed the distance until he kicked my behind, throwing me headfirst on the snow-covered road. He never said a word, just turned around and walked back into the center.

I sat there with an aching bottom, feeling both terrible for throwing a snowball at his bad eye and lucky that he didn't kill me. A few days later Gyuri was my partner in a friendly Ping-Pong match as if nothing had ever happened between us.

I often wondered what might have happened to me had I been a few years older. Perhaps I too would have ended up in Palestine, and my life would have turned out to be quite different.

I loved being at the center and hated going home to our tiny apartment. The food was great, we had lots of fun playing games, and I felt a sense of belonging there. This was also a great help to my mother, who didn't have to worry about what I did after school while she was still at work.

Our guardians, Moshe and Eszter, with the help of Rabbi Kálmán, tried to instill in us a strong sense of our Jewish identity. The wounds of the Holocaust were still fresh since almost all of us in the center had lost one or both parents simply for being Jewish.

Although we survived, we instinctively understood that we lived in an anti-Semitic society where our future as Jews was precarious, even under the communist regime. The exposure to Zionism's fundamental tenets of renewed pride of being Jewish, the right to our culture, and the use of our ancient language and learning self-reliance were critical in soothing our psychological wounds.

One day at the day care center, an amusing event made a great impression on me. As usual, I waited until the last minute before running to the toilet to empty my bladder. I dashed in and opened the door to one of the stalls; there were no urinals, and both girls and boys used the same bathroom.

I caught Eszter just as she stood up, with her underwear still around her ankles. I stood frozen like a deer in headlights and just kept looking at the black, bushy triangle that covered up the biggest mystery a nine-year-old boy could witness. Finally, she snapped at me and said, "What is the matter with you? Haven't you seen such a thing before?"

I don't remember how many years the day care center was operational, but I do remember those years very fondly. I will never forget the Ping-Pong table we played at for hours at a time, the yard with the large willow tree in the corner I used to climb, the soccer games with my friends, or Hanna, the beautiful blond teenage daughter of Rabbi Kálmán, who used to assist Moshe and Eszter with our homework.

Socialism/Communism

If you have read my story this far, you have some sense of what living under a communist regime is like. To appreciate the consequences of living in a totalitarian political system characterized by severe restrictions on individual freedoms and the covert and overt attempts to proselytize and to indoctrinate the population with communist propaganda, a little historical background is in order.

Stalin, with "boots on the ground," had total control of Hungary and the other Eastern European countries liberated by his forces in 1944–45. Contrary to public statements made by the leaders of the Western powers, they gave Stalin carte blanche as far as Hungary was concerned.

As a result, by 1949, the Hungarian Communist Party, led by Mátyás Rákosi, gained total control through intimidation, arrests, and even assassination of political opponents. There were political show trials, executions and exiles, forced resettlements of hundreds of thousands of people, collectivization of farms, and forced industrialization, all of which resulted in a severe decrease in living standards.

The final step in the communist takeover of Hungary was on August 20, 1949, when the Hungarian parliament passed a new constitution modeled after the one adopted by the Soviet Union. The name of the country was changed to the Peoples' Republic of Hungary, "the country of the workers and peasants."

Socialism was declared the main goal of the nation, a new national emblem was adapted—which included the communist red star, the hammer, and a sheaf of wheat, signifying the country's priorities of industry and agriculture—and Mátyás Rákosi became the new leader of the country.

Moscow turned Hungary into an important source of agricultural

21. Hungary's emblem from 1949 through 1956.

products, as well as of heavy industrial manufacturing for the Soviet Union, placing a much lower priority on the needs of the Hungarian population. After all, Hungary was the "enemy" during the war, and no love was lost between the rulers in Moscow and the general population of Hungary, which had expressed much more sympathy for the Germans than for the Russians.

Nationalization of large businesses began in early 1948 and extended to virtually all private enterprises in the subsequent years. Forced collectivization of farms began in the fall of 1948 with disastrous results in productivity of the agricultural sector, the main contributor to Hungary's GDP.

All the planning for Hungary's economy was centralized and followed the "five-year plan" cycle of the Soviet Union. Everything was top-down, from the allocation of resources for consumer goods to investment in heavy industry; all were dictated by the priorities set in Moscow. Political indoctrination and relentless propaganda affected the daily life of every family. All of society was turned upside down in terms of class structure.

My introduction to socialism/communism probably started in third grade in 1947–48 and ended as a freshman at the Technical University of Budapest in October 1956. I am sure that even if I had grown-ups around me to explain the consequences of living in a socialist society, I wouldn't have understood it and would have cared even less. The fact that all public media (newspaper, radio) were now under state control and espoused the communist propaganda had no effect on my life until I was much older in high school.

Students' indoctrination generally followed two parallel paths. One venue of indoctrination took place at the school, where we were taught revisionist history of the twentieth century. The virtues of socialism/communism were extolled by teachers, and students were "encouraged" to participate in group activities (special events, marches, etc.) organized by communist officials who had total control of the education system after 1948.

I joined the young "Pioneers," as everybody else did, but I never gave it a second thought as to why there was no other alternative for a youth organization. I listened to the relentless propaganda on the radio, but I didn't even recognize it as propaganda until I was older. In fact, I probably accepted some of it without thinking, not realizing what an impact it had.

I subscribed to the weekly government publication that targeted the youth population of the country, but the only thing I was interested in was the puzzle. I diligently worked on these, typically math or simple science problems, and often submitted a solution. I won a few times and was quite proud to see my name printed in the paper under the list of winners.

I must confess that I blindly absorbed most of the propaganda, probably through the eighth grade. I subscribed to the communist newspaper dedicated to schoolchildren, participated in whatever activities were handed down through school, and read all the "right" books that told us of the glorious victory of the Soviet Union against the Nazis during the war.

I accepted that Hungary owed its survival to the heroes of the Red Army and the frequent accusations against the Imperial West (a well-understood reference to the USA) for the miserable economic conditions we suffered. Unfortunately, I had no adult at home to set my political compass in the right direction and effectively counter this repressive propaganda.

My mother, who had an eighth-grade education, was not up to or decided not to give me "the other side" of the stories I was bombarded with for security reasons. In addition, as a seven-year-old Jewish boy who owed his life to the Red Army, which liberated me in the Big Ghetto of Budapest, I developed an emotional sense of gratitude to my liberators.

If the Red Army had liberated the Big Ghetto a few weeks later, I may not be alive today. This gratitude remains, but I now understand that saving me, a Jewish boy, from dying of malnutrition was an accidental result of the true objective of the liberating Red Army. Their real goal was to fulfill Stalin's orders to occupy Hungary and prepare for the ultimate political and economic domination by the Soviet Union that lasted for fifty years.

The second form of indoctrination was through the day-to-day living experience: constant propaganda on the radio and in the press, as there was no television in those days. All textbooks and any other books were censored for publication. Plainly speaking, life was under a totalitarian system, where everything was controlled by the Communist Party that existed in parallel and was imbedded into the official parliamentarian system of government.

However, the process of my political reeducation began around the time I started high school in 1952. I discovered strange bits of living in a socialist world that somehow didn't fit with the ideals and aspirations of the official bubble we lived in. I started to listen to Radio Free Europe and the Voice of America at night, behind closed doors with the window shades drawn.

I was old enough to understand that life in Hungary for most of us required lying, stealing, and cheating in order to survive. The joke went, "The government pretends to pay us and we pretend to work." Since the capitalist system of workers' exploitation was replaced with one where the workers owned everything, it was reasonable to steal since we took what was already ours. And so, the cycle continued.

Being an avid reader, I managed to get a hold of some "forbidden" books from an uncle and a friend of my mother who had a library full of Western literature. I consider my years in Hungary as my undergraduate study in political science, majoring in socialism/communism.

At a White House luncheon in 1954, Churchill famously stated, "The inherent vice of capitalism is the unequal sharing of blessings; the inherent virtue of socialism is the equal sharing of miseries." In Hungary I experienced the second part of this quote for eight years. Once I was in the West, I began my homeschooling of the inherent vice of "the unequal sharing of blessings" in capitalism.

The negative impacts of living in a totalitarian society came close to home when Aunt Klári, my Uncle Laci's wife, was jailed in 1949 when I was only eleven years old. Nobody ever explained to me what actually happened to her, and I wasn't particularly interested in such grown-up matters anyway. However, her story illustrates the communist system's brutality and paranoia in maintaining absolute control over its citizens.

Aunt Klári's sister Kati, together with her male friend, escaped from Hungary to Austria in 1948 with the help of a professional guide/smuggler. Escape typically entailed a dangerous walk across the border, which was protected by mines and watchtowers. Escapees could take with them only what they could carry on their backs and in their hands. Having successfully smuggled Kati to Austria, the smuggler was also retained for an additional fee to smuggle out additional personal belongings and deliver them to her in Austria.

These additional belongings were to be taken out of Kati's Budapest apartment, the keys to which she left with Aunt Klári, together with instructions for the smuggler to pack up whatever Kati wished for him to transport to Austria. Unfortunately for Aunt Klári, while escorting another group of would-be refugees, the smuggler had information on him that contained my aunt's name, address, and other incriminating information. Aunt Klári was promptly arrested by the Hungarian secret police and severely beaten at the police station. She was brought face-to-face with the smuggler, and prompt justice was served in typical communist fashion.

There was no prosecution, legal defense, or any kind of trial. She was to serve several years at an internment camp at Kistarcsa, a small village northeast of Budapest, designated for political prisoners. Unfortunately, because of all the beatings she suffered and the poor prison conditions, her health deteriorated and she developed a large infectious swelling on her neck that the doctors couldn't treat.

She was sent to a hospital under detention and eventually was released, partly because the doctors thought that she was ready to die soon. Fortunately, Aunt Klári recovered, and it was after her release in 1952 that I got to know her and her son Péter well.

The impact on Péter of his mother's imprisonment, of course, was devastating. In addition to the personal pain of losing his mother, Péter had to suffer the fallout of his mother's status as a political prisoner.

The year his mother was released from prison in 1952, Péter was to enter university with a desire to become a surgeon. However, his status changed to "class alien" and "politically unreliable," with no hope of gaining admission to the medical university. His dreams of becoming a surgeon were dashed, and my Uncle Laci had to move heaven and earth to get him into dental school.

Only in high school did I start to more clearly understand the ramifications of living under a closed society. I started to listen to the forbidden Voice of America and Radio Free Europe, and I gradually began to realize that there was a universe "out there" where life is completely different from the one I was living in Hungary.

I slowly became aware of certain restrictions imposed by the regime that limited my exposure to ideas and viewpoints other than the official ones promulgated through the media outlets. I discovered that certain movies made in the West couldn't be shown in Hungary. Certain books couldn't be found in the library. Certain music created couldn't be heard on the radio. Certain languages, other than Russian, couldn't be studied in high school.

Not that I ever considered the possibility of traveling, but journeying outside the Warsaw Pact[1] countries was impossible. I also realized one had to be careful expressing certain opinions about our national leaders or leaders of the Communist Party because of the harsh consequences. I gradually came to understand that we lived in a "make-believe" world, where we kept our private thoughts to ourselves and success was partially measured by how well we could exploit the system we lived in.

I knew that my ticket to success was education, and the "system" provided me with an advantage through the official communist version of "affirmative action." Because of my parents, I was a member of the "working class," and admission to the university was guaranteed, assuming that my grades were acceptable. Mine were excellent.

I also learned early on that the economic priorities under the communists were production and full employment. Soon after the takeover in 1948, the government introduced the Sztahanovista model in the workplace. It was named after Aleksey Stakhanov, a coal

---

[1] The Warsaw Pact was an organization of communist states in Central and Eastern Europe initiated by the Soviet Union in response to NATO and signed on May 14, 1955. Hungary was one of its members.

miner whose team increased its daily quota sevenfold by organizing a more efficient division of labor.

This movement began in 1935 in the Soviet Union and was aimed at ever-increasing industrial production by using efficient work techniques. Like the Soviet Union, the Hungarian government was eager to ensure its successive Five-Year Plans and promoted the Sztahanovista movement by offering higher pay and other privileges to workers. In many cases, the emphasis on speed and production resulted in poor quality and increased worker casualties, together with the whole concept being widely criticized by the West, specifically by the labor unions.

My mother, being a piece worker before she became party secretary, had to meet monthly quotas, the feared "norm," set by the factory management. She and everyone else in similar circumstances had to be careful to manage their own productivity and not to outproduce their quotas by too much lest they would see their quotas raised to ever-increasing levels.

Religion and its free exercise in public was an anathema to the communist regime. The communists always believed that "religion is the opiate of the masses,"[1] but more fundamentally, they perceived religion as something to be feared because it diverted people's commitment to the godless ideology of their system.

Consequently, I don't ever recall religion as a public subject of discussion. In fact, I don't recall this as a topic of conversation even in our home. Churches and synagogues existed, and many people observed some type of religious ritual, as I did with my family, but by and large it was kept out of the public light.

During one summer break following my sophomore year of high school, our literature teacher gave us an assignment to read a book of our choice. We were to write a brief report on it when classes started in the fall of 1955. Somehow or other I got hold of the Hungarian translation of a book titled *The Wandering Jew*.

---

[1] This expression was coined by Karl Marx (1818–1883), a German philosopher, political economist, historian, political theorist, and revolutionary credited as the founder of communism.

Legend has it that the book's main character is condemned to travel around the world as punishment for insulting Jesus on the way to the Crucifixion.[1] How I got hold of this book and why I read it I cannot recall now. I read a plethora of books that I could have written a report on. However, for whatever reason, I dared to talk about this book.

When I stood up in front of the class and relayed the title of the book, there was a sudden silence. The word *zsidó*, the Hungarian word for "Jew," had never been openly uttered during my four years in high school. My teacher was visibly stunned and my classmates were incredulous for picking a book with such a title. I suddenly realized that I crossed an invisible line of political correctness, and after a couple of minutes of trying to describe the book, I sat down, feeling quite embarrassed and foolish.

However, even with these limitations and lack of freedoms, I didn't feel that I was living a terribly oppressed life. I was too young and not sophisticated enough to understand the long-term consequences of living under communism. I surrendered to the fact that this was the country and the society I was going to live in forever, and I was determined to make the best of it.

Philosophizing about the long-term consequences of living in a dictatorship never occurred to me. I suppose I was like the proverbial frog in the pot of hot water. While some parts were inconvenient, a nuisance, or even upsetting, I was too comfortable enjoying my day-to-day life of school, friends, family, and sports to pay attention to the social, economic, and moral consequences of living under a totalitarian system.

It would be negligent not to mention the cultural opportunities that were made available to ordinary working people under the communist regime. Disregarding the political motivations,[2] the fact

---

[1] The origins of the legend are debatable, and there is no literary consensus about it. The book I read was probably the Hungarian translation of Morris Cohen's 1950 book called *Reflections of a Wandering Jew*.

[2] Since most freedoms that we are accustomed to in the free world were curtailed or eliminated, providing virtually free access to the arts was a gesture of accommodation by the ruling Communist Party.

is that all forms of "high culture," such as music, opera, theater, and ballet, were made available at a very low cost. Since the state owned and controlled everything, all cultural activities were subsidized to such levels that virtually everybody could afford taking advantage of them if they wanted to.

As I got older, my mother encouraged me to go to the theater or see an operetta or opera. I even had season tickets in my junior and senior years in high school to some events. By the time I graduated from high school, my repertoire of classic operas I had seen included Verdi's *Rigoletto, Il Trovatore, La Traviata,* and *Aida,* in addition to Puccini's *Madame Butterfly* and *Tosca.*

The fact that back in those days all operas were sung in Hungarian made it easier to appreciate the music since I could understand the story without reading the libretto. I particularly enjoyed seeing the light operettas, such as Franz Lehár's *The Merry Widow* and Johan Strauss's *Die Fledermaus.*

I shall never forget Act 5 of Gounod's *Faust* opera known as "Walpurgisnacht" or "A Night in Purgatory." It is actually a ballet performed by devils and witches in a fantastic underground setting to extremely haunting music. It is an orgiastic ballet depicting the revelry that continues throughout the night. Unfortunately, because it is so expensive to include this ballet act in the opera, most Western performances omit it. I also recall sitting through Shakespeare's *Hamlet,* which lasted almost five hours. After the third act I understood why some people in the audience brought pillows to sit on.

In addition to the arts, the regime also encouraged all children to participate in sports. The success of such state-sponsored programs was best exemplified by the consistently superior performance of the East German athletes in a variety of sports in the international arena. But we now know much of their success can be attributed to their use of performance-enhancing drugs and steroids.

Anti-Semitism

I covered the history of Hungarian anti-Semitism in some detail in my previous story; therefore, I will only touch on this shameful and regrettable national characteristic as it impacted me after the war.

A well-known Hungarian author, Imre Kertész,[1] once stated, "Before Auschwitz the anti-Semite was a latent killer, after Auschwitz a manifest killer." Anti-Semitism didn't suddenly disappear after the war; it was simply driven underground by the communist regime.

There was no open debate or discussion of the consequences of killing three out of four Hungarian Jews during the virulently anti-Semitic regime in Hungary in 1944–45. These topics were taboo and not to be addressed openly. Unrestricted discussions on this topic had to wait at least four decades until after the communist system fell in 1989.

What I was exposed to was the accidental public exposure to anti-Semitic sentiments. It could happen anywhere at any time. I might have been riding a crowded streetcar or a bus and overheard the words "stinking Jew" suddenly uttered or passing a drunk on the street raving about how the "dirty Jews" caused all of Hungary's problems, including the takeover of the country by the communists.

The general population's sentiment about the Holocaust and Hungarian Jews shortly after the war centered on the following claims:

- The number of Jewish victims were much fewer than six hundred thousand.
- There were no gas chambers and mass killings in the concentration camps.
- The various atrocities committed in the labor and concentration camps were fabrications by the Jews.

---

[1] Imre Kertész (November 9, 1929–March 31, 2016), Hungarian novelist, survivor of the Auschwitz concentration camp, and winner of the Nobel Peace Prize in literature in 2002.

- The Hungarians were not responsible for what happened to the Jewish victims.
- The non-Jewish Hungarians suffered just as much during the war.

It would be incorrect to say that as Jews we lived in fear of being accosted. Those days were gone. However, it is fair to say that I had an almost subconscious awareness of my surroundings. I was constantly on alert to being exposed to some anti-Semitic remark.

For me, the danger was that I didn't "look Jewish" at all. I was blond and blue-eyed and didn't fit the stereotype of a Jew. Therefore, people around me felt comfortable to let their guard down and make anti-Semitic comments.

Almost all Hungarian Jews had German last names. In my own family, we were Reichmanns and Spitzers. My uncles were named Grossman, Schwartz, and Stern. My wife's family name was Weisz, and her mother's maiden name was Blum. One of my grandmothers was a Rosenberg, and the other one was a Glück. These German names were easy identifications that we were all Jews.

It is fair to say that because of what happened to us Jews in 1944–45, I knew I was an outsider in Hungarian society, and it was impossible to hide my Jewishness because of my name. I wasn't ashamed to be a Jew—quite the contrary. I just didn't want to advertise it before anyone had a chance to get to know me. It is for this primary reason that I decided to change my name from Reichmann to Rátonyi in the spring of 1956.

I have no idea why the government decided to announce a program to allow people to "Hungarianize" their foreign-sounding names in early 1956. They offered a simple and free process. The changing of my name from Reichmann to Rátonyi was the result of a casual discussion with my mother, who didn't object.

I liked the name Rátonyi because it would be instantly recognized as an authentic Hungarian name. In addition, it was also popular because of a contemporary actor-singer and comedian whose name was Róbert Rátonyi. I filled out the necessary papers, and within a very short time I was officially notified of my new name, effective as of April 13, 1956.

The practical aspects of changing my name were simple. I got a new Personal Identification Document, something every person had to have in Hungary, and I notified my high school of my new name. The principal of my high school simply crossed out my old name and wrote in my new identity in my Student Report book that had all my grades for the past four years. With an asterisk he noted the change as of May 1, 1956, and that was that.

I could hardly wait to have a chance to introduce myself as Róbert Rátonyi. By the time I started university in the fall, I had gotten used to my new name, and everybody I met there knew me as Rátonyi. I thought I was all set for life. I would no longer have to spell my name every time I was asked and could hide my Jewishness from all the strangers I didn't feel should know about it. Being Jewish could be a private matter.

Within my own family, my Uncle Elek Reichmann changed his name to Révész. My Uncle Laci Spitzer ended up being Laci Szirtes, followed by my Cousin Gyuri with the same name.

It wasn't paranoia that drove thousands, if not tens of thousands, of Jews to Hungarianize their name starting in 1956. They all came to the same conclusion I did. My Cousin Gyuri Spitzer changed his name to Szirtes in 1969 when he was working at one of the largest and most reputable businesses of Hungary called Tungstram.[1] One day his boss told him that with a name like Spitzer, he wouldn't be able to advance in his career.

Regardless of the official taboo of discussing religion, or discriminating on the basis of religion, every Jew in Hungary knew the sad truth about the lingering anti-Semitism by the non-Jewish population. I wasn't naive to think that by the single act of name changing I would be protected against all future exposure to accidental acts of

---

[1] Tungstram was a light bulb manufacturing company. General Electric bought it in 1989 and invested hundreds of millions of dollars since then to make this their center of excellence for lighting products worldwide.

anti-Semitism. It was simply done to make life a little bit easier for me.

Had someone told me that changing my name would have lasting consequences for me just a few months later in Austria, and for my future children and grandchildren a few decades later in America, I would have broken out in laughter at the stupidity and absurdity of that observation.

I was convinced I would never be able to leave Hungary for the rest of my life. As it turned out, all these things came to pass, and I now want to apologize to all my descendants for not being more far-sighted and picking a more appropriate Anglo-Saxon name for them to bear. I also give my blessing to all future generations of Rátonyis to change their name to whatever name they think is more appropriate for them.

I must say that the sentiment of the average non-Jewish Hungarian about Jews has improved significantly fifty years after the Holocaust. A professional Gallup[1] research study conducted in 1995 about the Holocaust showed the following selected results:

> 74 percent of the population accepted the number of Jewish victims to be as claimed;
>
> 93 percent accepted the existence of gas chambers in the concentration camps;
>
> 92 percent accepted the atrocities conducted in the concentration camps;
>
> 52 percent accepted responsibility for what happened to the Hungarian Jewry;
>
> 67 percent believed that non-Jewish Hungarians suffered as much as the Jews did.

The above results, except for the last two points, show a marked improvement of sentiment about Jews in Hungary since shortly after

---

[1] The survey was conducted in 1995 through personal interviews with 1,500 statistically representative samples by Gallup and the Hungarian Public Opinion Poll Institute.

the war. I have personally heard Hungarians claim that the non-Jewish population suffered just as much as the Jews did, which is, of course, nonsense.

My own research indicates that there were about three hundred thousand to four hundred thousand non-Jewish Hungarians who perished, most of them soldiers fighting alongside the Germans, representing about 3 to 4 percent of the population of Hungary. How can this be compared to the loss of 75 percent of the Jewish population?

I didn't have to rely on a survey to know who suffered the most. As far as I know, not one of my non-Jewish high school mates lost a father during the war, but almost all my Jewish friends became fatherless.

Although I am a generally optimistic person, I have serious doubts that anti-Semitism in Hungary can ever be completely eradicated.

A Happy Childhood

It was a beautiful, crisp early morning, summer day. With four or five other fifteen- or sixteen-year-old boys, I had the summer job of digging a trench around an athletic field for the purpose of installing an irrigation pipe. It wasn't very far from where I lived.

I would get up around six thirty every morning to walk about forty-five minutes to get to the job. I would leave our house at 7 Fűzér Street and turn right to get to the corner of Kőrösi Csoma Road, where a small bakery shop at the corner was already open. I would buy a freshly baked roll and a liter of pasteurized milk in a bottle.

With milk and roll in hand, I would start my long walk to my jobsite. I wore my boots to handle the shovel and spade, short shorts, like we all wore in Hungary, and a short-sleeve shirt that I took off immediately when we started to dig.

I walked at a fast pace, munched on the still-warm crisp roll, and slightly slowed down to take a quick swig of milk. How I felt that morning has never left me, in addition to the complete clarity of the details. I felt the springiness in my steps and the energy in my body as I took in the crisp morning air. I felt happy to be alive, to be young and strong.

I looked forward to doing my daily job of eight hours of digging with an ax and a shovel. I considered this very physical job not as work but as a daily exercise to build some muscles on my rather slender frame and to get a great tan that I hoped would not go unnoticed by the girls in the neighborhood or at the public swimming pool I visited on the weekends.

This particular moment of happiness, and many others scattered around my childhood years, came after and despite the terrifying moments of the war and the Holocaust: the bombings, the forced separation from my parents, the hiding in safe houses and the ghetto, my father's death, and the loss of so many of my close family members.

In addition, as I have described, our standard of living following the war was near the bottom of the economic stratum. Given this background it would have been logical for me to turn into an unhappy or resentful child. However, why did that never happen?

One possible explanation is that all the bad childhood memories of 1944–45 receded into an obscure compartment of my conscious memory. They were to be locked up and very rarely opened up to feel remorse, anger, or sorrow. In addition, my mother instilled in me a sense of self-worth, completely detached from our economic or financial circumstances. From her I learned that who we were and how we fit into society had nothing to do with how little she earned through her physical labor or how primitive our living condition was.

My mother had only eight years of schooling, which was normal for girls in those days. She was not sophisticated or well-read and couldn't articulate complex ideas or theorems about world affairs or interpersonal relationships. What she taught me did not come from lectures, reading magazines, or sophisticated discussions, but through the day-to-day experiences of how we lived. Beyond the unconditional love she provided, she had a keen instinct for what I needed to be happy as a child.

Another important factor in my happy childhood was my large, extended family. Although many of my uncles, aunts, and cousins perished during the Holocaust or left Hungary afterward, I still had plenty of relatives who stayed in Hungary.

My interactions with my family had a positive emotional impact on me. They gave me a secure, comfortable sense of belonging. My mother and I, living in isolation on the outskirts of the city, were not alone, and I had many people who cared for and loved me. They motivated me to go far in this world by telling me that I was smart. And I believed it. Looking back at my childhood and adolescent years, I can clearly discern the forces and circumstances that shaped my character, my self-image, and the person I became over the ensuing decades.

I was brought up by a single mother who was able to provide very little of the guidance a growing boy needs to prepare him to be a man of sound mind, character, and responsibility. Luckily, I had others who filled the role of the missing father: my mother's older brother; my rabbi, who introduced me to the teachings of the Torah;

and my mother's best friend. They taught me important life lessons that I carried with me always.

One lesson is that early childhood tragedies don't necessarily have to have a negative impact on the rest of your life. In my case, the loss of my father and family members during the Holocaust made me stronger. All the pain, fear, humiliation, and loss evolved into ambition to become a "normal" person. Instead of looking back, it helped me look forward and make the best of my innate abilities and the opportunities that lay ahead.

My uncle repeatedly told me to remember, "Man must have both *sensitivity and sensibility*." At first I didn't understand what he meant, but as I grew older, it became clearer. He meant that we have to be both rational and logical while also sensitive and sympathetic to the people around us. I am certain that he meant that being smart is not enough to be a decent man.

Another lesson is that being poor didn't define my self-respect and esteem. Fortunately, I had some help in accomplishing this. My Uncle Laci, my mother, Manci néni, and my rabbi instilled ideas in me that helped me take responsibility for myself and for my widowed mother. From my childhood on, I always wanted to have a strong and healthy mind and body.

The lessons from living under a socialist/communist system are multitude. The whole system is a farce, with its tenets totally contradicting human nature and desire. I discovered somewhat later in life that under this political system the Ten Commandments of Moses were replaced by a single commandment that "the end justifies the means." I learned that all totalitarian systems are corrupt (the benevolent dictatorship of Singapore as a possible exception) and the system is based on lying, cheating, and stealing.

Most importantly, I learned that the worst part of the socialist/communist system was the moral corruption of the people. Many "true believers" of communism discovered later in their lives that their whole life was devoted to create, support, and build a utopian system that would never be achieved. To learn more about this, I recommend reading John V. Fleming's book *The Anti-Communist Manifestos*, published in 2009. According to Amazon.com,

The subject of *The Anti-Communist Manifestos* is four influential books that informed the great political struggle known as the Cold War: *Darkness at Noon* (1940), by Arthur Koestler, a Hungarian journalist and polymath intellectual; *Out of the Night* (1941), by Jan Valtin, a German sailor and labor agitator; *I Chose Freedom* (1946), by Victor Kravchenko, a Soviet engineer; and *Witness* (1952), by Whittaker Chambers, an American journalist. The authors were ex-Communist Party members whose bitter disillusionment led them to turn on their former allegiance in literary fury... Three of the four had been underground espionage agents of the Comintern (*Communist International*). All contemplated suicide and two of them achieved it. John V. Fleming's humane and ironic narrative of these grim lives reveals that words were the true driving force behind the Cold War.

Were it up to me, these books (which I have in my library) would be compulsory reading in every high school and college. The insidious moral effect of growing up and living under communism can take generations to clear out of people's consciousness. This is exemplified by the residual corruption and autocratic tendencies of the now-free former Soviet countries, like Hungary.

In addition to my family support, I enjoyed a healthy social environment as I grew up. I was and still am an extrovert who makes friends easily. I had several close friends in my neighborhood and was never lonely. I liked going to school, both for learning and for the social environment it provided. My teachers liked me because I was a quick learner, although I did have some behavioral problems because of my disruptiveness in the classroom.

I participated in all kinds of sport activities at school and outside school. My love of sports came from enjoying competition, the drive to win, and the physical aspects of training my body to allow me to perform to my maximum potential. Participating in sports and regular physical exercise contributed to my sense of well-being.

My brief overview of contributions to my happy childhood would not be complete without mentioning my exposure to the arts. Since affordable cultural events were a high priority for the government during the Communist era, there were many cultural events tailored for children. My mother made sure that I took advantage of this cultural opportunity. I am certain that my love of opera, classical music, and theater has its genesis in my early childhood exposure to these activities.

In summary, I can safely say that in spite of the fact that I and my extended family lived under the shadow of the post-Holocaust Communist era, I had a happy childhood.

The summer of 1956 came and went, and in September I enjoyed my new status as a university student. I obviously had no clue that within a few months my whole life would change drastically.

Gone would be the very modest but comfortable life I had gotten used to. Gone would be my mother and the close family support I enjoyed. Never would I have imagined that everything I knew and enjoyed would come to a sudden end.

I didn't know that I would celebrate the New Year in a strange land with people who spoke a different language. I didn't know that I would face a whole new set of life decisions to be made on my own with nobody to remind me of my responsibilities.

Had I been able to peek into the future, I would have been scared to death of what was coming. Yet, in a few short months, when the Hungarian Uprising began on October 23, 1956, my anticipated life as a student at the Technical University of Budapest came to an abrupt end.

Journey 3: The Hungarian Uprising of 1956

"If ten or so Hungarian writers had been shot at the right moment, the revolution would never have occurred." Nikita Khrushchev[1], December 1956.

Caught Up in the Revolution

On Wednesday, October 24, 1956, I awoke as usual around six o'clock in the morning. My mother had already gone to work at the nearby chemical factory, where her shift started at 6:00 a.m. I needed to get dressed, eat breakfast, and walk about ten minutes to reach the nearest streetcar stop by no later than 7:00 a.m.

I had to take three streetcars to reach the Budapest Technical University in Buda,[2] and if everything went well, I could make my 8:00 a.m. class. My trip would take me across the Liberty Bridge from Pest to Buda, where I would get off at the first stop on Béla

---

[1] Nikita Khrushchev (1894-1971) was Stalin's successor and was the First Secretary of the Soviet Communist Party.

[2] Buda and Pest were unified on January 1, 1873, under the name of Budapest. Hungarians still refer to the two parts divided by the Danube River as Buda on the west and Pest on the east.

Bartók[1] Road. The university was located behind Béla Bartók Road, overlooking the Danube, another five-minute walk from the stop.

Leaving our building on 7 Fűzér Street, I turned right and walked to the very first corner, where our street crossed Kőrösi Csoma Road. At the corner, I turned left in front of the building that was the Communist Party headquarters for our district. The streetcar stop was only a five-minute walk from this corner to the most commercial intersection of Kőbánya.

I looked to the right at the corner to see if the familiar yellow streetcar was coming. Because the road was straight for over a mile, I could spot the streetcar quite a distance away, helping me make an on-the-spot decision whether to run for it. Nothing was visible this morning, so I took my time walking to the stop.

I was standing at the streetcar stop for a few minutes already when I began to feel that something was out of the ordinary. There were fewer people waiting at the stop than normal, no streetcars were coming from either direction, and no buses or trucks were rumbling down the cobblestone road. There was an eerie silence, devoid of the usual cacophony of noises at this time of the morning.

The Budapest public transportation system was excellent, and streetcars and buses usually came every five to seven minutes during rush hour, but not on this morning. As I waited impatiently, I noticed a group of people across the street on the sidewalk, facing a wall that had large placards posted on it. I began to wonder what was going on, so I decided to cross the street to see what everybody was looking at.

Taped to the wall were handwritten posters proclaiming, "Russian troops, withdraw from Hungary!"; "We want a new gov-

---

[1]   Béla Bartók (1881–1945), Hungarian composer; lived in America for the last five years of his life.

ernment led by Imre Nagy!"[1]; "We want economic independence from the Soviet Union!"; and similar provocative demands.

A vague familiarity with the messages started to dawn on me, and I realized after a few minutes that these demands were excerpts from the Sixteen-Point Proclamation of the students, distributed to everyone and read aloud at a march the previous day. Still, I couldn't understand what these posters had to do with the fact that I had been waiting for more than fifteen minutes for my streetcar, which was nowhere in sight.

A man standing next to me quietly said, "Look over there," and jerked his head to the right, drawing my attention to the opposite direction from where I was expecting the streetcar to come. About fifty yards away, in the middle of the road, I saw an overturned military vehicle and two bodies next to it on the ground in what looked like Russian military uniforms. I was now beginning to connect the dots. I suddenly realized that what I was witnessing that cold Wednesday morning was somehow in some dramatic but yet unexplained way connected to the activities I participated in the day before.

Tuesday, October 23, the day before, was an unusual day for all of us students at the university. I hardly remember the morning except for the hustle and bustle of the large student body getting ready for an afternoon march to the statue of Joseph Bem, a Polish general who fought for Hungary's freedom during the 1848 revolution.

The march was to show solidarity with demonstrations that took place a week earlier in Poland, where a major confrontation involving the Polish workers, supported by their army and the political authorities, was averted in mid-October. Khrushchev personally

---

[1]   Imre Nagy (1896–1958) was a dedicated communist trained in Moscow during Stalin's era. He was prime minister when Khrushchev dismissed him in April 1955 for being too liberal and being too critical of the Soviets. He was stripped of all his political power, and when he refused to "admit his errors," he was expelled from the party. Many Hungarians revered him as a kind and people-oriented person.

flew to Poland to settle the crisis, agreeing to a number of concessions demanded by the Poles.

I was just milling around in the great hall of the university, eavesdropping on conversations, when I learned of another and apparently significant event that took place a couple of weeks earlier in Szeged, Hungary, a large city southeast of Budapest near the Yugoslav border. Students at Szeged University quit the Communist Youth Organization, a near-mandatory membership for all students, and established a new, previously banned student organization independent from the government.

Both events, the one in Poland and the one in Szeged, Hungary, were rather extraordinary, but they didn't mean much to me since I paid little attention to political events in Hungary and even less to events in Poland. I was a freshman just orienting myself with the new surroundings the past six weeks with no involvement in student politics. I had yet to build friendships with any of my engineering classmates, and I was not included in any of the meetings and discussions of the student body that planned the march for October 23.

Another factor explains but doesn't excuse my ignorance of the preceding events. Since 1948, when the communists finally achieved the political takeover of the country, we had undergone eight years of intense communist propaganda. After a while, most of the government's slogans, placards, meetings of the Communist Youth Party, demonstrations for and against various issues, newspaper headlines, and special educational courses extolling the virtues of communism over the Imperialist West's capitalism fell on deaf ears.

At the age of 18, the only things that got me excited were girls and sports—not necessarily in that order. If I wanted to know what was going on in the outside world, like most Hungarians, I listened to Radio Free Europe and the Voice of America, ignoring the risk of being jailed.

Another explanation for my political deafness was that I had no adult authority at home with whom to seriously discuss politics. My mother and I rarely ever discussed politics. I didn't know but later learned that her disinterest in any serious discussion was due to her complete lack of understanding of what was going on.

Beyond complaining about the ever-increasing "norma"[1] set by her factory managers, the best I could get out of my mother was that people in the Communist Party were "a band of stinking, lying, and stealing whores," a rather astute but less than scholarly assessment. Of course, she, too, was a member of the Communist Party, like everyone else. However, there must have been a subtle distinction to her membership that I was supposed to see.

Attending the university meant only two things for me: First, just by being admitted to the university I was fulfilling my ambition and one of my mother's dreams. I was brainwashed from childhood that I had to get a good education. The lessons of the Holocaust, only eleven years behind us, were not lost on my mother or her older brother, Uncle Laci.

Their words were etched into my consciousness: "Remember that you are a Jew and that they can take everything away from you, but they can never take away what is in your head." "They" in this message was a generic reference to the Nazis or fascists or any other people with the power to implement a threat. I must have heard this commandment hundreds of times.

These were not just empty words to me, but a stark reminder of my own Holocaust experiences, which didn't fade away. Having been accepted at the university, I at least partially fulfilled one of my obligations. I was now guaranteed, unless I completely screwed up my studies, that I could get a good education, which would assure me not only a decent living as an engineer but also the acquisition of something that could "never be taken away from me."

The second significance of being a university student was my monthly scholarship from the university. Hungary had its own "affirmative action" policy for students from working-class families. A basic tenet of the communist system was that the workers and peasants were in charge and not the former bourgeois class. As such,

---

[1] Quotas for piecemeal work, or norms. Tremendous pressure was put on workers to exceed the norms, but when workers regularly met or exceeded their norms, the norms were raised.

children of working-class families had preference in admission and in receiving financial aid.

This was essential in our socialist economic system since most working-class families couldn't afford to have their children go to college instead of bringing home a paycheck. My stipend of 270 forints[1] per month represented about 25 percent of my mother's monthly salary and made a big difference in our standard of living. My mother's weekly paycheck rarely lasted through the end of the week. If it hadn't been for her very best friend, I don't know how we ever would have survived the previous ten years.

Unfortunately, as I saw it at the time, the price of financial dependence on Manci néni was her meddling in my upbringing. I knew on which side our bread was buttered. Having my scholarship from the university freed us from financial dependence on her, and for me it brought a much sought-after degree of independence.

There was something else in the back of my mind that preoccupied me at this time in late October. I was still going through the culture shock of transferring from high school to the university. High school was easy for me, and I had good grades without too much studying, leaving plenty of time for sports. Out of the ten subjects we had to pass on a final oral and written exam, I ended up with the top grade of "Excellent" on eight and "Good" on two.

Nevertheless, in spite of my excellent grade in chemistry, I now had a huge problem looming over me at the university. I brought this on myself by cheating my way through my chemistry finals while learning the absolute minimum I could manage. I could blame my gym teacher for this, but being more mature now than in 1956, I can now fess up to my stupidity.

I was one of the star athletes all through high school. I was good at soccer, swimming, gymnastics, and most other sports. Primarily, I was a very good mid-distance runner. Miklós Bánki, my gym teacher,

---

[1] The value of the forint was not pegged to any hard currency, such as the dollar, and therefore no conversion is available. Based on its buying power, I would estimate that 270 forints was then equivalent to about $10. Today, 295 forints is approximately $1.

wanted me to continue to train and to race all through my junior year, the last year we had chemistry in high school.

I really didn't want to continue running for a number of reasons, one of them being my intent to prepare for my chemistry final that covered three years' worth of study. However, my gym teacher insisted, and we made a Faustian deal. I would continue to train and race; in return, he would find a way to make sure that I passed my oral and written chemistry exams.

Fortunately, my gym teacher held up his end of the bargain and I received the highest possible grade in chemistry. The downside of the bargain was that by the time I graduated a year later, I hardly remembered any of the material.

Nevertheless, it was shocking when I discovered that I would have to take advanced chemistry during my first year at the university. Not to mention that one of the toughest professors would be teaching it. I had been attending his classes since September, so I knew that I was in deep trouble.

Tests were coming up soon, and I had to brush up on three years of high school chemistry in just a few weeks. Thus, politics and what happened in Poland were the farthest things from my mind.

When I look back at this not-so-proud moment in my early life, I must admit that the moral issue of cheating on my high school chemistry final exam didn't disturb me much. Of course, I knew it was wrong, and I never told my mother about it.

I don't wish to make an excuse for myself by claiming that society was responsible for my immoral upbringing. However, the reality was that I lived in a world where cheating, lying, and stealing were, as my mother was fond of saying, normal events in the ordinary course of one's daily life.

I hadn't yet heard of Friedrich Hayek, the economist and political philosopher who so eloquently argued that socialist societies and their totalitarian propaganda "are destructive of all morals because they undermine the foundations of all morals: the sense of the respect for the truth."[1]

Anyway, I was somewhat preoccupied with my academic problems on October 23 as I tagged along with about five thousand of my fellow university peers and enjoyed the day off from classes. A sheet of paper was distributed to everyone with the following Sixteen-Point Proclamation:

1. We demand the immediate withdrawal of Soviet troops from Hungary in accordance with the Peace Treaty.[2]

2. We demand an election of new leaders of the Hungarian Workers' Party[3] by secret ballot on the local, intermediate, and central levels. The Party Congress should be convened and elect a new Central Committee.

3. The government should be reorganized under the leadership of Comrade Imre Nagy. All guilty leaders of the Stalinist-Rákosi era must be relieved of their duties.

4. We demand a public inquiry into the criminal activities of Mihály Farkas and his accomplices. Mátyás Rákosi, who is the person most responsible for all the crimes of the recent past, and for destroying our country, must be brought back to Hungary for trial before a people's tribunal.

5. We demand general, secret elections in the country in which all political parties may participate with the purpose of electing a new Parliament. We demand that the right of the workers to strike be assured.

6. We demand revision and readjustment of Hungarian-Soviet and Hungarian-Yugoslav relations in the fields of politics, economics, and cultural affairs, on the basis of complete

---

[1] Friedrich A. Hayek (1899–1992); born in Vienna, Austria; became a British citizen; Nobel Prize winner in Economics in 1974; author, *The Road to Serfdom* (The University of Chicago Press, 1944), page 155.

[2] The Peace Treaty was signed between Hungary and the Soviet Union on February 18, 1948, after the communist takeover.

[3] The Communist Party.

political and economic equality and of noninterference in the internal affairs of one by the other.

7. We demand the reorganization of Hungarian economic life with help of our experts. The entire economic system, based on a planned system, must be reexamined in light of conditions in Hungary and in the vital interests of the Hungarian people.

8. Our foreign trade agreements and the exact total of reparations that can never be paid must be made public. We demand precise and exact information on the uranium deposits in our country, on their exploitation, and on the concessions accorded to the Russians in this area. We demand that Hungary have the right to sell uranium freely at world-market prices to obtain hard currency.

9. We demand the complete revision of the norms in effect in industry and an immediate and radical adjustment of salaries in accordance with the just requirements of the workers and intellectuals. We demand a minimum wage for the workers.

10. We demand that the distribution system be reorganized on a new basis and that agricultural products be utilized in a rational manner. We demand equal support for independent farmers.

11. We demand reviews by independent tribunals of all political and economic trials as well as the release and rehabilitation of the innocent. We demand an immediate repatriation of prisoners of war and of civilian deportees in the Soviet Union, including prisoners sentenced outside Hungary.

12. We demand complete recognition of freedom of opinion and of expression, of freedom of the press and of radio, as well as the creation of a new daily newspaper for the MEFESZ.[1]

13. We demand that the statue of Stalin, a symbol of Stalinist tyranny and political oppression, be removed as quickly as

---

[1] Acronym for *Hungarian Federation of University and College Student Association.*

possible and be replaced by a monument to the memory of the martyrs of the 1848–49 Revolution.

14. We demand the replacement of emblems that are foreign to the Hungarian people by the former Kossuth arms. We demand a new uniform for the army conforming to our national tradition. We demand that March 15 be declared a national holiday and that October 6 be a day of mourning on which schools will be closed.

15. The students of the Technological University of Budapest declare unanimously their solidarity with the workers and students of Warsaw and Poland in their movement towards national independence.

16. The students of the Technological University of Budapest will organize local branches of the MEFESZ as rapidly as possible and have decided to convoke in Budapest on Saturday, October 27, a Youth Parliament at which all the nation's youth will be represented by their delegates.

Some of the proclamations made sense to me and I could relate to them. However, others I could not. For example, I didn't understand why Rákosi, who was officially revered in Hungary for the last eight years, as Stalin was in Russia, was suddenly a criminal. The famous denouncement of Stalin by Khrushchev had taken place just a few months earlier, and I hadn't paid any attention to it. I didn't understand any of the proclamations dealing with our economic and trade system.

Imre Nagy's name sounded vaguely familiar, but I didn't know who he was. I wasn't aware that our relationship with Yugoslavia needed to be "revised" and "readjusted." I knew Hungary had bauxite mines, but what did that have to do with uranium? Maybe if I had paid attention in chemistry class, I would have known.

And who was Mihály Farkas?[1] I had heard his name in connection to the Hungarian secret police, but I didn't know his role. Overall, I was mildly excited about the Sixteen-Point Proclamation, but I couldn't imagine how any of these declarations would change my life one way or another had they been attained.

There was talk that the authorities didn't approve of our march. Nonetheless, following a lot of commotion, the march finally began in the middle of the afternoon. General Bem's statue was a mile north along the Danube at the Margaret Bridge. Along the way we passed by the Elizabeth and Chain Bridges. The march started out slowly but then picked up some speed.

22. Technical University students marching to General Ben's square on October 23, 1956. I am in the back with all the other freshmen.

Many bystanders and ordinary workers joined us, young and old, swelling our ranks. Singing started of the "Internationale" and

---

[1] Mihály Farkas (1904–1965) was the sadistic head of the secret police that designed, organized, and operated much like the Russian KGB. He fought in the Spanish Civil War and settled in Moscow, where he became the secretary of the Communist International of Youth Workers. Upon Rákosi's request he was transferred to the Hungarian party.

the French national anthem, "Marseillaise," but I knew only a few words and couldn't sing along.

The mood then changed from the initial silent march to more zeal, and I noticed that some Hungarian flags were flown from the balconies of the passing houses with the communist symbol, the hammer and a sheaf of wheat, cut out from the center. We cheered a man on as he was trying to remove the red star adorning the top of one of the buildings.

No policemen were seen, but we knew there were plainclothes ÁVH[1] men around. The Sixteen-Point Proclamation was handed out to everyone along the way. It was a lively yet peaceful demonstration without any violence.

Our march was coordinated with other universities on the Pest side of the city, whose students marched along the Danube and

crossed over to Buda at the Margaret Bridge. Our destination, where General Bem's statue stood, was very crowded when we arrived. There must have been tens of thousands of people there and most of us couldn't even get close to the statue to hear the reading of the Sixteen-Point Proclamation.

After each point was read aloud, applause rippled through the crowd, even though most of us couldn't hear the speaker

23. Statue of Joseph Ben, October 23, 1956.

---

[1] "ÁVH" stood for National Defense Bureau, which was like a combination of the CIA and the FBI, and had extraordinary powers over the life of ordinary citizens. It reported directly to the Communist Party leadership and not to the proforma political "elected" leadership of the country.

since there was no public address system. Well-known nationalistic poetry was read and patriotic songs were sung, including the then-forbidden national anthem, which starts with the words "Isten áld meg a Magyart"—or "God bless the Hungarians." While the music of the national anthem wasn't forbidden, singing the lyrics was due to the fact that they included the word "God."

This was to be the end of the official march, but nobody seemed to want to disband and go home. By now, we were all fired up. It appeared that every single display of defiance, like flying the Hungarian flag without the communist symbol, the removal of the red star from a building, or singing the national anthem, further emboldened and strengthened the crowd, urging us to continue this mass expression of desire for change. Never had I been witness to such spontaneous emotional dynamics before.

There was shouting to go and march to the Parliament. Others wanted to march to Heroes Square, where Stalin's statue stood. I decided to join the marchers to go to the Parliament, and crossed over the Margaret Bridge to Pest with thousands of students and other marchers. There were so many people on the bridge that all the streetcars and buses on the bridge were trapped and motionless as we crossed. After crossing the bridge, we turned right and continued to march to the Parliament, located on the Kossuth Lajos[1] Square, where the same proclamations, speeches, and songs were repeated.

By now, what started out as a student march with a list of objectives had evolved into a mass demonstration of at least one hundred thousand people. Tens of thousands of students from other major universities joined in, as did many ordinary Hungarians. The workday typically ended around four o'clock, and many office and factory workers from around the city joined the demonstration.

---

[1] Kossuth Lajos (1802–1894) is one of the most famous Hungarian patriots who actually traveled to the United States in 1848, asking for American financial help to win the revolution. He dedicated his life to the freedom and liberty of Hungary, fought to end serfdom and aristocracy, and to establish Hungary's independence from Austria. Kossuth's statue is in the US Capitol building in Washington, DC.

I was never in a crowd as big as this before, except the compulsory traditional May Day parade. That parade was always well organized, and everyone was told exactly when and where to march. We sang officially approved songs and carried officially approved signs and flags. At the end, we were all happy to go home. This march was nothing like that. You could feel the energy, the excitement, and the spontaneous dynamics of the crowd in the air, as if the whole city had come alive.

24. Mass demonstration in front of Parliament, October 23, 1956.

Radios blasted from open windows, mixed with singing and loud speakers that amplified slogans and encouragements to the demonstrators. I felt energized and was riding the emotional wave of the crowd. The march turned out to be more exciting than I thought it would be. This was the first time in my memory that I saw people freely expressing their feelings in public, not caring about the potential consequences. It was a thrilling and exciting experience, a rare moment of genuine happiness.

It was getting dark, and I was alone without close friends to share the excitement of the day. Thus, I decided to stay close to the Parliament, where I was familiar with the neighborhood. I knew my mother would also be anxiously waiting for me if I didn't show up soon.

As darkness fell, I hopped on the number 2 streetcar that ran right in front of the Parliament building and I was on my way home. I realized then how tired I was. We had marched for hours; I was hoarse from singing, and I was hungry. But most importantly, I was elated. This spectacular day opened up some new possibilities I would never have thought existed. I was eager to see what tomorrow would be like back at the university.

I got home shortly after ten o'clock and told my mother my experiences of the day. I went to bed with innocent thoughts of the next day's classes. We didn't have a telephone, a luxury and privileged possession in those days, and there was no way for us to find out what was happening in the city after I left. And that is how I missed the most crucial and historic part of the evening, which marked the turning point for the transformation of a peaceful demonstration into a bloody uprising. I often wondered what might have happened to me if I had stayed with my fellow students and participated in what was yet to come.

A few hours later, at seven o'clock in the morning on October 24, as I stood there looking at the dead Russian soldiers, I realized that something extraordinary must have happened the night before after I left the crowd at the Parliament. I had mixed emotions; I felt a mild excitement as I began to recall the events of the previous day, but I also felt a deep anxiety about what all these unimaginable events would mean for my mother and me.

What did happen last night? Maybe the overturned jeep and the dead Russian soldiers were some kind of a freak accident and things would be back to "normal" in a few days. Was the university closed? If so, how long before things turned back to normal and I could return to the university to receive my stipend of 270 forints that was due any day now? I rushed home to turn on the radio.

As I hurried along on the main road, I noticed a petite old woman who rushed, almost ran, just a little bit ahead of me. She was dressed in a long black skirt and had a black kerchief on her head, more like a peasant than a city dweller. I was staring at her back when suddenly a window opened in front of her on the right and a portly lady with disheveled hair stuck her head out and asked the old lady, "What's going on?"

The old woman turned right so that I could actually see her wrinkled face and replied in a squealing voice, "We are killing the

Jews! We are killing the Jews!" She said it twice as if for emphasis and continued to hurry on without even pausing. Then she crossed Fűzér Street, where I turned right.

I was stunned. What was this all about? I was accustomed to hearing anti-Semitic remarks once in a while. I knew that anti-Semitism didn't die out with the Soviet liberation of Hungary from German occupation in 1945; it was only driven underground during the communist regime. I was on the streets just the day before for twelve hours, surrounded by thousands of people, and didn't recall one anti-Semitic slur. I shrugged off her comments and went home to listen to the news, although the image of the old lady has remained frozen in my memory.

I went home and turned on the radio, our primary source of news. There were some very unusual and rapid announcements the morning of October 24:

> 8:30 a.m.—Repeat of an earlier broadcast from 4:30 a.m.: Imre Nagy was appointed as new prime minister; "fascist, counterrevolutionary elements have launched an armed attack on our public buildings and on our armed security formations." The announcer said it was signed by the Council of Ministers, the organization headed by the prime minister.

> 9:15 a.m.—Ernő Gerő[1] delivers a speech: "The dastardly armed attack of the counterrevolutionary gangs during the night...and have therefore applied for help to the Soviet formation stationed in Hungary under the terms of the Warsaw Treaty."

---

[1] Ernő Gerő (1898–1980), first secretary of the Hungarian Communist Party, was a lifelong communist and spent most of his life in the Soviet Union, but unlike Imre Nagy, Gerő was universally hated, like his predecessor Rákosi, and was characterized as a "soulless Stalinist technocrat, a cross between an inquisitor and a computer."

9:30 a.m.—Martial law has been proclaimed with summary death penalty for troublemakers. The announcer mentions that Imre Nagy, new chairman of the Council of Ministers, signed the order.

These announcements were confusing. I wasn't a fascist or counterrevolutionary. I wondered where all these fascist or counterrevolutionaries came from. Were the demonstrations taken over by others after I left Parliament Square last night? That didn't make sense.

Both Radio Free Europe and Voice of America repeated the same announcement made on Hungarian radio stations, thereby giving them credibility. This was a serious blow to whatever hope Nagy might have had to use his personal popularity and prestige to achieve some semblance of order in the streets, exactly as Gerő planned it.

Around noon, Nagy made a long speech, promising amnesty to all "freedom fighters" that laid down their arms by 2:00 p.m. Afterward, Hungarian Radio broadcast several messages, all of them trying to rouse popular support against the counterrevolution, and then another curfew was announced.

I wasn't politically savvy enough to read between the lines, but I understood that something went very wrong the night before. "Death penalty," "counterrevolutionaries," help requested under the "Warsaw Pact" were ominous words, and I could sense the panic in the air. The announcements also portrayed Nagy as the "bad guy," which didn't make sense based on what I had heard the day before.

Since the demonstrators demanded to have Nagy as the head of a new government, why was he now antagonistic and seemingly angry with the insurgents? After all, the student proclamations asked for significant changes, but they didn't repudiate the communist system.

My mother came home from work and told me that there was chaos at the factory. They were forming new "revolutionary committees" at work. She was worried; based on her experiences, any political upheaval represented a potential physical danger to us. However, I was less concerned, even though the image of the old peasant-looking woman I encountered earlier that morning was fresh in my mind, which I never told my mother about.

By the end of that day, through the radio and the local grapevine, I knew that something major and unprecedented had happened the night before and had continued throughout the day. However, I couldn't form a clear picture of the state of affairs in either the city or other parts of the country.

The next day, Thursday, October 25, brought other surprising news. In the early morning, the Hungarian radio announced, "The Army, the State Security Forces, and armed workers guard have liquidated, with the help of Soviet troops, the attempts at a counterrevolutionary coup d'état."

No doubt that this announcement sounded strange. When did the armed workers guard join forces with the ÁVH and the invading Russian tanks? I heard the day before that revolutionary committees had been created all over in support of the Uprising. It was painfully obvious that what I heard on the radio was not the truth. Then, around ten o'clock in the morning, we heard on the radio that Gerő had been dismissed, and János Kádár,[1] whom I had never heard of before, was appointed as the new first secretary of the party.

In our neighborhood, people on the street were going on about their business as usual. I decided to visit an old friend, Gabi Erőd, who lived just a few blocks from us. I needed to find out more about what had been happening in the city. His father married another young woman, so Gabi ended up having a half-brother more than ten years his junior. His new stepmother was kind and always welcomed me in their home.

---

[1] János Kádár (1912–1989) had been a staunch communist since 1931, when he was nineteen years old. He spent many years in prison under the prewar Hungarian regime, under the German occupation, and later under the communist regime from 1951 through 1954. He was "rehabilitated" and became a member of the Hungarian Politburo in July 1956. He ruled Hungary for the next thirty-three years, and the expression of "Goulash Communism," referring to the mildest form of a repressive Soviet satellite regime, was associated with his name. His regime ended just about the time the Iron Curtain fell. He died shortly after that on July 6, 1989.

No sooner had I found Gabi at home than he told me that the local police station had been broken into and they were handing out guns to anybody who wanted one. "Do you want to go and get one?" he asked. "Sure, why not?" I responded, and off we went to the police station. Of course, I didn't have the foggiest idea of what to do with a gun, but declining the invitation would have been embarrassing.

Indeed, when we got to the police station, we found several people milling about and an older person without a uniform was handing out guns to everyone who lined up. We joined the line, and before I knew it, I had a gun in my hand for the very first time in my life. It was a heavy bolt-action rifle, probably Russian-made WWII vintage, and it was long enough to reach up to my shoulders.

The man handing out the guns asked everyone to sign a book he had on the table next to him, which scared me for a moment. Nonetheless, by then I was committed, and with the gun in one hand, I signed the book as "Róbert Reichmann," which was no longer my legal name.

I then realized that perhaps I had made a rash decision to obtain a gun, not having thought of the consequences. Additionally, I was aware that putting down my original name instead of my relatively new one would not provide much cover for me. After living in the same place for eighteen years, virtually everyone in Kőbánya knew me as Róbert Reichmann and not as Róbert Rátonyi.

However, it was too late to worry, and Gabi and I marched to his place to figure out what to do next. It then dawned on us that we had no ammunition, and even if we did, we had no idea how to load the guns. We didn't care. The last thing in our minds was firing a gun at somebody.

Gabi and I decided to go into the city the next day and explore what was going on. We would listen to the radio in the morning and take stock of the situation before we took off. There was no public transportation at all, so we had to prepare for a long walk into the city and back. We were going to start early and walk all the way to Gabi's mother's place in the city, a good four-hour trek. I had never been there before, but Gabi assured me that she would welcome us and feed us lunch when we got there.

I went home with the gun on my shoulder to wait for my mother to come home. As I walked through the gate of 7 Fűzér Street, an older woman, perhaps in her forties, came toward me. Her face was familiar to me, but I didn't know her name or who she was.

As she approached me, she stopped. Her facial expression suddenly changed with recognition, and she loudly admonished me, "You, Róbert Reichmann, a Jewish boy, a university student. Your mother is a party secretary, you now carry a gun to defeat the system? Shame on you!" Next, she lifted her right hand and slapped me hard across the face, then turned and disappeared through the gate.

I stood there stunned, not knowing what to do. I looked around, hoping that no one else had witnessed this event, and hurried to our apartment, where I disappeared inside. I put the gun in the corner near the kitchen door and tried to collect myself.

Who was this woman? Was she a friend of my mother? How did she know so much about us? What did my having a gun have to do with being Jewish? She certainly didn't seem intimidated by the sight of the gun. The whole situation with the gun started to give me an eerie feeling. Who knows what trouble I would cause my mother and her position as party secretary if word got around that I was seen with a gun.

But my troubles this day were not yet over. When my mother came home, she almost fainted when she saw the gun in the kitchen corner. She started to cry, and with a painful expression on her face, she exhorted me, "My dear son, why did you bring a gun into our home? What are you planning to do with this gun? What if people find out?" She continued on, and I was stunned. This was the second time in one day that my gun got me into trouble, and now I felt terribly guilty for making my mother cry.

I made the lame excuse that it was Gabi's idea, but nothing could console her or appease her emotional distress. It occurred to me much too late that the sight of the gun brought back terrible memories for her. It was almost exactly twelve years earlier when she was forcibly removed, literally at gunpoint, from this very same two-room apartment and ordered to march out the gate, leaving me behind, her only child, and not knowing if we would ever see each other again.

I was stupid and inconsiderate. As I grew older, I simply added this incident to all my other infractions that caused my mother a great deal of pain during her life. Having children of my own, I now understand that the downside of living a long life is that your children can hurt you for a longer period of time.

I tried to console my mother and told her not to worry, that Gabi and I just wanted to go into the city and see for ourselves what was going on. We felt that it was safer to do this with a gun than without one. However, I conveniently neglected to tell her that I signed my name in a book at the police station, as well as about the incident with the strange woman in our gateway.

Another significant change was that there were suddenly a number of newspapers available that we had never seen before. I was familiar with the most popular papers called *Szabad Nép* (Free People) and *NépSzava* (Voice of the People) that normally carried the same stories and were the propaganda organs of the state. Conversely, a number of papers with different political viewpoints and positions became accessible, all of which were in support of the Uprising.

We finally had other media sources, in addition to the radio, about the events that took place on the night of October 23 and the subsequent couple of days on the streets of Budapest and in other cities. It was from these papers that all of Hungary learned the eye-witness details of the tragic events that took place at the Hungarian Radio building on the night of October 23.

On that day, about simultaneously as I hopped on a streetcar to go home, a large number of students marched to the radio building and demanded that our Sixteen-Point Proclamation be broadcast. Earlier in the afternoon, in anticipation of a potential problem, the ÁVH sent reinforcements of three hundred men to the radio building. By 8:30 or 9:00 p.m., the ÁVH men, positioned at the upper windows and on the rooftop of the building, were getting more and more nervous as the crowd got angrier and continued to demand access to the radio.

First, warning shots were fired. Then, shortly after 9:00 p.m., tear gas canisters were thrown from the upper windows of the building, and one or two minutes later ÁVH men opened fire on the crowd, killing a number of people and wounding others. The first innocent drop of blood was shed, and there was no turning back.

The crowd stormed the gates, and when they broke through, the ÁVH men were ready in formation with bayonets fixed. More shots were fired, and more students fell. The government ordered both police and nearby army units to head for the radio building to contain and disperse the crowd. Some four hundred policemen assessed the situation and declared that they were not going to fire on their fellow Hungarians. The army units went even further. Not only did they refuse to fight the crowd, but they also decided to join and provide the people guns and ammunition.

25. Canvas attached to the balcony says, "Free Hungarian Radio," with precommunist-era Hungarian emblem.
October 24, 1956.

The siege of the Hungarian Radio building continued until about 3:00 a.m. the next day. When it was over and in the demonstrators' control, there were dozens dead, including many ÁVH men. By midnight, the news of the killings at the radio building had spread across the city, and angry crowds demanded revenge on the hated

ÁVH. There was a full-scale armed revolt in Budapest, clearly the turning point from a peaceful demonstration into a bloody revolt.

The papers also reported on another noteworthy event that happened simultaneously with but independently of the storming of the radio building. Thousands of demonstrators gathered around the statue of Stalin near Heroes Square and tried to topple the huge seventy-five-foot-tall bronze statue. Workers from a nearby lamp factory used blowtorches to melt the statue around its knees. With the aid of steel ropes tied around Stalin's head being pulled by a tank, the statue was toppled, an event that I wish I could have witnessed.

26. Stalin's severed head on the street, October 24, 1956.

The severed head of Stalin was displayed in the middle of the street. By Thursday evening, it was evident that earlier radio announcements of the last two days concerning the joint efforts of the Soviet forces and the armed workers "to eliminate the counterrevolutionaries" were completely false.

The real story entailed Gerő losing his nerve on the evening of October 23 and calling for the Russians to intervene and move their troops into Budapest to restore order. With that decision, the die was cast to use violence to end the confrontation.

There were two Soviet tank divisions, the Second and the Seventh Mechanized Divisions, stationed about forty miles from Budapest. Following Gerő's invitation, the Russian tanks began to rumble across the cobbled streets of Budapest around 2:00 a.m. on Wednesday, October 24. The introduction of these tank units into Budapest had the unintended consequence of turning the people's anger from the hated ÁVH to the invading Russians.

Still, nobody had any idea of the political situation developing behind the closed doors of Parliament, party headquarters, or in Moscow, where the Russians were nervously watching the events unfolding in Hungary. We relied on Radio Free Europe and the Voice of America to provide insight as to what was happening in Budapest and around the world in reaction to the Uprising.

Apparently, the general strike that shut down all businesses, factories, farms, and all governmental units held, forcing the Russians to enter into discussions to withdraw their troops. Also, since both the army and police sided with the revolutionaries and the ÁVH men were in hiding, there was no one to enforce martial law as well as the curfew.

On Friday morning, October 26, the radio announced there would be no school that day. In addition, it broadcast that strikes continued at many places in the country and amnesty to the freedom fighters that was to end by 2:00 p.m. that day was extended to October 26 at 10:00 p.m. This was welcomed news for us if we were going to be in the city with guns on our backs. Also, the appointment of Kádár to replace Gerő was reiterated.

I walked over to Gabi's house, where we finally started our long walk into the city. We walked directly past the spot where I first saw the overturned military vehicle and the two dead Russians just a few days earlier. The vehicle and the bodies had disappeared without a trace.

We took the most direct route into the city along the Kőbányai Road to Orczy Square and continued straight, but the road was now named Baross Street. The closer we got to the city, the more destruction we saw. Several broken-down vehicles and a couple of burned-out tanks remained along the way. Trucks were going by with ordinary people in the back, flying the Hungarian flag minus the communist symbols. The number of people I saw with guns made me feel more comfortable with mine. After all, we were just a couple of ordinary Hungarian kids who took up arms against the Russians.

This walk was long, and we passed the time catching up on each other's recent life events. I divulged all my experiences at the university, and Gabi disclosed to me his lifelong ambition to become a professional soccer goalie. He was a year behind me, had not graduated from high school yet, and had no real desire to spend the next five years studying at a university. The fact that his family was well-heeled might have contributed to Gabi's lack of desire to pursue an education.

27. Young revolutionaries.

His life was consumed with playing soccer. Seldom did we get together without a soccer ball to kick around on the street or in the courtyard of his house when we were younger. He trained hard and played regularly all through high school. I saw him at matches, and he was impressive. He was fearless, had good reflexes, and could jump very well.

I often wondered how far he might have gone had he stayed with it. I suspect that his size, at about my size of five feet, six inches, was too small to become a superstar soccer goalie, considering the official goal size of twenty-four feet by eight feet.

As we got closer to the inner city, we didn't hear of any shootings and everything looked safe. We reached the Nagykőrut, or Big Ring, which was the outer ring of Budapest called József Boulevard.[1] Everything changed rather suddenly. It was as if we had entered a movie scene portraying the aftermath of war.

Several houses were heavily damaged with gaping chasms where windows used to be. Bullet holes were everywhere. Portions of the street looked like a tornado had swept through, turning everything

---

[1] ¹The Nagykőrút, or Big Ring of Budapest, is a complete circle of boulevards crossing over the Danube at the Petőfi and the Margaret Bridges. There is also a Kiskőrút, or Small Ring, which is more like a semicircle, going from the Freedom Bridge to the Chain Bridge in Pest.

upside down or on its side—yellow streetcars, trucks, military vehicles, and burned-out tanks.

More armed young people like we were appeared on the street in groups. We approached one group and started a conversation. I told them I was a Technical University student, which really impressed them. Everybody knew that the spark of the revolution was lit at our university. I conveniently neglected to tell them that I had virtually no part in planning the original demonstrations on Tuesday, much less the subsequent events on Tuesday night and Wednesday.

They asked us where we came from, and we told them we were from Kőbánya. They wanted to know if we had heard of any fights in our neighborhood, but we had nothing to report. I later learned that there was heavy fighting at the Dreher beer factory, not too far from where we lived, between armed workers and some Russian tanks. The boys told us about fierce fighting at the Kilian barracks, just one block away on Üllői Road. The Russians had mounted a major offensive at the Kilian barracks, but 1,200 Hungarian soldiers, under the direction of Colonel Maléter, held them back and destroyed a number of the tanks. Thus, the Russians finally withdrew.

28. Destroyed building at Baross Square and Rákóczi Road, October 29, 1956.

It was at this time that Gabi and I first heard about the massacre at the Parliament the day before. According to the boys, and later confirmed by the radio, a big crowd gathered there in the morning. There were a number of Russian tanks at the square, minding their own business. Some of the Russian tank commanders actually engaged in conversation with some Hungarians, many of whom had sufficient command of the Russian language after years of compulsory Russian education.

Suddenly, some ÁVH men stationed on top of the buildings facing the Parliament opened fire with automatic machine guns, aiming indiscriminately at everyone, including women, children, and even one or more of the Russian tank crews. The Russian tanks aimed their guns at the rooftops, eventually silencing the ÁVH killers. More than a hundred people had been killed and injured by the time the ÁVH guns ceased. This was quite a story to track down, but we decided not to go there because it was too far from where we were. Instead, we headed toward Gabi's mother's home.

We continued on Üllői Road, reached the Small Ring, and turned right onto Múzeum Boulevard. The street was full of people, many of them armed. We also noticed that several street names, typically secured on the corner walls of buildings, were crossed over diagonally with red paint and new street names were posted. As a small symbol of freedom and defiance, people had begun to reclaim the old street names used before the communists changed them.

The physical destruction was isolated yet ruinous. Many street shop windows were broken, but the merchandise was untouched. The Hungarian flag of red, white, and green was flying from windows and balconies in every building. Sections of the street were marred with cobblestones ripped off the pavement. Still, the worst sight was yet to come.

Suddenly, we came upon a number of bodies lying on the sidewalk. As we got closer, we could tell from their clothes that these were ordinary people. The

Hungarian civilian victims of the communist repression

29. Dead civilians, October 25, 1956.

dead included men, women, and young children. The bodies were sprinkled with lime and some flowers were placed on top of them.

Some of the dead were on their backs and their faces were frozen grimaces. The bizarre part was that ordinary people simply walked by, as if stepping around corpses on the sidewalk was a normal, daily routine in Budapest. Other than the two dead Russians I saw on the morning of October 24, this was the first indication of the deadly and violent nature of the Uprising. Gabi and I didn't speak to each other; we just pushed on.

As we reached another corner, an even worse sight appeared. At first it looked like some kind of long black sack hanging from a lamppost with some people milling around it. As we came up right next to this shapeless object, neither of us could make out what it was. Someone who noticed our puzzled looks simply stated, "ÁVH man." Then, I overheard fragments of a conversation.

A young guy standing around with what looked like a Russian-style submachine gun in his hand explained to another young man next to him, "He was hiding in...and we found him...he was an

30. Revolutionary justice, October 25 1956.

officer...stripped to his waist, hung him by his ankles, and started a fire under his head." His manner was rather casual as if it had been most ordinary for him to participate in this sordid affair. I doubted that he had had anything to do with this. To me he looked like he was just bragging and trying to build some respectability with his friends.

I was stunned, and I am sure Gabi was too, as we studied this lifeless, shapeless form that was a living, breathing human being just a few hours earlier. I was straining not to show the shock on my face in front of these strangers. All of a sudden, the little old lady shrieking "We are killing the Jews!" came to my mind. Is this what she meant? Were ÁVH men Jewish? I had no idea.[1] We silently walked away to make our way to Gabi's mother's place.

I was upset, maybe even scared, but I didn't know of what. Such brutality was displayed before us, and I just couldn't comprehend what could bring about such an act. Perhaps it was jarring to discover that ordinary people can commit such violent acts. Was the hatred against the ÁVH that intense? Was this revenge for years of brutal treatment, imprisonment, and even executions? If this unfortunate man was the victim, did that mean that Gabi and I were the victors? What are the acceptable limits of violence?

I had no answers then and still don't have them today. Those images of the dead lying on the sidewalk with their frozen expressions and what used to be a human being hanging from the lamppost have never left me. They have just been added to the ones from my days in the Budapest Ghetto in 1944–45. I was rapidly becoming accustomed to experiencing man's inhumanity toward his fellow man.

With our appetites gone, we continued to walk toward Gabi's mother's place. We heard sporadic gunfire and made sure to stay away from the sounds. Our whole mood had changed. We had to walk all the way to Népköztársaság (People's Republic) Road, a majestic, wide boulevard that runs like a spoke from the Small Ring toward Heroes Square near where Stalin's statue once stood.

As we arrived, we saw that its name had changed. The old name, Andrássy Road, was posted again. As promised, Gabi's mother prepared lunch for us and filled us in on some of the latest news. The West was more and more vocal about supporting the Hungarian Uprising. There was talk of food and medicine being brought in from Austria and other countries. The whole country was on strike. There was talk of the UN investigating the goings-on.

---

[1]   The idea of many Jews being in the upper echelons of the ÁVH is not far-fetched. After all, the top four political and intellectual leaders of Hungary since 1948 were all Jewish: Rákosi, Gerő, Farkas (the head of ÁVH), and Révai. This, combined with Hungary's strong anti-Semitic tradition, probably influenced the sudden anti-Jewish sentiment.

Gabi's mother confirmed the news we had heard about the large-scale killings at the Parliament. She offered to let us stay there for the night if we wanted to, but I declined because I had to get home. I used the excuse that we didn't have a telephone and my mother was expecting me. We said our goodbyes and started on our way back in the late afternoon because I wanted to get home before it got dark. After what we had seen, I no longer felt as safe as when we had left Kőbánya that morning.

We walked by the Kilian barracks on Üllői Road and saw the damage. We walked most of the way in silence, each of us immersed in our own thoughts. I had seen enough, and I needed time to digest all the events of that day. I began to realize the idiocy of walking into the city with unloaded guns on our backs. Additionally, there was something else bothering me that I couldn't put my finger on.

In hindsight, I felt somewhat alienated from what I witnessed. While I enthusiastically marched and shouted, together with thousands of my fellow students on October 23, the carnage and death I saw on the streets had a sobering effect. I then understood that revolutions are chaotic affairs; people get killed. We arrived home just as it was getting really dark. We shook hands and parted at the Zalka Máte Square, where I had waited Tuesday for the streetcar that never came. This was the last time, Friday, October 26, I saw Gabi in Hungary.

My mother was anxiously waiting for me, and I sat down to tell her what we had seen and experienced that day. Manci néni was also there and wanted to know what was going on in the city. She was distraught when she found out that I had a gun, and she predicted dire consequences for me. She was absolutely convinced that the Uprising was organized, launched, and managed by communist-hating, fascist reactionaries, just as the radio described during the first few days of the Uprising. She predicted severe retribution to all involved and urged me to dispose of the gun.

My argument that I didn't see any fascist or Western imperialist agents inciting the innocent crowds was countered by a dismissive gesture and by her conviction that I was clueless as to what was going on behind the Uprising, which was true. She also argued that foreign reactionary forces instigated it all, which of course was not true. And finally, she maintained that the Russians would return with unimaginable consequences, which also turned out to be true. We reached a stalemate, and my mother, like a referee at a Ping-Pong match, just watched the debate.

On Saturday, October 27, the Hungarian Radio building passed into the hands of the new Revolutionary Council, and with that, the news took on a different tone. Real information about what was happening all across the country was being reported. The strike continued; workers were demanding more and more reforms. Revolutionary Councils were formed in factories, government offices, the army, the police, and the unions, as well as among writers, poets, and at universities. Music from two popular and nationalistic Hungarian operas, *Hunyadi László* and *Bánk Bán*, were played throughout the day.[1]

The day after our trip into the city, I joined a group of armed young men and women who gathered at the post office, located next door to our house. This was the first time I was involved in an actual organized effort to defend against a potential Soviet counteroffensive. I was assigned to be stationed on the flat roof of the post office with a couple of other young guys I didn't know. We were given ammunition, and I was finally shown how to load my gun.

Defending the post office was probably a symbolic gesture, since there was not much of value there. The real action, if any, would be just down the street at what used to be the Communist Party headquarters. Now it was occupied by revolutionaries equipped with heavy machine guns. I was relieved to not be assigned to guard that building.

In the meantime, various events were unfolding in the political arena. In the afternoon of October 27, Imre Nagy announced

---

[1] Ferenc Erkel (1810–1893), the most significant Hungarian composer in the nineteenth century and the creator of Hungarian opera. His two most famous operas are *Hunyadi László* (a Hungarian statesman and warrior from the fifteenth century) and *Bánk Bán* ("Bán" denotes the rank or feudal title of viceroy, of a thirteenth-century nobleman named Bánk in this mediaeval tale). Both reflect universal tales of love, betrayal, fidelity, treachery, and struggle against oppression. Moreover, they express the Hungarian people's aspiration for independence from foreign rule. Erkel also composed the national anthem in 1844.

his new "provisional" government. The remarkable news was that it included, for the first time since 1948, six noncommunist out of a total of twenty-seven members. This was a minority of only 22 percent, but still an impressive number. At the same time, rumors were spreading that ex-party chief Gerő, predecessor to Kádár and ex-Prime Minister Hegedűs, predecessor to Nagy, had hurriedly fled the country for Russia.

Things seemed to be quieting down in the streets. There was a feeling of a cease-fire. The Russian tanks were no longer fighting, although they were still very much present at major points in the city. The biggest concern of most people, including my mother, was how to get food. Shops were empty, and we needed bread and other staples.

On Sunday afternoon, October 28, Nagy announced that the Russians agreed to withdraw their forces from Budapest. He informed the nation that negotiations had begun to settle the relationship between Hungary and the Soviet Union, that the ÁVH would be dissolved, and that a new, single police organization would be formed. The

31. Szent István Ring, Soviet troops temporary withdrawal from Budapest, October 31, 1956.

only demand Nagy made was that all fighting against the Russians and the scattered ÁVH stop immediately.

This was quite significant. It appeared that the Russians had conceded some of the key elements of the Sixteen-Point Proclamation, a major victory for the revolution. Ultimately, an immediate cease-fire was announced.

It is hard to describe the feeling of elation most of us had upon hearing this promising news. It seemed too good to be true that the

Uprising was successful and that the Russians had backed down and were willing to negotiate. Most Hungarians, including myself, still didn't have a clue about the political dynamics that took place behind closed doors.

News from the outside, through Radio Free Europe and Voice of America, kept pouring in, which was confusing and many times inconsistent with the news from the official state radio. I understood little of what was going on while my mother understood even less. Manci néni held fast to her views that the end was coming and the Russians would be back.

It was around this time that I decided to forsake my gun and once again become a civilian. I was just hoping I would be back at the university soon and life would return to its normal routine. As it turned out, much more excitement lay ahead.

Just when everything seemed to be going well—the cease-fire was holding, the Russians were seen to withdraw from the streets of Budapest, formal negotiations were going on for a final settlement with the Russians—we heard the news that war had broken out at the Suez Canal[1] on the Sinai Peninsula. Clueless as to what this meant for Hungary, I later learned this was bad news for us.

The events of the next few days were both sensational and confusing. Historic events were taking place in Hungary, but we only knew what we were being told on the radio from both within and outside the country:

---

[1] The Suez Canal crisis was precipitated by the Egyptian blockade of the Straits of Tiran, a vital trading route for Israel. On October 14, the president of Egypt, Gamal Nasser, made clear his intent and announced, "There is no sense in talking about peace with Israel. There is not even the smallest place for negotiations." Less than two weeks later, on October 25, Egypt signed a tripartite agreement with Syria and Jordan, placing Nasser in command of all three armies. The continued blockade of the Suez Canal and the Gulf of Aqaba to Israeli shipping, combined with the increased fedayeen attacks and the bellicosity of recent Arab statements, prompted Israel, with the backing of Britain and France, to attack Egypt on October 29, 1956.

Radio Free Europe and Voice of America encouraged fighters to hold on to their arms and fight until all the communists were driven out of the government. They called Nagy a communist,[1] and warned people not to trust him.

Israel was bombing the Suez Canal, and the UN was in emergency session to debate what to do. France and England decided to act unilaterally and joined the war.

Hungarian radio announced that earlier broadcasts (referring to the previous Gerő government) were full of lies and apologized to the nation.

Nagy announced a new cabinet and the decision to abolish the one-party system.[2]

Russians formally agreed to pull their troops out of Hungary.[3]

Voice of America and Radio Free Europe announced that the French and British forces were bombing Egypt.

The Hungarian cabinet was meeting to discuss implications of the Suez Canal crisis.

---

[1] Of course, he was a communist. Everybody in Hungary knew that. This commentary reflects the ignorance of the Western media and their attempt to stir up an anticommunist sentiment.

[2] Just a few days after the "provisional" government was announced, half of the new cabinet members were not communists, reflecting the tremendous pressure exhorted on Nagy to compromise. This was a major setback for the party loyalists, and it may have triggered the betrayal committed by Kádár a few days later.

[3] The cover story for stationing Russian tanks around the airports and cities was to assist in an orderly withdrawal of all the remaining forces and their families.

*Broadcast was made to the nation: the new cabinet
decided that Hungary would declare neutrality and
withdraw from the Warsaw Pact.*

This last piece of news was monumental. Even I could understand the unprecedented nature of it. It was hard to believe that we could go from full-scale, hard-core communism to a multiparty, democratic, neutral country in one week. We were all in a state of denial, except for Manci néni.

In the face of obvious signs of Russian determination to regain control of the political and military leadership, we all rejoiced and trusted Nagy, his government, and the international community to save us. The whole country was glued to the radio, listening to Voice of America and Radio Free Europe, anticipating that at any moment we would see the UN troops or the American paratroopers drop from the sky to help us secure the freedoms we had achieved.

By Saturday, November 3, the buses and some of the streetcars had started running again and the radio announced that plans were being made to open the schools. I was still wondering when I could return to the university. According to Hungarian radio, the situation in Budapest was calm; people were visiting restaurants and cafés and standing in line for food. Nobody on the street had any idea of the crisis that was brewing in Parliament and at the party headquarters. On the surface, it was the calm before the storm.

The next day, on November 4, we woke up at dawn to the sound of heavy gunfire not too far away, and I turned on the radio immediately. Shortly after, Imre Nagy came on the radio and announced in a somber voice:

This is Imre Nagy, president of the Council of Ministers of the Hungarian People's Republic. At dawn today the Soviet forces made an unprovoked attack on our capital with the clear intent to overthrow the legal democratic Hungarian government. Our troops are resisting; the gov-

ernment is in its place. This is my message to
Hungary and to the entire world.

Next came the same broadcast in German, which I recognized,
and then in another language that I didn't recognize at the time but
was probably English. Within a few minutes, another announcement
was heard:

> This is the Hungarian Writers Association speak-
> ing to all writers, scientists, writers' associations,
> academies, and scientific organizations of the
> world. We appeal for help to all intellectuals in
> all countries. Our time is limited. You all know
> the facts. There is no need to review them. Help
> Hungary! Help the writers, scientists, workers,
> peasants, and all Hungarian intellectuals. Help!
> Help! Help!

This was the beginning of the end of our revolution. The
sounds of gunfire were getting closer and closer, and my mother and
I decided that it was time for us to go down into the cellar, the same
cellar where we used to spend days and nights in during the Allied
bombings of Budapest in the fall of 1944. The cellar was damp and
cold and was primarily designed to provide extra storage space for
the residents. Residents from the other apartments were already there
with anxiety apparent on their faces.

Nobody understood what was happening. Why did the Russians
attack us all of a sudden? We were led to believe that negotiations
were underway for a diplomatic compromise. Everybody thought
that peacetime was just around the corner. What was going on?

A couple of hours later, when things quieted down outside, we
all clambered up the wooden steps and returned to our homes again.
We later learned that the radio went dead around eight o'clock in
the morning, most likely marking the end of the Nagy government.
This was Sunday, November 4, exactly twelve days since October 23,

but to me it seemed like a lifetime ago since I had marched with my fellow students to General Bem's statue.

Later that day, we heard the most bizarre news through a radio broadcast from János Kádár, a member of Nagy's new government. He informed the nation that he had formed a new Hungarian Revolutionary Workers-Peasant government and had asked the Soviet Union for military assistance.[1]

Feelings of nervousness started to take hold of me. The images and actions of the past ten days were coming back to haunt me. Signing my name in the book at the police station, being seen with a gun, the lady who confronted me at our house, and Manci néni's predictions were beginning to nag at me. Manci néni may be right again, and sure enough, it was not long before she showed up and self-righteously proclaimed, "I told you so."

During the next few days we spent more time in the cellar until we heard the radio announcement that the "counterrevolution" had been decisively defeated by "patriotic Hungarians supported by our historic friend, the Soviet Union, in a heroic struggle against the Western-inspired reactionary elements." Strangely, I didn't feel that I belonged to either side of this struggle. If anything, I felt sad and let down.

As the revolution had unfolded, I had begun to feel more and more enthusiastic about the potential outcomes, even though I couldn't fully comprehend what changes might take place. I was too young and naive, but I sensed that the promise of what might have been was a freer and happier life than the one we had been experiencing for the past eight years.

I could relate to getting rid of the Russians, to being more independent, and to some of the economic benefits promised. But the

---

[1] None of us knew it at the time that Kádár had become a turncoat and betrayed his friends and comrades in the new government, including Imre Nagy, his longtime friend and comrade. He had contacted the Russians a few days earlier and was secreted out of Budapest and flown to Moscow, where he made a deal: with Russian military support, he would bring the Uprising under control and return the Hungarian Communist Party to its former unrivaled leadership in exchange for the Russians installing him as the new leader of the country.

more subtle emotional, moral, and spiritual benefits of living in a "free society" had completely eluded me at the time. Living behind the Iron Curtain most of my life up to this point had robbed me of all conceptual and practical grounding in a "free society."

It took me many years, perhaps decades, to understand the moral damage the Stalinist-era communist dictatorship perpetuated on ordinary citizens. The lies we lived every day; the coercion to say, do, and even think as we were told; the official encouragement to spy on each other under the label of "proletarian vigilance" to protect us from the "imperialist" West; the daily signs of the personality cult imposed by Stalin and his pupil Rákosi in Hungary; the unwritten rule of the land that "everything was forbidden unless it was specifically allowed"; the fantasy that we were building a true socialist democracy and that the workers and peasants owned everything.

All these aspects had gradually, day by day, month by month, and year by year, infected our minds and souls, whether we were aware or not. I couldn't have come close to articulating these thoughts back in 1956, but deep down in the pit of my stomach I sensed there was something wrong with the system. And, as the sounds of the Soviet Army crushing the revolution became louder, I was saddened that whatever changes might have been were not to be.[1]

It took only about a week for the Soviet Army to crush the revolution, resulting in a heavy toll on human lives and significant damage to the city. This time, unlike on October 24, the Russian tanks came with additional reinforcement troops and were merciless in shooting at anything that moved on the streets. The Hungarians were no match for the superior Russian forces, and the much-desired help from the West never materialized.

The next time I ventured out to the corner of Fűzér Street and Kőrösi Csoma Road, the very same short walk I had made just about two weeks earlier to catch my streetcar to the university, I was taken

---

[1]　As it turned out, thirty-three years later, all the aspirations and hopes of the 1956 revolution became a reality. Hungary became a fully democratic country in 1989, the Soviet Army left Hungary in 1989, Hungary joined NATO in 1999, and she became a member of the European Union in 2004.

aback. What used to be the Communist Party Headquarters building was now just a pile of rubble with not even a single wall still standing. Workers and students took over the building on October 24 and used it as a center for coordinating the Uprising in the district.

I don't know if anybody ever fired a shot from that building, but the returning Soviet tanks had simply pulverized it. Now there was a military truck parked right in front of what used to be the building, and a Soviet soldier stood guard with his submachine gun at the ready. What exactly he was guarding is still a mystery to me. Perhaps it was a symbolic gesture to demonstrate that even the footprint of the party headquarters was to be defended at any cost.

As I walked by him and turned around to look in his face, I got scared. I had never seen a face like that, with the high cheekbones characteristic of people from Soviet Asia. He had a dark face, a long Fu Manchu mustache, and a weary look in his dark, piercing eyes. He wore the familiar Russian army hat with the red star in the middle and the ankle-long green winter coat as he stood on the truck bed looking down at me with his finger on the machine gun trigger.

I must admit I was quite intimidated. I always wondered if he saw me as the enemy he was told to fight in Hungary: the hate-filled fascist reactionary, hell-bent on destroying the democratic People's Republic built on the principles of Marx, Lenin, and Stalin. Perhaps he was more scared than I was, being thousands of miles from home, not knowing from which direction a sniper would aim at him.

I later found out why these strange-looking Soviet soldiers were in Hungary in November. The Russians didn't trust the troops they had stationed in Hungary prior to the Uprising. Events during the first few days of the revolution, when many Russian tank commanders refused to fire on the Hungarians, proved their suspicions right. Many of

32. Russian tanks returning to Budapest, November 4, 1956.

those troops had lived in Hungary for a long time, had established friendships with Hungarians, and were not to be trusted to accept the commands of their officers to shoot at the general population. That is why Russians brought in troops from Asia, who were soldiers mostly made up of rural people. They were told that they were in Hungary, a place on the map most of them had never seen, to crush a fascist Uprising.

During the last two weeks of November, we continued to hear sporadic shootings in our neighborhood and some innocent bystanders were killed. The most exciting news was that some of my friends had left the country and escaped to Austria. The first was Tibi Lesko, who had lived in our building ever since we moved there when I was a year old.

One day in late November, Tibi showed up and I had a chance to speak with him. He had been drafted into the border patrol two years earlier and was stationed on the Austrian border. His not-so-secret wish was to escape Hungary and live in the West, where he could pursue life as a jazz musician.

Tibi informed me that when the news of the Uprising reached the border guards, many of them got out of their uniforms, left their weapons behind, and escaped across the very border they were supposed to guard against Hungarians fleeing the country into Austria. Tibi said he came home to say goodbye to his mother and to his girlfriend and that he and his best friend, someone I also knew from the neighborhood, would shortly be on their way to Austria. He knew exactly where to cross the border and felt confident that they could easily escape.

The next day Tibi, my friend for seventeen years, was gone and I never saw him again. Some years later I learned from my mother that Tibi realized his dream and became a bass player in a London jazz band, and his best friend became a doctor in London.[1]

---

[1] I did find Tibi Lesko through the internet in the fall of 2003. He turned out to be a well-respected bass player, playing at different nightclubs and restaurants in Palm Springs, California. He has been in the US for almost thirty years.

A couple of days after Tibi left, my mother had heard that Gabi Erőd had left the country, which was quite the surprise. Just two weeks earlier we were walking the streets of Budapest together and now he was gone. It was then that the idea of leaving Hungary occurred to me for the first time.

Next, it was time for me to see my best friend, Vili Fodor. Other than Gabi Erőd, whom I had known for most of my life and was now gone, Vili Fodor was one friend I really trusted and respected. We grew up in the same neighborhood and became very good friends during our high school years.

Following graduation from a technical high school, Vili went to work as an electrical technician in Pécs, a small city 120 miles southwest of Budapest, near the Yugoslav[1] border. Following the Uprising on October 23, he returned to Budapest to be with his family and to see the outcome of all the turmoil. The timing was perfect. If Vili was interested in joining me, it would give me the confidence I needed to risk the escape.

---

[1] In February 2003, Yugoslavia became the Federation of Serbia and Montenegro.

The Uprising Drama

My participation in the Uprising was minimal, hardly worth mentioning. If I were to describe the 1956 Hungarian Uprising as a Shakespearean drama, then I was just a bit player in it with no speaking part. The characterization of the Uprising as a drama is fitting for its unrealistically complex theme, the extreme description of the players, both heroic and vile, and for the naiveté and stupidity displayed by many of its characters.

The necessary parts for a drama were all present. The play had villains and heroes, conflicts, examples of cruelty and vengeance, a great deal of dead people, many of whom were murdered, plots and counterplots, deception and betrayal by trusted friends and allies, extreme self-sacrifice and heroism, and many missed opportunities and bungled attempts for stopping the violence and the killing. However, I understood very little of this until decades later when I did some research for my story.

To follow this line of thinking, the Uprising drama can be described in five somewhat overlapping acts defined by time frames in chronological order.

Act I of the drama takes place on October 23, when a peaceful demonstration turns violent and full-scale rioting primarily directed against the hated secret police, or ÁVH, breaks out in Budapest and many other cities across Hungary. The government, made up of 100 percent communist representatives, panics and reflexively decides to call in the Russian tank units stationed outside Budapest for help. I play the role of an "extra" as part of a mob and retire at home for a good night's sleep before the day's actions are over.

Act II follows on October 24 when the demonstrators become armed insurgents and turn their anger against the invading Soviet tank units. The insurgents, led mostly by students, intellectuals, and workers, are joined by the army units and supported by the Budapest police. The whole country is in turmoil and "freedom fighters" begin to press for unprecedented changes in the political and economic system, as well as the relationship with the Soviet Union.

In Act II I am glued to our radio, trying to piece together the events as best I can from the Hungarian Radio and two forbidden broadcasts—Voice of America and Radio Free Europe. To everyone's surprise, including the freedom fighters', the Uprising achieves significant victories in chasing the ÁVH into hiding and stopping the invading Russian tanks.

Moscow, shaken up and upset at the Hungarian leadership's weakness, decides to take action via personal representatives of Nikita Khrushchev, who are flown into Hungary. Behind the scenes, negotiations begin between the various power groups with irreconcilable goals.

As we enter Act III on October 25, no one knows how to bring the Uprising to a peaceful end. Nor does anyone know what the limits of a negotiated deal with Moscow are, not even the Russians. The Hungarian political leadership is clueless in how to unify, control, and direct the multitude of the Budapest and provincial forces demanding more and more concessions from their own leaders and the Soviets. No concession seems to be enough.

The Russians employ a safe and proven method of handling problems that threaten their hegemony and the sacrosanct principle of Communist Party leadership: they prepare for a massive invasion and at the same time enter into an Oscar-winning performance of honest, respectful negotiations for a peaceful solution.

By the end of Act III, on November 3, the Hungarian government has evolved three times since October 23 and is now comprised of only 25 percent communists. A multiparty system is announced. The Uprising has taken on a dynamic of its own, hurling the whole country toward certain defeat. But nobody, not the leaders of the Uprising, not the politicians in Moscow or Budapest, not the armed forces on either side, can do anything to end it peacefully.

I play a minor role in the third act, first as a bystander in the back row with weapon in hand but no ammunition or instruction on how to load it, and later as a "revolutionary guard" protecting our next-door post office, which nobody bothers to attack. I am desperately trying to comprehend what is going on with little success.

Act IV begins at midnight on November 3 when the new Hungarian defense minister is led into a trap and arrested by the Russians. Within hours on November 4, fresh Russian tank units roll into Budapest ahead of a brand-new Hungarian government formed in Moscow and made up of 100 percent communists yet again.

Politically, Hungary has come full circle since October 23. It takes only ten days to crush the Uprising on November 14, but the costs are high. Major parts of Budapest are left in ruins, close to 20,000 Hungarians and 2,500 Russians are dead, and more than 100,000 Hungarians flee across the border into Austria. I lie low in our cellar, waiting for the fighting to end.

Before Act V begins in mid-December, I leave the stage during the intermission and escape to Austria as one of 200,000 refugees at that time. This prolonged, final act doesn't end until June of 1958 when all of the Uprising's political and military leaders, and their closest associates who didn't flee the country, are tried, executed, or imprisoned. Those hanged include Imre Nagy and Colonel Maléter. Prior to that, tens of thousands of Hungarians are imprisoned, and many are exiled to work camps in Hungary and Siberia.

The role of the Western democracies, and specifically the United States, is worth mentioning. Other than verbal encouragements piped into Hungary through Radio Free Europe and the Voice of America, nothing tangible was done to help the Hungarians. The Western powers were too busy fighting the war over the Suez Canal, where real and tangible economic interests lay, not principles of freedom and democracy. Eisenhower[1] even made discreet hints to

---

[1] Dwight David Eisenhower (1890–1969), American military leader and thirty-fourth president of the United States (1953–1961). Before becoming president, Eisenhower had called for liberation of the communist-dominated countries in Eastern Europe. Once in office, however, Eisenhower accepted the "containment" policy, which is why he made no offensive moves against the Soviets, even in 1956 when Khrushchev sent his tanks into Hungary to crush the Uprising. Eisenhower's refusal to intervene in Hungary was based on his most profound insight—that nuclear war was unthinkable. He believed that Communism was an unjust system that would eventually collapse on its own.

Khrushchev that he didn't intend to get involved in the Hungarian struggle for freedom.

I often wonder if the West had missed a historic opportunity to dismantle the Iron Curtain in 1956. The risks were high, given the nuclear standoff between the two superpowers. However, the Russian leadership was weak, recovering from the "de-Stalinization" led by Khrushchev, and their economy was in shambles. A show of political will and force by the United States and the United Nations could have created a free, democratic Hungary in 1956. As it turned out, Hungary had to wait another thirty or so years for its freedom.

Journey 4: The Escape

A Life-Altering Decision

I was sitting on a train going nowhere. Not even a locomotive was attached to the two passenger cars that sat on a railroad siding, quite a distance from the center of the railroad station. We were in Győr, an industrial city about eighty miles west of Budapest and fifty miles east of the Austrian border.

There were around thirty people in this railroad car, most of them young or middle-aged men and women, as well as a few young children. Besides our stationary status, and the fact that there was no engine attached, something else was peculiar about our compartment. Unlike the typical train rides I took in my childhood, there was hardly any luggage accompanying the passengers on this train. Here, everyone had one or two small suitcases while the overhead luggage bins remained virtually empty. Some of the people, like me, appeared to have no luggage at all, except for a briefcase.

Our group of seven was the largest on this train. I had just met two young women, Zsuzsi, and the other whose name I cannot recall, back in Budapest when we all gathered in front of our house around five o'clock that morning. Their goal was to end up in Australia, a place known to us for being on the far side of the world and for having kangaroos, in addition to a shortage of women. Their destination made sense when I looked at Zsuzsi, a dark-haired girl with a remarkably unattractive face. The blonde, on the other hand, was quite pretty, making the pair pleasant company to be around.

The oldest and the youngest members of our group were Mrs. Erőd and her eight-year-old son, András. Mrs. Erőd was the step-mother of my friend Gabi, who had left Hungary a couple of weeks earlier. The fact that she was leaving Gabi's father behind surprised me, but I wasn't about to inquire about her decision.

Then, there were three of us guys, all about the same age. Pali, whose last name I cannot remember, was a kind, quiet guy I had recently met in our neighborhood through my close and trusted friend, Vili Fodor. Vili and I were the "leaders" of the group. We had planned the trip as much as was possible in advance and were charged with providing "protection" to the others.

We must have been sitting there for hours with the hope that as night fell, an engine would miraculously show up and transport all of us to some unknown crossing point along the Austrian border. I had no idea, and it is doubtful that anyone else on this train did either, exactly where along the border our train would arrive or how we would eventually cross it.

It was December 6, 1956, the date my mother would refer to many years later as that "cursed day." I always wondered why that day troubled her so. Was it because I left her, or was it because she didn't leave with me? Was it because that day marked the turning point in our lives when our physical and emotional relationship changed forever? I never found out, because as the years went by, we became more and more emotionally separated, never discussing any sensitive topic.

It was a dreary, rainy, and cold day, and as darkness enveloped our train, the elevated anxiety level was apparent in the gradually fad-ing faces of my fellow travel companions. I was nervous too. We all had put our faith into the hands of the Győr railroad stationmaster, who promised that after dark, there would be an engine attached to our cars, and we would be transported to the border.

We were given instructions on what to do in case the train encountered Russian patrols along the way. The conductor was going to blink the lights three times as a warning and slow down the train in order for us to jump off and escape. How the conductor would know what lay ahead, and how we would manage to jump off the train with the two girls, a mother, and her ten-year-old child was not clear. Moreover, why was the stationmaster so kind as to assist in our escape?

None of this was evident until many hours later as events were unfolding. In the back of my mind, I was worried that the railroad master had lied to us. What if, instead of an engine to transport us to the border, the local police would show up, or the Russians, who by now had taken control of most of the major transportation facilities in Hungary?

I was getting cold; we had been sitting there for hours, trying to stay quiet, and the late-afternoon cold of winter was creeping inside the railroad car, in spite of the closed windows and doors. However, there was nothing to do but wait and hope for the best; we were committed. Since conversation was out of the question, I could only ruminate about exactly how I got here.

Only a few weeks earlier, although somewhat traumatized by the events of the October 23 Uprising, I was anxiously waiting to return to the university and continue my studies. And now I was just a short train ride away from leaving behind forever—possibly with no chance ever to return—my mother, my country, the rest of my family and friends, my own comfortable little universe I had known for the past eighteen years, and embarking on a whole new life in an unknown place.

The sequence of events during the last two weeks of November and the first week of December are fuzzy, but I do know that the idea of leaving Hungary came to me after hearing that two of my friends, Tibi Lesko and Gabi Erőd, had escaped. It is unclear whether I first discussed the idea of escaping Hungary with my mother and then talked it over with Vili, or the other way around.

Thinking of Vili as a companion with whom to plan a joint escape to Austria was natural. Our friendship goes so far back that neither of us can recall when we first met, but chances are that we knew each other while in elementary or middle school. However, our friendship didn't develop until we were in high school. Although we went to different high schools, there were several things that brought us together during those four years, and by the time we graduated, we had become close.

We were teenagers, so our friendship had few requirements. Back then, I knew instinctively that the two of us had suitable personalities. In retrospect, after decades of continued friendship, I can see why. Vili's more reserved and conservative personality complemented my more risk-oriented and easygoing character. His close to six-foot height and corresponding weight was also a nice balance to my more slender five feet, six inches—giving me significant peace of mind whenever we went to a party together, where the risk of a fistfight was always present.

Another important thing that brought us close together was our love of sports. Although we pursued different sports during high school—Vili was into rowing and I was into track and field—there was one sport, European-style handball, which we played together for the junior Vasas[1] team. As it turned out, our playing handball for the Vasas significantly influenced our escape.

I also enjoyed the rest of the Fodor family. The Fodors and my family were pretty much on the same rung of the socioeconomic ladder, near the bottom. During high school, Vili was living with his parents and younger sister in a two-room apartment just as tiny as ours, about a twenty-minute walk from my place. I was a frequent visitor to the Fodors, and Vili's mother was the kindest lady I ever knew.

I spent many happy hours at the Fodors', sharing a meal with them, fighting with his tomboy younger sister, Mari, or playing cards with Vili and his dad. The fact that Vili was a Roman Catholic and I was a Jew was never a factor in our friendship. We never discussed religion or talked about our experiences during World War II.

Fortunately, following the Uprising on October 23, Vili decided to leave his job in Pécs and return home to Budapest. When I proposed the idea of the two of us leaving the country, he agreed to it

---

[1]   Acronym for the Hungarian Locomotive Association.

right away. His support was critical to me. I truly don't know what I would have done had he refused.

I might have looked around for another friend to join me or gone by myself, but it is also possible that I might have just forgotten the whole idea. I'm not sure what Vili would have done had I not approached him, but it's possible that he would have stayed put.

Once we agreed to proceed, we had had several discussions on the topic. But the only one we can both recall today is one that took place on a dark late-November night, way past the official curfew time. We sat on a wooden bench in one of our neighborhood parks.

The walkways in the park were covered with small pebbles, and a water fountain sat in front of the bench about fifteen yards from us. The fountain had a concrete or steel bowl, making it the perfect target for throwing pebbles. Since it was pitch-dark, the sound the pebbles made as they hit the bowl was the only indication that we had hit the target. Those are the only specifics that we can both recall about this meeting.

All that was discussed were the mechanical and logistical aspects of how to escape to Austria, without ever touching on the emotional aspects and consequences of our decision. Here we were, about to forever leave behind our mothers, a sister, the rest of our families, friends, home, country, and everything we knew and were familiar with, while playing a friendly game of "hit the water fountain."

In addition to not thinking through the emotional consequences of our decision, we didn't contemplate a lot of the pragmatic difficulties of starting a new life in a strange land, such as our inability to speak any of the major European languages like German, French, English, or Italian.

Looking back now, more than fifty years later, it is unnerving to think of how we approached this life-altering decision. We discussed the pros and cons of leaving as two eighteen-year-olds would do: superficially and without any consideration of the real reasons why we decided to leave, much less the emotional impact on us and the loved ones we would leave behind. The only part we had focused on was the physical aspect of getting to and crossing the border, which was already being shut down by the occupying Soviet forces.

I don't think we were unemotional about our decision; we just couldn't articulate our feelings. In truth, it has taken me several decades to write down this story and to focus on the emotional aspects of our decision to leave Hungary.

In preparation for writing this story, I traveled to Grand Rapids, Michigan, in the fall of 2003 and spent three days with Bill[1] Fodor and his wife, Nicole. I recorded about six hours of conversation, in which we each learned much about each other that was previously unknown.

I guess the conventional wisdom about men applies to us. We had been friends for a lifetime but had rarely discussed anything sensitive or emotional about each other. Therefore, that year, we filled in many of the gaps we each had in our recollections of what happened on December 6, 1956, as well as on the days preceding our departure and the subsequent weeks. We also had some good laughs discovering how different our recollections are of several events and places we had experienced together.

I found out how unhappy Vili was with his life as an electrical technician in a small town called Pécs, following graduation from a technical high school in Budapest in the spring of 1956. Vili had no choice where he was going to work or how much he was going to make for the rest of his life. The "state" dictated this for him. He felt trapped in his job and in the system, with no opportunity for significant individual achievement.

For Vili, leaving Hungary was an escape from what he perceived as a gloomy future. His father's death in January 1956, making Vili the de facto head of the family, made his decision to leave rather difficult. He had to reconcile his sense of obligation to assist and support his newly widowed mother and sister with his aspiration to break free from our closed society and give himself a chance for a better life.

Following the outbreak of the Uprising on October 23, 1956, Vili came back to Budapest, and he and I connected with each other shortly after. My enthusiasm about leaving, combined with his state

---

[1] Vili formally changed his first name from Vilmos to William when he became an American citizen in 1974.

of mind about his career prospects, undoubtedly influenced his decision to leave the country. However, being a cautious man even at this young age, Vili wanted to seek the advice of his sister's godfather, Uncle Béla, an older man with relatives living in Austria.

We went to visit Uncle Béla, who happened to live just a few blocks down on Fűzér Street. He told us that life in the West was unlike ours in Hungary. Young men like us would have plenty of opportunities to make decent lives for ourselves. This input was sufficient for Vili to make up his mind. His mother strenuously opposed his leaving, but Vili decided to leave no matter what, knowing that both his mother and sister would resent his decision and never forgive him.

I now know that Vili's decision to leave Hungary was more difficult than mine. Consistent with our personalities, temperaments, and educational backgrounds, Vili was much less certain of his future prospects in a new life outside Hungary than I had been. While I was absolutely certain that I would finish my university education no matter where we ended up, Vili was far from certain that he had the academic background and talent to do the same.

As it turned out, he underestimated himself, characteristically. In addition, Vili was riddled with guilt about leaving his recently widowed mother and ten-year-old sister behind. His mother was vehemently opposed to his leaving, while mine was supportive. By now, I think Vili had surrendered to leaving his family behind. I'm sure that his mother, like most mothers do, forgave him long before she passed away. However, I suspect that his sister's undiminished resentment, even after decades have passed by, still causes him a lot of pain.

My reasons for leaving were dissimilar. I had a great career in front of me as an engineer in Hungary, which would have been acceptable for me. Engineers were paid top salaries in all the communist countries. Building and running factories to produce capital goods, not consumer goods, was the most important national priority, much higher than the other "soft" sciences, such as medicine. Engineers were making the same or more than doctors in Hungary.

Frustration with my professional future was not a reason for my decision to leave Hungary.

There was the probability of retribution by the new regime for all those who were associated with the Uprising, one way or another. While this factor occurred to me, I never fully believed that anything serious would happen to me had I stayed.

Then, there was the fact of my being Jewish. The communists followed the edicts of Karl Marx, who declared, "Religion is the opiate of the masses." As a matter of state policy, the practice of religion was strongly discouraged, and religious discrimination was forbidden.

In Christian Hungary, a traditionally religious country, the communist edicts simply drove all religious practices and all expressions of traditional anti-Semitism underground. The feelings, biases, and prejudices still existed, but they couldn't be openly expressed.

This state policy brought great relief to all non-Christians, mostly the Jews, who lost close to three-quarters of their population during the Holocaust, by officially suppressing the primarily Christian religious activities and influence in the political, civil, and socioeconomic life of the country.

I would be safe as a Jew under communism, but I would also be forever surrounded by Hungarians, the real Magyars, who would just as soon see me disappear from "their country." Still, this factor alone would not have made me leave.

So, if it wasn't the fear of retribution or the discomfort of continued living in an anti-Semitic country, what was it that made me leave my family and home and give up admission to Hungary's most prestigious technical university? It all came down to being almost nineteen years old. The idea of leaving a closed a society, discovering what lay beyond its borders, and facing new challenges and opportunities was exciting.

My experiences during our student march on October 23, a sense of freedom, and the thrill of free expression were still fresh in my mind. It was more intuition than a well-informed opinion of a better life outside Hungary that fueled my desire to leave. The opportunity to break through the "iron curtain" was too good to miss, particularly as I learned that some of my friends had already tried and succeeded.

In addition, my self-confidence played a significant role in facing the uncertain future. This was not justified by any prior life experiences. Rather, it was the result of family encouragement I had received as a child that I could accomplish just about anything I wanted to do.

I had a very close, emotional connection to my mother, who single-handedly raised me since my father died in 1945. She was the only person in the world with unconditional love and care for me. I admired her willingness to work hard, sacrifice much, and provide me with many material things way above our economic ability. It was an unspoken understanding between us that once I became an educated professional, she would never have to worry about her own future. To simply turn around and say goodbye to her forever was unthinkable.

When I first approached her with the idea of leaving, I was thinking of both of us leaving together. Initially, she didn't object to the idea, but after discussing it with Manci néni and her older brother Uncle Laci, she suggested a different approach. I should go first, and after crossing the border, we could figure out a way for her to join me. The crossing may be dangerous, and I might be better off without her, which sounded logical.

I was too naive to see through her transparent logic. It never occurred to me to question her reluctance to undertake the dangerous journey, while at the same time she asked me to assist Mrs. Erőd, her son, and two other young ladies.

Many years later, Uncle Laci confessed to me that he thought I would be a lot better off without my mother to take care of myself—not just in crossing the border, but also in settling down in an unknown country, continuing my education, and building a new life for myself. I believe my uncle was really looking out for me, and in retrospect, he was right. However, I was hopeful that my separation from my mother would be temporary and brief.

In the end, Vili and I made up our minds. The plan was simple; we would leave as soon as possible, within days, and make our way to Győr, find a train or other transportation to the Austrian border, and walk across.

Hungary is a landlocked country, and in 1956, it was surrounded on three sides by other communist countries: Czechoslovakia[1] to the north, Romania to the east, and Yugoslavia to the south. The only safe escape was toward the west into Austria. No additional planning was necessary since it was impossible to plan out the details of "how" and "where" until we got closer to the border.

Time was of the essence. The Soviet forces had begun to seal the borders in mid-November after crushing the remaining fighting forces of the Revolution, so escaping was becoming more and more difficult. That was the plan, simple and no hassle, just the two of us. Thus, we agreed on the date of December 6.

---

[1] Czechoslovakia, a country formed in 1918, following the First World War, when Slovakia announced its independence from the Austro-Hungarian Empire and incorporated the Czech lands of Moravia and Bohemia. It was replaced in January 1993 by two independent countries: the Czech Republic and Slovakia.

Crossing the Border to Austria

Transportation to the Budapest Eastern Railroad station was provided by one of Vili's neighbors, with whom we used to play cards. He was a supervisor at a trucking company, so he would provide a truck and driver to take us to the railroad station in the city. He assured us that the driver knew what was going on in the city and suggested we leave around five o'clock in the morning to avoid any problems. Vili would come to our house with the driver and truck to pick me up.

A few days remained before our departure. Only essentials would be packed for the trip; everything had to fit into a briefcase. To bribe our way through some Russian patrols along the way, we agreed that each of us would carry a couple of bottles of vodka and a few cartons of cigarettes. I think my mother procured the vodka and Vili's aunt, who ran a tobacco shop on the Kőrösi Csoma Road, provided the cigarettes.

I was ready to leave immediately, but my mother had one request before we left. She wanted me to see Uncle Elek, one of my father's younger brothers, to say goodbye to him. I didn't understand why she singled out Uncle Elek; after all, I had several other uncles and aunts living in Budapest, but I saw no problem with it. Maybe her request had something to

33. Destruction in Budapest; József Ring and Üllöi Road; end of October 1956.

do with the fact that Uncle Elek had a special relationship with us, since he ended up in the same Austrian forced labor camp with my father in 1944.

Uncle Elek lived in the city, so it entailed dedicating a full day for this visit because transportation was still not back to normal. I vividly recall my saying goodbye to Uncle Elek and his family. Before I left them, I asked them if they had thought about leaving Hungary. My uncle made a gesture with his two palms turned facing up, shrugged his shoulders, and said, "How could I? With these two small children?"—while pointing toward my little cousins. Both he and his wife claimed that it was too dangerous. I went around the room, kissed everyone twice on the cheeks per the custom, and said goodbye. They all wished me good luck, and I left for home.

The trip into the city was my second since Gabi and I had walked into the city with guns on our backs a few weeks earlier. This was the first time I had seen the destruction caused by the Russian forces invading the city on November 4. Although the fighting had stopped almost two weeks earlier and all the dead had been removed from the streets, the rubble and physical destruction were still visible everywhere.

On my way home, I was thinking that this might be the last time I would see these family members, in addition to all the others I had not told goodbye. I thought of several other uncles, aunts, and cousins from both sides of the family I might never see again, and I felt a little tightening around my throat. Nevertheless, I was glad that Vili and I had decided to leave.

Just a few days before we were ready to take off, we encountered some unanticipated surprises. Word got out in the neighborhood that Vili Fodor and Robi Reichmann (most people still didn't know me as "Rátonyi") were going to escape. The first companion who asked to join us was a young man of our age named Pali. He was the adopted son of a friend of the Fodor family in Kőbánya. Vili and I had no problem with Pali joining us; in fact, it made us even stronger as a team. However, the other volunteers were of a different type.

Gabi Erőd's father visited my mother and asked that we take his wife and their small child, a boy of about ten. Apparently, when Gabi left just a week earlier, his stepmother wasn't ready to leave with him. It was clear that my mother and Gabi's father had already discussed this, and my mother expected me to agree. I had no choice but to go along with the deal. Gabi's stepmother was a kind lady; her plan was to end up in Buenos Aires, Argentina, where she had some family. All of a sudden, there were five of us, including one child, ready to make the dangerous trip across the border. We weren't done yet, however.

Just one day before our departure, my mother informed me that two young women around the age of twenty or twenty-one would like to join us. They were the daughters of a friend of a friend, and the argument was that it was too dangerous for the young women to go by themselves, knowing what the Russians were likely to do to them were they to be captured.

I naively ignored the fact that should we run into some Russians equipped with machine guns, there was little Vili and I could do to defend our companions. If anything, the girls were better equipped to barter their way to freedom than we were. Things were getting a little bit out of hand, but I couldn't refuse my mother. Therefore, the two girls also joined us.

Finally, the day of our departure came. It was a typical cold, overcast December day with a light drizzle. I put on my only suit, the beautiful tailor-made dark-blue one I had gotten for my high school graduation. I had my long, winter overcoat and hat and the brand-new briefcase I had received as a present to carry my books to the university. My mother packed an extra nylon shirt and underwear for me, a couple of sandwiches, and my toothbrush and shaving kit. I hesitated to take my shaving mug and brush since they were heavy and I only needed to shave once a week at most.

My mother gave me two hundred forints for the road—less than one dollar at today's exchange rate—and two bottles of vodka, in case I needed to bribe my way across the border. With briefcase in hand, I looked like I was ready to hop on a streetcar and attend my classes at the university.

At the prearranged time at dawn, my mother and I went to our gate to meet the others, who were already there. Before we went outside, my mother took a small gold ring off her finger and gave it to me to have as a keepsake. She said it would remind me that I had a mother left behind. It never occurred to me to question this sentimental gesture of hers, in light of our understanding that she would be joining me soon. Now as I reflect on this incident, it seems to me that she already knew that our separation was going to be a long one.

I laughed and assured her that I didn't need a reminder, but she insisted that I keep it. The ring had a tiny diamond set in it, probably of very low quality, and was so small that it only fit on my pinky finger. With that done, we went outside to meet the others.

To Vili's great surprise, there were six of us waiting for him when he arrived with the truck and the driver. I had not had a chance to tell him of the additional company we were supposed to chaperone to Austria. However, he took the news calmly, as I had expected.

I kissed my mother goodbye. Then, we all got on the truck and headed toward Kőrösi Csoma Road, the main road leading to the Eastern Railway station[1] in the city. As we pulled away, I looked back at my mother standing in front of our house, waving to us, her tears no longer visible in the dim dawn light. I will never know what went through her mind.

The driver let us off at Baross Square in front of the railway station. It was getting lighter, and as I looked around, I could see the second-floor balcony of my Aunt Vica's apartment on Baross Street, right next to the station on the north side. It was here in the summer of 1955 or 1954 when Vili and I, working for the railroad, took the train around five o'clock every morning from this station to some place outside the city to shovel coal all day. I had stood on this balcony many times, admiring the busy square and station entrance below.

When we got inside the station, it was already a beehive of activity. The platform was crowded with people, most of them hugging their small carry-on luggage. Neither Vili nor I can recall exactly how

---

[1]   The station was built in 1884 and for decades was Central Europe's most modern railroad station. The station has four pairs of railroad tracks under a glass cover.

the idea of finding the stationmaster came to us. Vili remembered that he was a big fan of our handball team—his association was our sponsor, after all—and came to many of our matches back in 1955, when we both played handball for Vasas. Nevertheless, we did find him on the busy morning on December 6, and he indeed remembered us. We asked him for help to get us to the border. He told us which train to get on and what to do when it arrived in Győr.

There were several trains waiting to leave. We didn't have trouble finding which train was heading west. Somebody was shouting "Vienna Express!" in front of one of the trains, and all of us climbed aboard—three guys, two young women, Gabi's mother, and her child. I don't recall even bothering to purchase tickets. It seemed like nobody really cared.

I have no recollection of anything noteworthy during our train ride to Győr, which is somewhat strange. I must have been in some kind of mental daze. It took us several hours to reach our destination, only eighty miles away. Today, the same trip would last one hour and forty-five minutes and cost a very reasonable six dollars.

We all disembarked at Győr in the afternoon, and Vili and I went to find the local stationmaster, whose name we were given in Budapest. We found him, and after introducing ourselves, he gave us the number of a railroad siding at the very far end of the rail yard, where we would find two railroad cars. We were to wait there until after nightfall when a locomotive would hook up and take us to the border. He told us that the engineer would blink the lights three times should we run into a roadblock set up by Russian or Hungarian soldiers. The train would slow down, and we could all jump off.

And that is how we got here, sitting on the train, waiting for some unknown locomotive engineers to show up, connect us to an engine, and take off in the middle of the night for the Austrian border.

If I read about this in a novel, I would judge this story to be a rather weak plot with many holes. Who told all these people which train to take to the border? Did they all ask the same stationmaster we did? Why did we all trust this man? And what motivated these railroad engineers to take off in the middle of the night to transport total strangers to the Austrian border?

Why would they risk their necks? Did the other people on the train have to pay for their transport, and we just got lucky because of our connections? And how were we supposed to jump off the train should we run into soldiers, with two girls, a mother, and a child? I had no answers then, and I don't have them now—but some light was shed on these questions as events transpired during the night.

Finally, around ten o'clock, we heard some noises, and our railroad car suddenly jerked forward. We had just gotten hooked up to an engine. Without any further ado, we just started rolling. It was now pitch-dark, and I could barely make out the faces next to me. Unlike the train we took this morning in Budapest, this one didn't stop at all, to either let off or take on passengers. It had a single destination: a small village perched on the side of a large, swampy lake[1] that straddled the border between Austria and Hungary.

As we approached our destination, my anxiety level was rising, and I could feel the adrenaline flowing in my body. This was it. We would find out shortly if we would succeed in crossing the border into Austria.

Although it was dark, and I could hardly see anyone sitting next to me, I could sense the tension rising in our compartment. There was no conversation, not even a whisper. After about an hour, the train started to slow down and finally stopped. Not a thing could be seen through the windows. It was pitch-dark inside and out.

Suddenly, the door to our compartment opened, and a commanding voice declared, "Everybody out, form a single line." We had arrived, but I had no idea where we were. Who was this man ordering us to get off the train? Are we going to be arrested, or even worse? We had no choice but to follow the order we were given.

We all grabbed our belongings and, carefully, so as not to trample the person in front of us, stepped down the steps of the railroad

---

[1] The Austrians call this Neusiedler See, literally translated as "New Settlers Lake." We Hungarians always called it the Fertő tó or "Slough Lake."

car and into the total darkness of the night. Since we had absolutely no idea of what to expect upon arrival, there was some confusion about what to do next. This was not a regular railroad station; there was no building or a platform to step down onto. We were in the middle of nowhere, and I could tell by the feel of it that we were standing on some kind of dirt road.

The same voice ordered us to line up single file, which we did, with me in front of our group. I thought Vili was right behind me, and I assumed that all the others were following. I was nervous. This was not how I had imagined our escape, although I couldn't exactly describe what I had anticipated.

Who was this man ordering us to get off the train? Was he armed or not? Was he alone, or were there more of them? It appeared that they were waiting for us. What were they going to do with us? Why the single line? These and similar questions raced through my mind as I was desperately trying to figure out what was going to happen.

I was straining my eyes, trying to pierce the darkness for some sign of life or something familiar up ahead when the line started to move. As we walked away from the train, our last protected shelter, some flickering lights appeared about thirty yards ahead. And then I saw two soldiers in uniform.

I couldn't make out whether the uniform was Russian or Hungarian, but both were bearing machine guns slung over their shoulders, a flashlight in one hand, and what looked like papers in the other. The soldiers then looked at the papers and stuffed them into their coat pockets. Next, a person in front of them moved out of the narrow, bright beam of the flashlights. It was then that I connected the dots.

The soldiers were not handling papers; they were counting money. It was clear that we were about to be shaken down by enterprising soldiers to pay our exit fare from the country. Every single passenger from our train had to stop before the soldiers and negotiate a transaction.

My mind was racing at warp speed. What if I didn't have enough money? Would they turn me back? Or worse? I also felt angry that these mercenaries, taking advantage of our tenuous situation, had trapped us. Whether it was out of sheer defiance or anger, I made a quick a decision, and there was no time to have a conference with my fellow traveling companions.

Having made my decision, I passed it on to Vili, whom I assumed was right behind me. "Let's go around the soldiers. I go left and you go right. The others can follow us," I whispered, not waiting for his acknowledgment. In retrospect, I might have been slightly hasty and perhaps selfish for not waiting for his response, but we were getting closer and closer to the money-collecting soldiers, and time was of the essence.

What I didn't realize at the time was that Vili was nowhere near behind me. As I later learned, he was making his own plans to avoid this trap and purposely fell back to the very end of the line.

I stepped out of the line to the left and started making a wide arc, while keeping my eye to the right on the flickering flashlights to give me a point of reference. I needed to calculate how far I had to swing to the left in a semicircle in order to end up out of sight from where the soldiers were standing.

My mind was so focused on getting the distance and the angle right that everything else was blocked out. I paid no attention to who was following me. The only thing I was conscious of was the rough terrain under my feet. It felt like a plowed field, and my ankles were turning and twisting as I made my way forward.

Apparently, the pathway where the train stopped was in the middle of farmland. The cold December weather made the dirt under my feet feel like solid rocks. I looked back, but I could see and hear nothing. Not having given Vili a chance to respond to my decision, I had no idea where he was and who, if anybody, was following me. But there was no turning back. I was committed and had to find my way around these soldiers.

It took just a few minutes of walking, and I could see that I was now in line with the faint flashlight beams to my right. I still couldn't hear anyone following me, and I pushed on to continue in a circular arc so that my directional signal, the flashlights, would be behind me, approximately in line with where I started from.

I must have been about thirty yards beyond the soldiers when I suddenly heard some conversation, and I began to make out the shapes of several people standing around in a group. I had actually managed to avoid the soldiers. I felt relieved, but not for long, as I suddenly realized that I was all alone. Nobody in my group had followed me.

I walked up to the people I saw ahead, some of them being recent arrivals from the train, with luggage in their hands. The others were unmistakably local peasants, with their high boots, thick over-coats, and rugged faces. I joined the first group I saw, and one of the peasants, an older man, told me to wait a while and that we would all be leaving soon. Nobody questioned how or why I had emerged from the darkness instead of coming directly from the line where the two soldiers were conducting their business.

I kept looking back, left, and right, waiting for others in my group to show up, but nobody came. I told the old man that I was with a group of seven and they should show up any minute. He nod-ded, which gave me the impression of an agreement to wait a while.

Minutes went by, but none of my fellow travelers appeared. The old peasant probably noticed my nervousness, so he told me not to worry and that the others would arrive later in the village. I wasn't sure what he meant. Why were we going into a village? I thought we were here to cross the border, but this was no time to ask for an explanation.

Clearly, our arrival at this spot was expected, and a routine had been developed for organizing the escapees into groups of about ten persons. I stayed close to the old man, and he soon motioned us to follow him. I don't remember how long we walked, this time on a well-trodden dirt path, but we were soon in a small village with houses on both sides of the single road ahead. We stopped at one of the houses, where he ushered us inside.

The entrance opened into a large room, which seemed like a combination family room, kitchen, pantry, and who knows what else, with a huge fireplace against the opposite wall. An older lady, presumably his wife and dressed in dark traditional peasant garb, welcomed us. There was a young man, probably their son, who also happened to be our guide across the border.

I looked around, surveyed my fellow travelers, and recognized the young couple I saw on the train with their two small children. There must have been about eight or ten of us in this group, including the children.

It was warm inside the house, and it felt good to warm up my cold feet and hands after so many hours on the train and out in the open field. The old lady was asking the young couple with children if they would like to have some milk, to which they both agreed. I don't recall if she offered all of us something to eat or drink. My mind was still preoccupied with the whereabouts of Vili and the others in my group.

I was irritated that my quick decision to avert the soldiers had caused me to separate from the rest of my group. I was getting more and more nervous and fearful that I might never find them again. Here I was, still on the Hungarian side of the border, and had already lost my best friend and companion.

Two different emotions raced through my mind. The first was fear of being alone, while the other was guilt for having inadvertently abandoned the rest of my travel companions. Why had I acted so rashly? After all, I was entrusted with the safety of Mrs. Erőd, her son, and the two young women. Did I let my best friend and cohorts down? What to do now? I finally decided to approach the young man who was to be our guide.

I said to him, "Excuse me. I came with a group of people on the train, and I cannot find them. Could you do me a favor and see if they ended up in someone else's house? I have only two hundred forints on me, but I will be glad to give you a hundred if you could go and look for them."

I had yet to develop my negotiating skills, which would serve me quite well later in life. No sooner had I spoken to the young man than I realized that I shouldn't have told him how much money I had. I immediately regretted my oversharing, but it was too late.

He looked at me and responded, "Sure, not a problem." Suddenly, I got a whiff of a strong aroma of alcohol on his breath as he spoke. This made me uneasy, but I couldn't retreat at this point. I had gone too far.

"My friend's name is Vili Fodor, and he is with another guy, two girls, a mother, and her child," I told him. He seemed to have lost interest in my detailed description of the group, pocketed my money, turned around, went to get his coat and hat, and disappeared through the door.

I could feel perspiration forming on my neck and back. Perhaps the room was getting too hot, or I was getting tenser, finding myself all alone with strangers about to cross the border. This was not the plan. Vili and I had designed this trip together and promised to stay together, come hell or high water. I also realized that trusting this already intoxicated young man was not such a good idea, and now half my money was gone.

Suddenly, I didn't have much confidence in my handling of things, and this sudden loss of self-assurance caused a near-panic attack. I was just hoping that the young man would turn up soon with news of my fellow travelers.

In about half an hour or so, my guide finally showed up by himself. He said he had looked everywhere, but nobody knew of Vili Fodor. However, he assured me that he was probably safe and that we would meet once we were across the border. I then realized that the guide probably had marched right to the local tavern and spent my money on more drinks to fortify himself for the arduous task of taking us to Austria.

I was now resigned to the fact that I was alone and that I had to simply face whatever challenges were ahead without my group. There was still a good chance that Vili and I would meet once we were in Austria, but I had some nagging doubts about that.

What I didn't know at the time was that even if he tried, my guide could not possibly have found Vili and the others because they were still wandering around in the fields, completely lost in the total darkness. But that's Vili's story, which I will come to later.

Finally, around midnight, our guide gathered everyone and gave us brief instructions for the road.

He explained, "Everyone has to follow me in single file. The road is narrow, and there is a swamp on both sides. If someone needs to stop, pass the word to me up front, and we will take a break. Otherwise, do not talk while we walk. If I see or hear any disturbance ahead, we stop and wait. If we see Russian soldiers or hear gunshots, we have to lie down on the ground and be very still."

He then walked over to me and asked, "Would you mind helping me carry one of the children? I will carry the older one, and you could take the younger one. And you don't have to pay me." I realized that this was an offer I could not refuse. He also offered to carry my briefcase, but I told him that I would carry it myself and ask him for assistance if necessary. This guy was smart. He already knew that I had only a hundred forints left, and he needed help with the children, whose transportation was probably funded by the parents.

We all put our coats on, and the father of the little girl helped to put the child on my shoulders, with her two little legs dangling in front. The guide was up front with the older boy on his shoulders, I was next, and behind me was the father, carrying two small suitcases. Behind him was the wife, also carrying some luggage, with the others following her.

We started walking, and I was surprised how light the little girl was on my shoulders. This wasn't going to be as much effort as I had anticipated. Of course, I was clueless to the actual length of the walk ahead.

I didn't have much business experience back then, but I could already see the shape of an enterprise in front of me. I have no proof to back up my assertion, but I think what we stumbled into was a well-organized business. It was made up of the locomotive engineers that drove the train, the stationmasters who were so kind to us in Budapest and Győr, the men in soldier uniforms, and the local peasants patiently waiting for everyone to pay the "toll" before they took over as our "hosts."

This was definitely not a setup run by the Red Cross or some humanitarian organization to help the Hungarians fleeing the renewed oppression by the new communist regime. Rather, it was run by some greedy Hungarians taking advantage of the desperation of their fellow countrymen seeking freedom in the West.

By the time we got to the border in early December, almost two hundred thousand Hungarians had crossed into Austria and Yugoslavia.[1] The demand for transportation to the border and expert guides to navigate across into Austrian territory was present. The anxiety caused by the physical danger of border crossing and the emotional burden of fleeing one's home and country provided customers who were willing and happy to pay whatever it took to escape.

We started walking, and I actually began to feel better. The physical act of moving toward our destination was gradually restoring my badly shaken sense of self-confidence. Our leader set a steady pace as if we were off on a weekend hike in the forest. The little girl on my neck held her gloved hands together around my cheeks, and we marched on.

I followed our leader only two paces behind and kept my eyes on the ground in front of me. We must have walked for about ten or fifteen minutes when I suddenly felt the burden of the extra weight on my shoulders. I was surprised how quickly my body had reacted to the weight of maybe forty to fifty pounds. I now started to feel the pressure on my shoulders, but I wasn't worried. I was in decent physical shape, and my legs were strong from all the running I had done.

We walked silently, and I couldn't ignore the weight on my shoulders. The slight pain from earlier had now gotten a bit stronger, and I could feel the stress on my lower back and my legs. I reached into my briefcase, took out the bottle of vodka, and had a nice swig. The vodka burned my throat as it went down, and within seconds I could feel the warm sensation in my stomach, which felt good.

Our leader and the father of the little girl behind me noticed my indulgence, but neither of them said anything. I repeatedly yet

---

[1] While Yugoslavia was still considered a communist country under the dictator Tito (born as Josip Broz, 1892–1980), there was a serious rift between it and the Soviet Union. Tito, the only communist leader to do so, achieved political and economic independence from Moscow and the freedom to pursue his style of socialism. Rumor had it that Hungarians fleeing their country would be provided free passage through Yugoslavia.

gradually shifted the weight of the vodka from the briefcase to my stomach. I lost track of the amount of time we had been walking as more and more of my attention was on the little girl I was carrying. Her weight had seemingly increased by the minutes. The mental anxiety I had about losing my friend Vili was gradually replaced with concern of my physical ability to carry the little girl.

The muscle pain kept getting more pronounced, and I wished that our leader would give us a brief rest, but he kept on moving steadily ahead. I thought about asking him to stop for a rest, but my pride wouldn't let me admit that I was unable to bear the burden on my shoulders. After all, we made a deal, and I had to keep my end of the bargain.

It was about this time that my years of training as a runner came in handy. Anyone who ever seriously trained to be a distance runner knows that the biggest challenge in a race is managing physical pain.

The first thing I learned was that pain is natural and simply the body's way of communicating that the muscles are working hard. I knew how pain felt, and I learned to accept it. Now in the middle of the night, as we approached the Austrian border, I imagined myself in a race where I had to overcome the natural desire to ease up on the ever-increasing bodily pain by slowing down my pace. Instead, I had to focus on my breathing, as well as on a steady rhythm of putting one foot forward at a time.

From time to time, I fortified myself with the contents of my bottle of vodka until it was empty. The strange thing was I didn't feel the least bit drunk for having polished off at least a half liter of vodka. The physical exertion, the level of anxiety, and the cold December weather all must have affected my metabolism so that the alcohol was simply burned off.

We must have been walking close to an hour when our leader finally stopped, turned around, and told us that this was as far as he was going with us. He said that the Austrian border was less than fifty meters ahead, and all we had to do was to continue on the same path we had been following. The father of the little girl lifted her from my shoulders, and it took several minutes before the relief registered on my aching body.

Everybody except me concluded his or her financial transaction with our leader. He wished us "Jó szerencsét"—or "good luck"—and disappeared into the darkness from where we had come. Although I'm not a skeptic, the idea of us being tricked and left in the middle of nowhere did cross my mind.

I offered to carry the little girl again, thinking that we were only minutes away from crossing the border. No matter how tired I was, I figured I could carry her for another fifty meters. We all continued walking ahead, this time I was in the lead and the father was behind me. We had walked for only a few minutes when suddenly out of the darkness, a deep, male voice called, "Gute Nacht!"[1] We had made it to Austria.

The Austrians were well organized and waiting for us. An Austrian border policeman in uniform, with a flashlight in hand, emerged from the darkness and immediately directed us to a horse-drawn wagon, which had a thick layer of hay on the bottom. He said something in German, which I didn't understand. However, I didn't have to. We all climbed onto the wagon and were moving within minutes.

It all happened very quickly; I was already sitting in the wagon, sensing the rough terrain the wagon wheels were slowly traversing, when the idea of being free finally struck me. I had made it! The sense of elation I felt was diminished quickly by the thought of separation from Vili. I was still hopeful that somehow soon we would meet on this side of the border.

Physical exhaustion, together with the effect of the vodka, soon took over, and I actually began to doze off in the wagon. We probably had traveled no more than half an hour when we arrived at a very small Austrian village near the border. We were escorted into a building with several rooms prepared for our arrival. I think this was the local school building temporarily converted into a night shelter.

There were straw-filled mattresses on the floor, where we would spend the rest of the night. Somebody explained to us that we were to stay here just for the night and that tomorrow we would all be trans-

---

[1] "Good evening!" (*literally, translation: Good night!*).

ported to Eisenstadt, where a large camp was set up for Hungarian refugees. I literally collapsed on the mattress and immediately fell into a deep, dreamless sleep.

Soon after I awoke, I was told that another Hungarian boy named Vili Fodor was looking for me. I cannot recall the details of our reunion, but we found each other in this tiny Austrian village on the western side of the Fertő Lake, which straddles both Hungary and Austria. Unfortunately, I never memorized the names of the two villages, one in Hungary and one in Austria, which served as our crossing from east to west, from *communism* to *freedom*.

Whenever I think of our escape, I remember the little girl I carried over the border. I never learned her name, and I have no idea where she ended up in the world. She is probably in her early seventies now and married with kids of her own. She may even tell her children the story of her escape from Hungary when she was five years old—how she was carried to the border on the shoulders of a young man whose name she never learned.

Over the years I learned in bits and pieces of how Vili made it across the border, but I never got the full story until we got together many years later at his house in Grand Rapids, Michigan. If I thought my crossing the border was full of excitement and adventure, it was nothing compared to his.

Clearly, I was mistaken when I thought that Vili was right behind me as we got off the train. Like me, he also decided to take the initiative and not stay in single file and pass through the two soldiers that collected a "toll" from everyone.

Vili decided to stay in the very back of the line and, taking a calculated risk, struck up a conversation with the Hungarian soldier who was in charge of getting us off the train. I am almost certain that this soldier was by himself, his only job being to get everyone off the train, line everybody up, and march them through the other two soldiers who were the money collectors.

Vili made up his own mind about finding a way out of this situation, just like I did. He didn't know what waited for us up ahead and didn't want to take any chances. He offered all his money, two thousand forints, to this soldier if he would let our group step out of line. The soldier gladly pocketed the money and agreed to let Vili and his group go.

Apparently, the two girls and Pali were close to Vili, but Mrs. Erőd, her son, and I were not. Vili maintains that he had asked the soldier to go up the line and find me. Not surprisingly, the soldier returned and told Vili that I was nowhere to be found since by this time I had already stepped out of the line and was circling around the money collectors.

Without Mrs. Erőd and her son, Vili, Pali, and the two girls went off to the left, the same direction I had taken, and soon found themselves completely lost in the woods. They stumbled through the woods for hours, not knowing where they were heading. Finally, they came upon a house, still on the Hungarian side of the border and, after debating the risk of exposing themselves as potential escapees, they knocked on the door and asked for help.

While the man who opened the door was not very sympathetic to their situation, he did point them in the right direction to the nearby village, where everyone else had gathered from our train. It was in this Hungarian village that Vili, Pali, and the two girls were reunited with Mrs. Erőd and her son. Unfortunately, Mrs. Erőd had broken her ankle in several places on the rough terrain.

Vili's guide, much like mine, had given them instructions on what to do, and they took off toward the border. It is my guess that by this time I was already in Austria and probably sound asleep. Initially, Mrs. Erőd would lean on Vili or Pali to walk, but they eventually had to form a makeshift seat with their hands and arms between them and carry her while she hugged them by their necks.

They also had trouble with her son, who was complaining that he was too tired to walk. He incessantly whined and cried despite his mother's repeated pleading to stay quiet. The guide finally took matters into his own hands and told the little boy that they would all be shot if he didn't shut up. This less-than-gentle approach worked; the poor boy was stunned into silence, probably scared to death, until they crossed the border.

After a while, their guide told them to go ahead and continue on the same path but that he would be turning back. They pleaded with him to stay until they got to some civilization, but to no avail. It isn't clear what happened after their guide left them.

Maybe his instructions on the direction to follow were not clear. Perhaps they were too exhausted to pay attention. In any case, they continued to walk until they came to what seemed like an irrigation canal with no bridge to cross it. Finally, after failing to find a safe way to cross, they managed to get across on floating logs, but not without getting soaked up to their ankles in the near-freezing muddy water.

Yet again, Vili and his group found themselves in the middle of nowhere, exhausted, and not knowing if they were still in Hungary or in Austria. It was around dawn by the time they found a haystack as a shelter. They all collapsed in it and slept for a few hours. Shortly after that, they were found by an Austrian border guard and were escorted into the same village where I had spent most of the night sleeping in the shelter.

Even after all these years, I still feel guilty for having lost my friend. After hearing Vili's story of how he and Pali had to carry Mrs. Erőd over the border, I felt even worse for not having been there to assist them. However, the good news is that everyone made it across safely, except for Mrs. Erőd's broken ankle, and we were reunited.

The next day, December 7, we were taken into the Eisenstadt refugee camp. Eisenstadt was a small town—its population is currently around ten thousand—with its most important claim to history being that it was the hometown of composer Franz Joseph Haydn[1] for many years. Unfortunately, I didn't know much about Haydn at the time; otherwise, I would have visited the famous Eszterházy Palace, where Haydn spent most of his life as music director.

More importantly for Hungarian refugees, Eisenstadt had a large post—World War II American army camp with its barracks still in place. It was hastily converted into a refugee camp in early November 1956, as tens of thousands of refugees flooded the Austrian border.

---

[1] Franz Joseph Haydn (1732–1809). He became the Kappelmeister (music director) of the very rich and famous Eszterházy family in 1776, and he worked for the family until he died. Haydn's remains still lie in the Berg church in Eisenstadt.

By the time we got there on December 7, it was teeming with refugees of all ages.

In Eisenstadt, we were "registered." I told them I was a first-year engineering student at the Technical University in Budapest and wanted to continue my education. Vili and Pali were high school graduates, who also wanted to continue their education. Someone took down our names, duly noting that the three of us were students.

Our orientation was very brief, consisting of pointing out where the kitchen was, when the meals were served, and where we could find some cots to sleep on in the empty barracks. We were also informed that the International Student Council[1] would arrange transportation for us to Vienna, where we would be properly looked after. Additionally, we were told in which part of the camp most of the students were congregating.

Each of us was given two blankets and left to find our temporary quarters. We checked a number of barracks before concluding that no more empty cots were available. We went back to where we got our blankets, but they couldn't help us. They offered us a few more blankets to sleep on, which is what we ended up doing.

We made our "beds" on the floor; the two girls were next to each other with their blankets touching, and Vili, Pali, and I were in the other corner. Mrs. Eröd and her son were no longer with us. She was in the infirmary with her broken ankle and was being attended to by the camp physicians. We also discovered the shower room, so for the first time in forty-eight hours, we took hot baths.

Two days later, on the evening of December 9, we celebrated Vili's nineteenth birthday. We still had one bottle of vodka left, which the five of us proceeded to polish off. Neither of us has much recollection of the party details, Vili the least of all since he passed out. My nineteenth birthday, on January 11, was coming up, and I was hoping that I wouldn't have to celebrate it in Eisenstadt.

As I now recall these events with some help from Bill Fodor, I try to remember how I felt and what my frame of mind was after

---

[1] Neither Bill nor I can remember the exact name of the organization. We do know that it had the first two words "International" and "Student" in it.

having gone through some extraordinary circumstances during the preceding forty-eight hours. The truth is that I remember very little. The subsequent fifty-plus years have blurred many of the impressions and feelings of those days. I am pretty certain, however, that our earlier anxiety about crossing the border had been replaced by an even more daunting angst about our immediate future.

Crossing the border was challenging and tiring, both emotionally and physically, but it was just a small step in the long road ahead of us. And at this stage we had no clue as to where that road would lead. Nevertheless, I do remember that I wasn't in the mood to celebrate our successful border crossing. If anything, my level of anxiety concerning the future was heightened by the fact that major decisions lay ahead, and I was not at all in control of my own destiny.

I was anxious to get going. I felt that the actual experience of being "free at last" could wait. I had my whole life ahead of me for that. But finding a host country to settle in and restart my life was an urgent matter. We left Hungary later than others, so there were tens of thousands of refugees ahead of us who had already preempted some of the choices for a new homeland. Also, I had to get to Vienna to contact my mother to let her know that I was safe and to try to make immediate arrangements for her to join me.

While we waited for our transportation to Vienna, I decided to find the barracks where most of the young people were living. When I found them, they were full of young men and women, most of them older than I, and the place reeked with cigarette smoke so thick that I could barely breathe. Everyone was in a jovial mood, and I felt like I had stumbled into a New Year's Eve party.

I'm not a prude and certainly loved to party, but somehow this scene had turned me off completely. I wanted nothing to do with these young men and women, so I turned around and never went back. The last thing I wanted to do was join a party. Crossing the border into Austria was not worth a celebration. I only wanted to know how soon we could get to Vienna so we could start our new lives.

After we had settled in, we had some time to kill and decided to go into the town of Eisenstadt and look around. There was nothing remarkable about our brief visit except our chance encounter with a local citizen. As we were walking along the street engaged in conversation, an older man was coming toward us from the other direction. He must have heard us speaking Hungarian, so he stopped in front of us.

He asked us a question in German, and the only word I understood was *ungarish*, which means "Hungarian" in German. I responded, "Ja." I knew very little German, and I wondered if we had done something wrong. The man reached into his pocket, pulled out several paper bills, and handed them to us. I was barely able to say a "danke schön," which translates to "thank you very much," and the man walked by us.

I was stunned. The gesture of this total stranger giving us money because we were Hungarian refugees was so impressive that I shall never forget it. This object lesson in generosity was something I wasn't used to, and it taught me that even the simplest and most modest charity could greatly affect someone's life.

Finally, about three days after we arrived in Eisenstadt, a bus came to take a bunch of us "students" to Vienna. We said goodbye to the girls and Mrs. Erőd, and the three of us were ready to go.

This was the most luxurious bus trip we had ever taken in our lives. Everything impressed us. Never had we been in a bus where the luggage compartment was under the seats and accessed from the outside, or where the seats reclined to a preferred position and were covered with soft fabric.

There were reading lights above each seat, and a piece of white cloth covered the top of each seat, where we could rest our heads. To top it all off, there was music coming out of speakers above. Things were looking up for us, and we were in good humor while awaiting our next destination: Vienna.

Vienna

The bus took us directly to one of the universities where the International Student Council had a desk set up to assist us. We all ogled the beautiful buildings, many of them looking architecturally similar to the buildings in Budapest, with the exception of an absence of ruins and bullet holes in the facades.

We registered for the second time at the Student Council desk, where they gave us a green identity card with our name on it. The words "Katholik Hochschule," or Catholic University, stamped on each card caught my attention, but I didn't give it a second thought. Since most of Hungary is Catholic, it made sense that a Catholic religious organization would provide assistance to us.

Nobody ever asked us what our religion was, which was just fine with me. The idea of looking for a Jewish agency assisting Jewish refugees had never even occurred to me. We all got meal cards to be used once a day at a cafeteria chain called WÖK. In addition, we received free passes for the streetcars number 1 and number 2, which ran along the Ringstrasse, one of the wide boulevards that surrounded the inner city, an area of approximately five square miles with the Danube flanking the northern part of the area.

We learned that the only accommodation available was at one of the monasteries in the older part of Vienna, in District I. Unfortunately, neither Vili nor I can recall the name of the monastery. There are close to a dozen of them located in the central part of Vienna, including the Franciscans, the Maltese, the Dominicans, the Minorities, the Capuchins, and others. Since all we cared about was having shelter in the dead of winter, we gladly accepted whatever was available.

We also learned that there was opportunity to work, which involved putting together care packages for refugees. Payment for our services was two schillings a day, and the three of us eagerly volunteered. Work was good; it gave us a sense of purpose and some pocket money. Putting together care packages also provided a few fringe benefits that gradually appeared.

It was at the Student Council desk that we informally heard that the immigration quotas for new Hungarian arrivals were already filled for many countries, including the United States. The three countries mentioned with open quotas were Sweden, Australia, and Canada. We knew that our very first priority once we located our shelter in the city would be to find a country that would welcome us as students.

Based on the directions given to us, we found the monastery that was to be our home for the next two and a half months on a small square with very narrow streets surrounding it. We rang the bell, and a friar, dressed in an ankle-length brown tunic with a white cord around his waist, greeted us. After looking at our papers, he showed us our quarters.

The friar led us into what used to be their dining room, where two rows of ten to fifteen rubber mattresses were lined up on the floor along the walls. A woodburning stove stood near the end of the row on the side where all the windows were. Vili, Pali, and I quickly claimed the first three beds near the stove, a smart move on our part as the winter of 1956–1957 turned out to be exceptionally cold. No meals were to be provided in the cloister, and there was one bathroom with a large old-fashioned cast-iron bathtub available for us.

We did have an unpleasant surprise, though; no warm water was provided for either bathing or washing our clothes. Washing my underwear and nylon shirt was a finger-numbing experience. Vili, having had some practical bachelor experience while living in Pécs, offered to iron shirts for anyone who was willing to wash his laundry.

The strict rule that the doors to the monastery would be closed at ten o'clock in the evening was consistently enforced. Anyone who didn't make it back by that time would be locked out until the next morning. Fortunately, we missed the curfew only once during our stay.

We continuously rang the bell for about an hour, hoping that they would take pity on us and let us in. Finally, one of the friars in his nightgown and nightcap and a candle in his hand opened the door. He was rather upset and admonished us in German, which went right over our heads. However, the message was clear, and we never missed curfew again. Once we had settled into our temporary home at the monastery, it was time to find the country that would welcome us as students.

Despite rumors we heard, we decided to first go to the US Embassy and find out about the possibility of immigration. The official word we got there simply confirmed what we had already expected: that the US quota for Hungarian refugees had been met. The truth is that I don't recall having any preference to come to the United States. The only quality university I had known about was the Swiss Federal Institute of Technology, where I would have liked to study; unfortunately, Switzerland was also closed.

We didn't have too many choices, so by process of elimination, Vili and I decided on Canada. Pali had no say in our decision since he had no ambition to continue his formal education no matter where we ended up. All we knew about Australia was that it was far and on the other side of the world, it was an island-continent, and there were fewer women. Thus, we quickly dismissed that option.

Sweden was somewhat appealing, but the Swedes wanted us to sign an agreement that in exchange for assistance with education, free tuition, and a guaranteed job after graduation, we would remain in Sweden for ten years. At the time, we didn't know much about Sweden's reputation for its beautiful blond women, and it is possible that we made too hasty a decision in dismissing it as our future homeland. As a result, our final choice was Canada, which we knew nothing about save for it was in North America bordering the US and that they spoke English.

I had very briefly considered Israel as a possibility. After all, this was the Jewish state, and some extended family resided there, all of whom were survivors of the Holocaust, except my Aunt Rutka, who left Hungary before the Holocaust. I even visited the Israeli Embassy once, where I talked to a Hungarian-Israeli soldier who was sent there specially to recruit Hungarian Jews.

Israel offered six months of intensive language and cultural training followed by two years of service in the Israeli Defense Forces (IDF). Being a Jew, citizenship would have been granted immediately, and I was offered a full scholarship to any of the universities after discharge from the army. This wasn't a bad deal. However, I didn't want to "waste" more than two years before resuming my education.

This would have been in addition to the academic year of 1956–57, which I considered a lost year already. In addition, there was Vili, a Roman Catholic, who had absolutely no reason to be a part of the Israeli Army. I must admit that many decades later, with anti-Semitism rising all over the world, including in America, I occasionally wonder if I made the right decision not going to Israel.

The Canadians had welcomed us with open arms and told us that as soon as air transportation was available, they would fly us to Montréal. In preparation for living in Canada, we bought ourselves a small bilingual English and Hungarian dictionary and started to memorize some words. I wanted to learn ten new words every day. This was my first introduction to the language of Shakespeare, and my motivation to learn English had been far greater than learning Russian during the prior six years in Hungary.

The Canadians had asked each of us to produce some kind of documentation to prove that we were enrolled in a university in Hungary or that we had completed high school there. I immediately wrote to my mother and asked her to mail the necessary papers for me, as well as to visit Vili's mother to secure his technical school graduation document.

Once we committed to Canada, we quickly settled into a daily routine. I can't remember how many days a week or how many hours a day we worked, but the days we did were rather pleasant. We were in a place with heat, and we stuffed oranges, chocolate bars, and cans of sardines into bags to be given to fellow refugees, who had by now flooded the city of Vienna.

Seeing oranges in winter was strange for us. As far as I knew, nobody in Hungary, other than those in the regime's elite class—Communist Party leaders, members of the secret police, or national sport heroes—could ever have such delicacies as oranges in the wintertime. Even in the summer, oranges were considered luxuries.

We realized quickly that we could eat as many sardines and chocolate bars as we wished. In addition, nobody paid any attention to what was in our winter coat pockets when we left our workplace. Vili had been thoughtful enough to buy some bananas and prepare a package of tropical fruits that he mailed home to his mother and sister.

The mornings were not pleasant at the monastery. We washed ourselves in ice-cold water, shaved if necessary in ice-cold water, and quickly got dressed. Breakfast was either sardines, chocolate, or both. Vili, being the most practical of us, noted that an unintended benefit of our steady chocolate diet was that we had a much less frequent need to use the toilet at the cloister, which had an ambient temperature similar to the inside of a meat freezer.

To round out our dietary needs beyond our once-a-day hot meal at the WÖK, we went to other aid agencies in the city. We found one agency that provided fresh bread, while another provided large chunks of cheddar cheese. The fresh bread and cheese were a welcomed alternative to our sardines and chocolate diet in the morning and at night after dinner. Fortunately, this diet didn't do any permanent damage to our digestive systems. However, it did have a temporary psychological impact on Vili. He claims that after we had left Vienna, he couldn't even look at, much less eat, a can of sardines for at least ten years.

I'm not sure where I wrote my first letter to my mother to inform her of our safety; it might have been in Eisenstadt. Now, with two shillings every day, I could buy stamps and write her frequently, sometimes twice a week. I had an address in Vienna so she could write to me, which she did. She answered all my letters right away, and we had a constant flow of communication. Whereas there were no more than 175 miles between us, it felt like we were a world apart.

I kept her abreast of the day-to-day discoveries we made in our new world, in addition to our progress in finding a home for ourselves. She didn't have much news to tell me, but it didn't really matter. The physical presence of her letters and her usual warnings to be careful and to take care of myself were profoundly meaningful. I felt that I wasn't alone and was still very emotionally attached to her even though I didn't realize it at the time.

In one of her letters, my mother sent me the address of Mrs. Erőd in Vienna. We went to see her, and a few nights later she offered to prepare us our first home-cooked meal in her small apartment since we left Hungary. It also happened to be the last one for a long time to come. Mrs. Erőd thanked us for helping her across the border and even offered to help us should we decide to go to Argentina, where she had planned to go.

As soon as we had accumulated some money, Vili and I bought two identical suitcases for twenty schillings each. They were cheap lockable suitcases made out of pressed paper, but served their purpose. We needed to protect the food treasures we hoarded: the oranges, chocolates, and sardines. In addition to holding our food, we needed the suitcases to store our belongings because all we left Hungary with was our briefcase.

We went to an organization similar to the Salvation Army and began to collect some additional clothes we needed for the winter, such as gloves, shirts, sweaters, warm pants, jackets, and shoes. Anything we couldn't find there, we bought for ourselves. We were soon well-dressed, even for long walks, for the bitter winter that descended on Vienna in late December of 1956.

Vienna is a walking city with sidewalks on every street, very similar to Budapest. As is typical for European cities, it has a great public transportation system. Buses, underground trains, and streetcars crisscross the city. However, we mostly walked everywhere. We enjoyed strolling around and seeing the buildings and observing the people on the street as they went about their business. In some way, we felt like tourists in a foreign land, taking in the sights, tasting the local food, meeting the natives, trying to speak their language, and anticipating our eventual departure to our new homeland.

We didn't yet have any concept of our future "home." One of my fondest memories of walking the streets of Vienna was occasionally buying ten pieces of scalding-hot roasted chestnuts picked one at a time off a smoking grill and handed to us in a small paper bag by the street vendor.

Vili and I compared our memory banks to see what we could recall from our Vienna days. It is interesting that we couldn't remember many important places, events, and names—like our friend Pali's last name—while we could recall insignificant incidents like the one about a cute girl we followed one day.

The three of us were walking on the street, studying a map for directions, while walking directly in front of us was a well-dressed middle-aged couple with a girl about our age. She was wearing a short, tight-fitting winter coat and a skirt, exposing her nicely shaped legs. We followed them for a block or two, while looking at street signs and debating our directions. At the same time, Vili and I started to rate the attractiveness of the young girl's physical features, such as ankles, calves, thighs, buttocks, etc., on a scale of 1 to 10. We gave her high marks all around as we spoke loudly in Hungarian, secure that nobody could understand us.

We caught up with the couple and the young girl at a red light, where we all waited for it to turn. While standing there, we looked at our map and started to discuss which direction to take. At this point, the father turned around and told us in perfect Hungarian which street would be our best choice. His sly smile on his face as he spoke told us that he heard everything we had said about his daughter. Naturally, we were embarrassed yet glad that we didn't make any rude comments. This incident, together with the fact that we still remember it, simply proves that while we had many grown-up decisions to make, we were still very much teenagers at heart, with raging hormones and one-track minds.

The proximity to Budapest, both in distance and elapsed time since leaving, was once again evident. One day while walking, we suddenly heard a loud rumbling, the unmistakable noise of a tank with its caterpillar tracks. Instinctively, we jumped into the nearest doorway, expecting to see a tank rolling down the street. Instead, what we saw was a snow removal machine on treads, which made us burst out in laughter. We must have still been conditioned to expecting military vehicles roaming the streets in broad daylight based on what we had experienced in Budapest just a few weeks before.

One peculiarity of the inner city of Vienna still brings a smile to my face every time I think about it. We braved the cold winter and walked to our workplace, taking us thirty minutes or so to tread along several smaller streets with many turns. Many of the Viennese apartment buildings are designed to have two, sometimes more, openings to different streets.

They are common in Budapest too and actually have the name *átjáróház*, which literally translates into "a house with a passageway," a rare occasion where the English expression is much longer than the Hungarian. Then, almost two months after we started working and shortly before we left Vienna, we discovered that if we had just walked through a couple of these *átjáróházak*, it would have taken us only ten minutes to get to work.

Our evenings following dinner at the WÖK were typically spent at the cloister, where we exchanged our daily experiences with our fellow Hungarians and discussed our plans for the future. Lights were turned out some time after ten with the conversations often continuing well into the night.

One night after everyone was settling down and trying to get to sleep, Vili started rubbing his finger on the rubber mattress, creating an ugly, ear-piercing, shrieking noise. After a while, a guy across the hall started to shout some Hungarian obscenities, including rather specific anatomical descriptions of the perpetrator's mother and other blood relatives, and asked that whoever was doing this stop it immediately or else. Of course, it was pitch-dark except for the glow of the woodburning oven next to Vili's bed, so nobody could see who was creating the noise or exactly where it was coming from.

This went on for a while until I suddenly heard someone stumbling around his bed from across the room. This was quickly followed by a whooshing sound that ended in a rather strange cracking noise and sharp cry from the bed next to me, where Pali was trying to fall asleep. The whooshing sound we all heard turned out to be the air disturbance following the trajectory of a heavy winter boot as it was flying across the room at high speed. The sharp cry on my side came from Pali after the boot hit his nose and broke it.

Ever since Pali joined us in Budapest, I always admired his composure when faced with adversity, but this moment was paramount. He calmly got up, took the boot, walked over to the oven, opened the latch on the door, and dropped the boot into the flames. He then closed the oven door, walked back to his bed, and lay down to sleep. Absolute silence followed, and eventually we all went to sleep. Had the boot landed on my nose, I doubt I would have had the presence of mind to react like Pali.

From this night on, Pali's nose was visibly out of joint, but not enough to significantly alter his otherwise pleasant profile. As far as I know, not once had Pali complained to Vili for causing his minor facial disfigurement. Nonetheless, Pali's broken nose didn't prevent him from marrying a cute French-Canadian girl less than a year later in a small rural town just southeast of Montréal.

One night about a week or ten days after arriving in Vienna, the three of us were sitting in a WÖK cafeteria having our dinner. Not wanting to make a major blunder in ordering, we probably chose similarly to what we did on previous nights, such as a wiener schnitzel. We happened to pick a table that was situated so that I was facing the main entrance to the cafeteria.

As I was eating my meal, I happened to look up as the door opened, and in came my Uncle Elek, followed by his two young boys, his wife Magda, and his mother-in-law. I instantly recognized him in his dark-brown leather coat that came down almost all the way to his ankles. Breathless by the sight of him, I jumped up and rushed toward him crying out, "Caga!"—the nickname we all called him in the family. I could feel the tears forming in my eyes as I hugged him. Having my uncle physically next to me in Vienna gave me such a tremendous sense of relief that is difficult to describe.

"What are you doing here?" I asked. "Just ten days ago when I stopped by to say goodbye in Budapest and asked you if you were planning to leave, you said no. What happened? What changed?" I demanded to know.

"We changed our minds," he replied. While the rest of the evening is unclear, my uncle told me that they were staying at a hotel paid for by a Jewish agency and asked me to stop by to see them the next night.

The next evening, I learned that Uncle Elek had found a guide who agreed to take all five of them from Budapest right across the border to Austria for two thousand forints per person. They came with another family, the Singers, who were somehow related to Magda. They explained that my uncle's mother-in-law's sister Ilus couldn't join them but that she was planning to come out within the next few days using the same guide. The idea struck me that my mother could join Ilus and leave Hungary under the protection of this guide.

My uncle made urgent phone calls from the hotel to Budapest, and arrangements were made to notify my mother—since we didn't have a telephone—of the plans for her to join me in Vienna. I was sure that my mother could collect the two thousand forints from Manci néni. Within the next twenty-four hours, the plans were firmed up. If everything went well, my mother and Ilus would cross the border the following night.

My uncle was to go to the Austrian village where they were to cross over and bring them back to Vienna. Plans were made for my uncle to phone us back at the hotel as soon as the two women were safe in Austria. The possibility of being reunited with my mother made sleep impossible that night.

I went to my uncle's hotel the next evening to be present when the call came with the good news. It was a small room, and I was anxiously awaiting the phone to ring. It finally rang, and my aunt picked up the phone. Her smile indicated that it was good news. She began to talk to Ilus, and I interrupted him to ask how my mother was. She asked, "Is Robi's mother with you?" and the smile on her face disappeared. I felt this strange sensation around my chest and throat as fear started to take over. My aunt put the phone down, turned to me, and said that my mother didn't show up at the appointed hour; thus, Ilus had no choice but to leave without her.

The subsequent moments are a blur. I vividly recall, as if I were watching a slow-motion picture, looking down on my aunt, her mother, the two cousins, and myself from a vantage point somewhere near the ceiling. I saw myself bursting out in tears and crying out, "Mother! Why didn't you come?"—repeating it over and over again as I turned to the wall and banged on it hard with both fists. It was anger, sorrow, and frustration all mixed together, and I couldn't stop either my sobbing or my pounding on the wall.

The whole time I saw myself in my mind's eye, I could see the shock on the faces of my family, including my two little cousins, who probably couldn't comprehend what was taking place. I can count on one hand how many times I lost control in my life, this being one of those times. The disappointment was unbearable.

My aunt tried to comfort me, but something in my heart was broken. It was almost as if I sensed that this was it, that I would never be reunited with my mother. If there is a moment in our lives when we suddenly turn from a child into an adult, then this was that moment for me. Although I didn't give up the idea of my mother joining me for years to come, somehow I knew that from now on, I was on my own.

The letter arrived two days later explaining that she couldn't get the necessary two thousand forints. I believed her because I needed to. I never questioned it until many years later. Why couldn't she ask for the money from Uncle Laci or Manci néni, who always had plenty of money? Or just simply borrow it from Ilus?

Just before Christmas, the whole city was blanketed with fluffy white snow. Christmas lights were hung on street corners, houses, buses, and streetcars, and holiday music filled the air. A joyous, festive mood descended on Vienna, something we weren't used to experiencing in Budapest. Not realizing it then, this was only the second Christmas that the Austrians could celebrate as an independent country and without the presence of any foreign troops since 1937.[1]

At one of the major traffic intersections in the city, two police officers were directing traffic at a stoplight. Near them was a large container, almost the size of a dumpster, that normally held sand to be used on the icy roads. Cars were approaching the policemen and actually coming to a stop, even when they had a green light. The car window lowered, and a small package, nicely wrapped in

---

[1] Hitler annexed Austria (referred to as the *Anschluss* or *Union* with Germany) on March 13, 1938. Following World War II, the four Allied powers—the United States, Britain, France, and the Soviet Union—basically controlled Austria until May 15, 1955, when a treaty was signed with Austria, formally reestablishing the republic.

Christmas paper, was handed to the nearest policeman. Greetings were exchanged, and the car moved on.

The policeman took the package over to the sand box on the sidewalk and placed it inside. I stood there watching, at first not understanding what was happening, and then in admiration at this public act of generosity. What planet were we on? If someone had told me two weeks earlier back in Budapest that this is how ordinary people express their appreciation of their public servants, I would have laughed. This was one of many culture shocks we experienced as we were introduced to a whole new way of life in Austria, and later in Canada.

From Uncle Elek, I found out the name and address of the Jewish agency that so generously provided them with a hotel room and meals. I decided I had nothing to lose, so I called on them. The person I met asked me for my identification card. He looked questioningly at my card as if something was wrong with it. Finally, he looked up and inquired, "Are you Jewish?"

"Of course, I am," I replied.

"Then why is your card stamped 'Katholik Hochschule'?" he asked.

Suddenly, I understood that I was confronted with an unfamiliar problem: how to prove my Jewishness.

I explained that I had left Hungary with a friend who is Catholic and that when we first entered the Eisenstadt camp, we were looked after by the Catholic student organization. However, the man wouldn't budge; it was clear that he didn't believe me. In an act of desperation, I asked him if he would like me to drop my pants to provide physical evidence of my being Jewish, which he declined. I left frustrated and feeling cheated, out of what I wasn't exactly certain.

Christmas, New Year's Eve, and then my nineteenth birthday on January 11, 1957, came and went fast. We were trying to learn new English words, phrases, and grammar every day. I was also speaking some rudimentary German just by interacting with Austrians on a daily basis. When the three of us were together walking around the city, asking for directions or negotiating a purchase, I was the one fumbling with the German language. Pali never opened his mouth, and Vili was shy, petrified of mispronouncing something. I wasn't fazed, so by the time we left Vienna in February, I could ask for directions, order food in a restaurant, and get around the city.

Obviously, we didn't have the means or the time to fully explore cultural life in Vienna, but we did manage to sample it a bit. One day, I decided to see an opera in the famous Vienna State Opera House.[1] Having had season tickets to the Budapest Opera back home, courtesy of my mother's indulgence to expose me to arts, I developed an affinity for operas. I had enough money to buy two tickets to Puccini's *La Bohème*, and I invited Jutka, the teenage daughter of the Singers, who came to Vienna with my uncle, to join me.

This turned out to be the beginning of a budding romantic relationship that was to continue many months later in Montréal, Canada. The singing was wonderful, even though I couldn't understand a word of it. However, I didn't need to. I knew the story because traditional Hungarian operas were sung in Hungarian, making them more popular with the younger generation. It was a delight seeing the ornate, gold-trimmed decorations and plush interior of the opera house. It reminded me of the Budapest Opera House, which was built around the same time and in a similar style as the original Vienna Opera House.[2]

We heard about the famous Schöenbrunn Palace from some of our more cultured and older friends and decided to make a visit. The palace was the residence of the Hapsburg emperors from the eighteenth century to 1918. It has the world's oldest, still-operative zoo, which opened in 1752. Fortunately, the buildings weren't destroyed during the Second World War. While there, I bought a small memento, a key chain attached to a small round medal that

---

[1] The *Staatsoper* or *State Opera* opened on May 25, 1869. It was totally destroyed on March 12, 1945, during an Allied bombing raid. It was rebuilt and reopened on November 5, 1955.

[2] The Budapest Opera House was opened on September 27, 1884, and was completely reconditioned in its original golden splendor for its centennial anniversary in 1984.

had the picture of the palace on it. I kept that key chain for years, but I unfortunately lost it some years ago.

Finally, in early February, we were told that our departure date for Canada was set for February 13. We were to be flown to Montréal, Québec. After spending more than two months in Vienna, we were eager to land in our new country. On the morning of February 13, we packed up all our belongings and were transported to the Schwechat airport on the outskirts of Vienna. There we were given a Canadian visa issued by the local Canadian Embassy.

Altogether, there were about thirty of us students waiting to be flown to Canada. The plan was to board the plane and take off that afternoon. We sat around in the departure lounge, waiting to board the plane, when we were informed that there was going to be a delay. At that point, we didn't care as long as we were going to take off soon. There was a buzz of excitement since most of us had never flown in an airplane before.

As the hours went by, we began wondering what was happening. Rumors started spreading that the plane was late arriving or that it had mechanical issues that had to be fixed. The Canadians in charge were trying their best to assure us that everything was fine, but as evening descended, we suspected that we wouldn't be taking off that night.

Everyone was hungry, yet there was no food to be had. Then we were told that our departure was delayed until the following day on February 14. The only problem was that there were no accommodations at the airport for thirty people to sleep. In the end, we ended up sleeping on the floor, with some blankets provided by the airport authorities.

Finally, at dawn while still dark, we all lined up to board our plane. Vili thought the plane was a World War II vintage, four-engine turboprop transport or a bomber, like a B-52, converted to carry passengers. As we lined up to board, Vili told me that the best seats are in the tail, where we ended up having the last two seats, with me in the window seat. I didn't think to question him, a mistake I soon regretted, since he claimed to have relevant experience in these matters, having done some flying in a glider plane back in Budapest the previous summer.

Finally, our plane took off with a deafening roar, and I was in near panic, staring out the window, looking at massive purple, red, and orange flames coming out of the engines as the plane slowly lifted off the runway. We were on our way to our new homeland. I was filled with mixed emotions: the fear of flying in this angry, fire-spewing monster; the sense of finality that one part of my life had come to an end; the anxiety of the unknown future awaiting us; and the excitement of a new beginning.

Reflections

The preparation and research for writing this story led me to reflect on the experiences my friend Vili and I had within a broader historical context of Austria.

I tried to portray the Austrians in this story as we saw them, a caring and generous people. The examples are abundant: the border guards who met us at midnight on the Austrian border, the total stranger who gave me money straight from his pocket, the citizens who stopped their cars in the middle of a Vienna road and gave presents to their policemen, the friars who gave us shelter in their monastery, and the volunteers at the Student Council who helped us to orient ourselves. Individually and collectively, the Austrians clearly demonstrated goodwill, kindness, generosity, and the willingness to accommodate and assist close to two hundred thousand refugees.

Vienna, the center of culture, architecture, art, and music for much of the nineteenth century, was enriching, even in our significantly constrained status as refugees. When Americans think of Austria, they may think of a country that produced Mozart, the waltz, Sacher tort, some of the world's best Alpine skiers, and even the former governor of California, Arnold Schwarzenegger.

However, there is also a dark side to Austria, of which many people are unaware. It is the country that produced Hitler and numerous other top Nazi officials who had leadership roles in planning and executing the Second World War and the genocide of six million innocent Jews. This is the country that, for almost fifty years after the Second World War, tried to perpetuate the myth that it was a victim of Nazism and not an active collaborator. However, the facts prove otherwise.

This is the country that murdered sixty-five thousand, or 80 percent, of its own Jewish population in the Holocaust. Vienna is the city where Hitler was cheered by hundreds of thousands of Viennese when he entered the city following the annexation of Austria to Germany in 1938, the year I was born. During the infamous *Kristallnacht*, on November 9–10, 1938, the German and Austrian Nazis terrorized their Jewish neighbors.

This is the country that took forty-five years after losing the war to publicly admit that Austria and its people were willing servants of the Nazis.[1] In addition, Austria has one of the worst restitution records of any country in Europe. While Germany has largely settled claims for property stolen from its Jews, Austria has returned only a diminutive part of the art, books, land, bank accounts, and other assets stolen by the Austrian Nazis.

However, one doesn't have to go back fifty years to find Nazi sympathizers in Austria. On March 7, 2004, Joerg Haider, an openly anti-Semitic, right-wing Nazi sympathizer, led his Freedom Party to victory in the elections in the Austrian province of Carinthia. Haider has been on the Austrian political scene since 1979. His Freedom Party achieved 22.6 percent of the vote in the 1994 national elections, winning the dubious distinction of gaining more votes in parliamentary elections than the gains of any other European far-right party.

Haider and his party are alive and well, as shown in the excerpts from an ADL[2] publication:

> Haider was reelected to governor of Carinthia by a landslide in 1999. Later that year, the Freedom Party finished second in the general elections with a stunning 27 percent of the vote. With the political leverage gained from the 1999 election, in 2000, the Freedom Party succeeded in joining the new Austrian government as a coalition partner. This development led to an outcry from many in Austria, the international community, as well as Jewish and non-Jewish organizations around the world, and finally culminated in Israel recalling its ambassador from Vienna. The European Union imposed sanctions on Austria.

---

[1] Chancellor Franz Vranitsky's statement in the early 1990s.

[2] ADL stands for Anti-Defamation League. The publication is "Joerg Haider: The Rise of an Austrian Extreme Rightist," March 9, 2004.

While Haider resigned as the head of the Freedom
Party in 2000, he continues to be a major influence behind the scenes, and retained his position
as Governor of Carinthia.

Is history repeating itself? I hope not.

Closer to home, I discovered that I was not the first one in my
family to visit the region of Eisenstadt the day after I crossed the
border on December 6, 1956. Both my father and mother were there
before me in 1944. The town of Lichtenwörth, just a few miles west
of Eisenstadt, is where my mother ended up as a prisoner, after a
dreadful six-week march on foot from Budapest.

Just a few miles east of Eisenstadt is Donnerskirchen, the home
of the forced labor camp where my father died. His remains have
never been recovered. My mother returned, barely alive, following
the liberation of Lichtenwörth in the spring of 1945. During the
time I was in Eisenstadt in December of 1956, I had no idea that I
was almost within walking distance of such sacred grounds.

I tried but could not find traces of these two camps. Searching
for "Donnerskirchen" on the internet leads to the WorldGolf.com
website for a "Scottish Links" golf course with the following description: "Good condition, difficult greens, very tight and extremely
tough course where it is always windy." Who knows how many
corpses are buried under the fairways of Donnerskirchen.

These two death camps are just two of the many smaller
ones that history has long forgotten. Only the larger ones, such as
Matthausen[1] and Gusen, near Linz, Austria, are recorded in historic
documents. From my research, I learned that the Mauthausen camp
was one of the most infamous in the entire alternate Nazi universe
of human destruction. Many people, most of whom were innocent

---

[1] Mauthausen was officially declared as a "forced labor" camp. It was in operation
from August 1938 through September 1944, when the US Army liberated it.
For a gruesome view of Mauthausen, you can visit http://www.remember.org/
camps/mauthausen/.

of any crimes, were tortured to death in its rock quarry and in the tunnels of Mauthausen-Gusen, the most infamous of the subcamps.

Prisoners were to be given only the most primitive tools and were to work with their bare hands whenever possible. This policy was known as "Primitivbauweise"—or "primitive style." In Mauthausen, it resulted in a harsh stone world, deprived of any human kindness and compassion. It is still there today, sitting on a small mountaintop in the astonishingly beautiful and bucolic Austrian countryside, maintained by the Austrian government. The number of prisoners at Mauthausen was estimated at 199,404, of whom 119,000 died.

To be fair, it is worth mentioning that not all Austrians were Nazi collaborators or silent bystanders. As of January 2018, the Yad Vashem Holocaust Authority honored 109 Austrians as "Righteous Among the Nations."[1]

So, what am I to make of these seeming contradictions? The same people who created, admired, and welcomed beauty and excellence in art, music, and architecture, the people who are devotedly religious, churchgoing Christians, are also the ones who were capable of committing mankind's worst atrocities or, at best, silently tolerated them in defiance of everything that is human. How could the same Austrians who demonstrated such kindness and generosity toward us refugees in 1956 commit or be complicit in such crimes only a short twelve years before I met them?

While I don't know the answers to these questions, perhaps, as I already mentioned in my previous story, there is good and evil in all of us and a thin line that separates these opposing sides of our human consciousness. As history has demonstrated, it may not take much to cross this boundary. If that is the case, then our foremost individual responsibility is to recognize good and evil and act accordingly in order to keep us on a righteous path.

---

[1] The principle memorial at Yad Vashem is the Hall of Remembrance. The approach to the Hall of Remembrance is lined with trees planted in honor of non-Jewish men and women—"Righteous Among the Nations"—who, at the risk of their own lives, attempted to rescue Jews from the Holocaust. A total of 22,765 people have been honored with the title "Righteous Among the Nations" as of January 1, 2009; 725 of them are Hungarian.

Journey 5: Immigrant Years

I must admit I struggled with this story because I wasn't certain what message I wanted to leave behind. My immigrant years in Canada and in the United States lack the tragedy, drama, and danger that characterize my previous stories. My life, as it unfolded during seven years, from 1957 through 1964, were typical of hundreds of thousands of immigrants coming into Canada and into the United States.

My life was not in danger. I didn't have to live under or escape an oppressive system, and I didn't have to survive a bloody uprising. So, why write about my immigrant years? After some reflection, the answer became clear. It is likely that none of my progeny will ever experience life as an immigrant—where they have to learn a new language or start a new life in a culture that is significantly, perhaps even drastically, different from what they had been accustomed to growing up.

While Hungary was certainly part of Western civilization in the 1950s, it was in sharp contrast to life in Canada or the US. Those differences were political, economic, social, as well as cultural. When I grew up in the midst of the Cold War in the 1950s, Hungary was a paradigm of the worst excesses of the Stalinist era. In order to ensure its survival, Hungary's totalitarian, state-controlled, one-party socialist system depended on political indoctrination, the population's constant fear of the state, backed by a feared secret police force, and the denial of any freedom of expression and of the many personal liberties that are taken for granted in the West.

The state owned, planned, and managed—or tried to—the economy of the whole country, denying the right of individuals to handle their own affairs. To put it simplistically and at the risk of dramatizing it, everything was forbidden unless it was expressly approved by the state—a stark contrast to our way of life where everything is allowed unless expressly forbidden. This state tyranny extended into the very fabric of life, such as freedom of speech, of religion, of education, in addition to where to live and where to work.

Like me, immigrants coming from such backgrounds and living in a free society had to go through dramatic adjustments to successfully adapt to our new country. I concluded that what I had to go through in order to become first a Canadian and then an American, while shedding my old habits, prejudices, and, to a major degree, my family connections, may be a part of the Rátonyi family saga that my grandchildren and future generations may find interesting.

There is another reason why I decided to write this story. Other than the first four years of living in Canada, I have spent the rest of my life in America. Through my own and my wife's personal experiences, I have learned and come to appreciate the historic importance of immigrants to the unique achievements of my adopted country in the areas of arts, sciences, technology, commerce, and industry. I am proud of being an American and of having been able to contribute to the welfare of my adopted country. In fact, I am sad to say, I often feel I am more American than those who were privileged to have been born and raised here.

I hope that the story of my immigrant years will help the readers appreciate how unique and wonderful our country is. I can think of very few countries in the world that are as inclusive of immigrants as the United States or Canada. The cornerstone of our national identity is that of being a country of immigrants, starting from our Founding Fathers to the latest immigrant arriving today. Where else could a refugee with no money, no earthly possessions, and no English start out and end up being a productive member of society?

I don't mean to sound melodramatic, but this country is truly the place where one can participate in the *pursuit of happiness.*[1] Both Canada and the US are unique in the sense that where you end up economically and socially doesn't depend on either where you came from or what you had at the start, but on your native intelligence, plus your willingness to work hard and make the necessary sacrifices along the way to reach your goals.

To me, the closing lines of the sonnet "The New Colossus," written by Emma Lazarus[2] and placed on a tablet at the pedestal of the Statue of Liberty in 1903, are not just some tourist attraction or political slogan, but the essence of who we are as Americans and where we all came from:

34. The Statue of Liberty.

Give me your tired, your poor,
Your huddled masses yearning to breathe free,
The wretched refuse of your teeming shore.
Send these, the homeless, tempest-tossed to me,
I lift my lamp beside the golden door!

---

[1] Excerpt from the Declaration of Independence, July 4, 1776: "We hold these Truths to be self-evident, that all Men are created equal, that they are endowed by their Creator with certain unalienable Rights that among these are Life, Liberty and the Pursuit of Happiness."

[2] Emma Lazarus (1849–1887), American Jewish poet and essayist born in New York City.

Journey to the Unknown

My previous story ended when I finally got on an airplane at the Schwechat airport in Vienna with Vili and Pali and was heading toward our destination in Canada. Naturally, I was nervous about flying since I had never been on an airplane before. In addition, I soon discovered that my stomach didn't take kindly to the sensation of my feet not set firmly on solid ground.

Adding to my already high level of anxiety and exacerbating my motion sickness, we were informed after about two hours of flying that the plane developed some mechanical problems, and we would have to return to Austria. It turned out that one of the four engines had caught on fire.

We stayed at the Schwechat airport for about eight hours before taking off again. Sitting in the last row of two seats of the airplane, I once again had to face the ordeal of flying. By now I was too tired, too worn out, and too exhausted both physically and emotionally to care much about what we were facing.

Our next refueling stop was in Glasgow, a seaport in southwest Scotland, where we arrived in the very early hours of the morning. I remember being ushered into a very spacious dining room with tables set up with china and silverware on white linen but completely empty of people. We were served a full breakfast with bacon and eggs, and Vili had no problem finishing off both his and my portion.

My stomach was too upset for me to eat anything. I still haven't quite forgiven my friend for talking me into sitting in the last row of the plane. Never having flown before and trusting his "experience" of flying a glider plane, I assumed that he knew what he was talking about—an assumption I greatly regretted, as I was airsick virtually the entire way to Canada.

We finally took off again and headed northwest in a wide arc to make our way to North America via Iceland, our next refueling stop. We landed at a US military base in Reykjavik, the capital, where the wind was so strong that military personnel drove steel pipes into the ice on the ground, to which they strung a thick rope from the airport building to our airplane in order to secure our disembarkation. We held on to the rope as we got off the plan to make sure that the wind wouldn't blow us off our feet.

The friendliness of the uniformed soldiers was impressive as they welcomed us with small bags of goodies that included a tooth-brush, toothpaste, and some Chiclets chewing gum. They all knew about the Hungarian Uprising and probably suspected that some of us had a part in instigating the upheaval and defying the Soviet army. Unfortunately, direct communication with the Americans was impossible because none of us spoke English, except for the few words we had learned back in Vienna.

I wasn't the only one who suffered throughout the flight. One or more of the students were swearing that they would never again get on an airplane, even if they had to spend the rest of their lives in Iceland. Of course, at the end of our short stay, all of us got back on the plane for our final leg to Montréal. Both Vili and I estimated that it took about twenty-two to twenty-four hours from the initial takeoff from Vienna to our plane arriving in Montréal.

Our first stop was Canadian Immigration, where they issued identity cards to all of us, labeling us "refugees." If we wanted to change our names, this was the time to do so, an offer I didn't take and greatly regret in retrospect. If I had had the presence of mind, I could have changed my name back to Reichmann or anglicized it to Richman or Rich or anything else that would have been a lot easier to pronounce and spell than the Italian-sounding Ratonyi. But who considers such things at the age of nineteen when the whole world is changing around you?

It was sufficient to drop the accents in my name to make it Robert Ratonyi from Róbert Rátonyi. Vili thought about changing his first name to William but decided to stick with Vilmos, a decision he also later regretted. In 1974, he officially changed his first name to William when he became an American citizen. I am grateful to my parents for choosing an English first name like Róbert, which I never had a problem with.

Following the processing at the airport, we took a bus to an immigration collection facility in the east end of Montréal, in St. Paul L'ermit. Unfortunately, we arrived in the middle of the night, so we were all starving. The place was deserted, except for a lone custodian, who opened a massive refrigerator and told us to help ourselves to whatever we could find. This was our first experience with white "cotton" bread, a staple of the Canadian/American diet. Bread and milk were the only food in the refrigerator, which we filled our stomachs with. In the morning, we were "processed" by the Canadian authorities.

They divided us into two or three groups, and Vili and I ended up going to what may have been a Franciscan monastery in the outskirts of Montréal's French district. Perhaps because "Catholic University" was stamped on my paper from Austria, the authorities assumed that I was a Catholic without ever bothering to ask me. This wasn't a problem until one of the Hungarians complained to the priest in charge that Vili's friend was Jewish.

The priest confronted Vili and asked if he knew that his friend was Jewish. Vili told him that of course he knew and that it was not a secret. Following this "discovery" of my religious identity, I vaguely recall a subsequent conversation with the priest, who kindly offered to convert me to Catholicism, an offer I politely declined.

The priests not only took care of our spiritual needs via the daily prayer services but also looked after our social needs. Young ladies from a French-Canadian girls' school were brought in on a Saturday night for a dance that we all enjoyed, in spite of the watchful eyes of the chaperones. This encounter with French girls may have had a fatal effect on our friend Pali.

Some weeks went by, and we were all asked if we wished to learn French or English, so we were divided into two groups accordingly. Most of us decided that English was the best choice, but there were a few in the group, including Pali, who chose French. A few days later, around mid-March, about ten of us were told that we were being sent to Kingston, Ontario, where we were to begin our formal education in the English language.

Indeed, the time came when we boarded a train to take us to our next destination, the campus of Queen's University in Kingston. This was when we parted with Pali, our companion since leaving Budapest, and we never saw him or spoke with him again. We heard many months later that he had married a French-Canadian girl from a small town in Québec, where they had settled down together.

Pali's decision to learn French instead of English, to marry so quickly, and to settle down in a small provincial town didn't surprise me. The journey had ended for him, while for Vili and me, it was just the beginning. Pali had modest ambitions, whereas I had dreams of enjoying the fruits of higher education that the Canadian government offered us.

Kingston was an important place for me, both physically and emotionally. I had had plenty of excitement in my life since I left Budapest three months earlier. But finally, I was able to focus for the first time on my immediate future and get ready to continue my education. In fact, I was so focused on being prepared to continue my college education that I probably overlooked many of the daily life happenings that I am now trying to recall more than fifty years later. Names of the six Hungarian fellows I bunked with escape me, except for Vili Fodor, of course, and another fellow named Jocó (nickname for József) Mezöfényi, who became a good friend later on in Montréal.

Kingston is a nice small town at the northwest corner of Lake Ontario, almost halfway between Montréal and Toronto. Queen's University is one of Canada's leading universities, established by the Royal Charter of Queen Victoria in 1841, right on the shores of Lake Ontario. Our living quarters were spartan, yet clean and safe. We were well fed, and all we had to do was learn enough English to be able to go to college in the fall.

Our home in Kingston was on the ground floor of the athletic center at Queen's University. We slept in one of the rooms that was equipped with bunk beds, where the football players stayed during their summer and fall practice. Our daily routine was simple.

In the mornings we had a professional English teacher to teach us, a nice young lady and expectant mother, showing visible signs of her pregnancy. She spoke no Hungarian, so each morning all we heard was four hours of English. The government hired a Hungarian professor of English to coach us in the afternoon and to help us with our daily assignments. In the evenings, we studied and tried to memorize about ten new words every day.

We got five dollars every week for spending money and meal tickets to the university cafeteria. Kingston is a small town, so word got out quickly that some Hungarian students, escapees from communist Hungary, were in town. Occasionally, we were invited to dinner by some of the locals, and we even had an invitation to a dance with girls from the local nursing school.

35. Queen's University, Kingston, Canada; spring 1957.
I am in the front, Jocó and Vili (*last*) are in the back.

There were six of us who formed a short-term friendship that unfortunately didn't last beyond our time in Kingston, save for Vili, Jocó, and me. I know I felt happy, except for the sadness of leaving my mother behind. What impresses me now, having looked at a few sixty-year-old pictures, is how nicely dressed we were in white shirts and ties, as if we had no worries in the world. What the pictures don't show is that we had few possessions other than what we wore and were living on the Canadian government's generosity.

We had the opportunity to start college full-time in the fall of 1957 at either Queen's University or at McGill University in Montréal. McGill University is one of Canada's best-known institutions for higher learning and the country's leading research-intensive university. The oldest university in Montréal, McGill was founded in

1821. The Canadian government offered us loans and scholarships, assuming that we had learned enough English and gotten decent enough grades to qualify for scholarships.

There was one major change in my plans to continue my education. My plans to start college full-time in September 1957 were interrupted after my mother and I reached an agreement through our frequent written correspondence that she would follow me to Canada as a legal immigrant as soon as possible. Following the Uprising, the Hungarian government eased up on the rules allowing family members, particularly older people, to leave the country.

Canadian immigration rules required that in order to bring my mother to Canada, I had to have a job and sufficient funds to guarantee support for my mother as a dependent. This meant that I had to have a full-time job, save enough money to bring my mother out of Hungary, and start my college education in an evening program. Fortunately, Sir George Williams University, now known as Concordia University, planned to start a new evening engineering program in September of 1957, which was tailored to McGill University's daytime engineering program.

Four years of evening engineering classes were offered at Sir George to cover the first two years of coursework at McGill. This was a reasonable solution for me to work while simultaneously restart my college education. The delay of two years in my graduation didn't bother me at all. I felt then, as I do now, that it was the least I could do for my mother. The changing roles in our relationship didn't escape me. Just a few months earlier, before I escaped from Hungary in December 1956, I depended on my mother to support me. Now I was ready to assume the financial and legal responsibilities for her.

Around May, we were told that funding for our program had come to an end and that we now had to get a job for the rest of the summer. A mining company from Timmins, Ontario, sent recruiters to Kingston, so Vili and I decided to sign up. Unfortunately, I didn't meet the height and weight requirements to haul one hundred pounds of dynamite and equipment up and down the mineshafts. Vili decided to go, and we agreed that we would meet in the fall in Montréal and start school together. Vili and two other Hungarian boys took off for Timmins, while I stayed in Kingston, looking for a job.

I fondly remember my first paying job in Canada. I was hired to wash windows at the Kingston General Hospital for $120 per month. As I told my children many years later, I started my career at the very top—the tenth floor of the hospital. I loved hanging out the window in my shorts and no shirt while I was secured by a wide safety belt hooked to the sides. I thoroughly enjoyed cleaning windows while watching the pretty nurses walk by. Life was good, and I was gaining confidence that everything would turn out well in the future.

After about a month of window washing, I decided to move to Montréal to start preparing for college entrance in the fall. I learned through my mother that my Uncle Elek, the one I met in Vienna a few months earlier, had settled in Montréal with his family. I contacted him, and he agreed to put me up in his apartment on Barclay Street in a northwest suburb. One day, I packed all my belongings into my suitcase and headed for the train station.

My trip to Montréal was memorable in many ways. At the station, in broken English, I asked and paid for my ticket. I asked the ticket agent which direction the train to Montréal would be coming from, but his response, which I'm sure was in perfectly good Canadian English, was incomprehensible to me. I was really worried that I might take the wrong train.

I saw a group of Canadian soldiers hanging around on the platform, and I gathered the courage to ask one of them which direction the Montréal train was coming from. He replied, which I had no trouble understanding, that they were all going to Montréal and I should just stick with them. Indeed, when the train pulled in, I went right along and ended up in a small compartment with about five of them. They were all young, perhaps the same age as I.

As soon as the train started moving, one of my companions pulled out a flask from his uniform, and they joyfully passed it around, which was accompanied by loud but friendly banter. I was offered to take a swig, which I couldn't refuse. After all, these guys were my age, and I didn't want to act prudish. Even if I could speak English well enough, I would have had a hard time explaining to them that the last time I drank hard alcohol was about six months earlier when I was crossing the Hungarian border into Austria. So, I shared their whiskey as if it were most natural for me to drink. Finally, we arrived in Montréal, where I bid farewell to my new Canadian friends.

I found the taxi stand and showed the piece of paper with my uncle's address on it to the driver. I closed my eyes in the back seat, thinking that so far everything was all right. Within about ten minutes, my stomach started churning, and I knew that I would throw up any second.

There was no sense in trying to explain my nausea to the driver and asking him to let me out to relieve myself, so I rolled down the window, stuck my head out, and projectile vomited outside the car. I don't remember the driver's reaction, but he didn't even slow down a bit. The good news was that by the time we got to my uncle's apartment building, I was feeling much relieved and in very high spirits.

It must have been past ten or eleven in the evening when I arrived, because everyone was asleep when I rang the doorbell. My uncle, his wife, Magda, and his mother-in-law, Bözsi, all got up, and we sat around the kitchen table, as I proceeded to tell them my adventures since we last met in Vienna about six months earlier. It was way past midnight by the time I got to bed. It never occurred to me that my uncle, who was a taxi driver, had to go to work in the morning.

Montréal: The Years of Struggle

I spent four years in Montréal, trying to establish an existence and to prepare myself for the wonderful future that I dreamed of. During this crucial period between 1957 and 1961, my confidence in what I was doing and my positive outlook for the future never wavered, no matter how little I had in terms of money or goods, how hungry I was at times, or whether I was working or out of a job.

I was willing to sacrifice everything in order to educate myself and to establish a solid base on which to build a career. I had two priorities: to study well enough to be accepted to the day program at McGill University in 1961 for the final two years of engineering, and to work in order to save enough money to bring my mother over and support us. Everything else, social activities, sports, etc., became a distant third priority.

In terms of lifestyle, I lived a life typical of non-English-speaking immigrants. I did nothing extraordinary that hadn't been done by thousands of others who came to Canada from different corners of the world to build new lives. Back in the 1950s, Montréal was the center of immigration inflow into Canada, which gave it a special allure, a sense of belonging and being welcomed that no longer exists there.[1]

I lived with my uncle and his family in a three-bedroom second-floor apartment on Barclay Street, where eight of us resided. My uncle and his wife slept in one bedroom. His mother-in-law, Bözsi, and her sister Ilus slept in the second bedroom; and another young relative on my aunt's side, Péter Halász, and I slept in the third room. I don't remember where my two little cousins Tomi and Gabi slept, but it might have been on the living room sofa.

---

[1]   In 1960, The "Quiet Revolution" ushered in an array of sociopolitical transformations, from secularism and the welfare state to a specifically Québécois national identity. The changes included the transformation of the national identity among Francophone Quebecers (from the Canadian Français to the Québécois). These changes drove most of the English-speaking immigrants out of Montréal. Today, Toronto is the melting pot, where most immigrants want to go when they first come to Canada.

I have many wonderful memories of living with my uncle. One of my fondest is of the evenings when we all sat around watching *The Ed Sullivan Show*, trying to guess what he and his guests were saying. I'm certain that Sullivan's very slow, deliberate style of speaking contributed significantly to our learning to speak English. In addition to improving our language skills, television also helped us to acclimate to the cultural life of Canada.

I was also extremely well fed while living there. My aunt's mother, Bözsi, was a typical "Yiddishe Momme,"[1] whose happiness consisted of keeping everyone well fed. Her greetings always started with asking if we were hungry, no matter the time of day, and she was always ready to put some food on the table and enjoy watching you eat. Bözsi never learned to speak English yet had no trouble communicating to the milk deliveryman how many bottles to leave at our door.

I am convinced that my renting a room at my uncle's place was a net loss to him, considering how much I ate while living there. However, no matter how good of a deal I had at my uncle's place, I knew that I would have to move as soon as I started college in September. The place was too crowded, and I couldn't possibly study there.

During the summer of 1957 and early fall, I had a succession of jobs. The ones I can still recall include selling costume jewelry door-to-door, washing dishes, and being a busboy at Ruby Foo's and Miss Montréal, two of the city's nicest restaurants then. Furthermore, I operated a huge diazo[2] printing machine in a room filled with poisonous ammonia gases being emitted from the printing press. But none of these jobs were steady enough for me to go to college at night and earn enough money.

---

[1] Jack Yellen (1892, Poland–1991, New York), pop lyricist who wrote "My Yiddishe Momme" for Sophie Tucker in 1935. This sad, melancholic song became one of Sophie Tucker's biggest hits.

[2] Diazo (blueline) printing was the mainstay of large-volume, large-size engineering drawing reproduction until new technologies such as xerography and digital printing made it obsolete. Ammonia was the basic chemical used to operate diazo machines.

Fortunately, in late 1957, I met some Hungarian engineers, also recent immigrants, who managed to get me a desk job at Northern Electric, one of Canada's largest corporations. It was then owned by Bell Canada and is now a public company known as Nortel. I was a mechanical draftsman, which was the perfect job for me.

The hours were eight-to-five, and I had to speak English, which helped me refine my language skills, and I sat at a nice drawing board in a clean office environment. Occasionally, usually after an all-night text translation and study session, I could even sneak a few minutes of sleep while my supervisor wasn't present. I am forever indebted to the two Hungarians, Jancsi Török and Bandi Kramer, who helped me get this job.

36. My first desk job at Northern Electric, Montréal, fall 1957.

By pure chance, in July of 1957, I bumped into a friend at a bus stop on Barclay Street, Jocó Mezöfényi, whom I had met while living in Kingston. We discussed our living accommodations and realized that both of us were looking for a change. Jocó was also living with a Hungarian family with children and needed more privacy. He had a steady, well-paying job with Bell Telephone Company, so we could afford to rent a nice room somewhere downtown close to both his work and to Sir George.

By the time our bus ride ended, we agreed to move and live together as soon as we could find a suitable place. Shortly after, we moved to Westmount, a western suburb of Montréal. After a couple of moves, we ended up at 3429 Drummond Street, on the corner of

Drummond and Sherbrook. It was a three-story house, owned by a dentist who had his practice downstairs.

A spiral staircase led to the second and third floors. Each floor had three rooms for rent with a common bathroom and a small kitchenette. Single women rented all the other rooms, which provided some enlightenment and occasional diversion in my fairly routine and socially disadvantaged life. Sir George Williams University was just down the road on Drummond Street, making this location extremely convenient for me.

Jocó was a great roommate, and we got along well. He worked the night shift at Bell Telephone and had the room all to himself during the day, so I could study all night without bothering him. We even had a telephone at a special discount rate because of his affiliation with Bell. He was crazy about classical music, and I enjoyed listening to his collection of classical and popular records. I still recall listening to Sarah Vaughan, one of the most famous jazz singers of all time, sing "Tenderly."

Jocó had decided not to continue his college education in the fall of 1957 but changed his mind a year later, so he, too, ended up going to Sir George Williams at night. He started in September of 1958 and earned his BS degree. He claims there were almost ten Hungarians in his class. According to Jocó, Péter Csákány and I were the pioneers in 1957 that proved the feasibility of getting a higher education to the rest of the Hungarian community.

Jocó's full-time job paid him enough to purchase a used car, and one day he showed up with a 1948 black Oldsmobile that we immediately christened as "Cyrano," after Cyrano de Bergerac, due to its huge "nose." The car had no first gear, but it still ran. Although I didn't own the car and didn't even have a driver's license, having a car in our "family" was thrilling. We now had mobility on the weekends and ventured to explore Montréal and its surroundings.

Unfortunately, the reverse gear soon failed, so we had to be more careful about where we would drive. I will never forget the weekend afternoon when we accidentally went into a one-way, dead-end street in a residential neighborhood. People were sitting outside their apartment houses and looking at us as we drove up to the end of the street. Without a reverse gear, we had no choice but to shift into neutral, get out of the car, and push it backward until we could turn it around and drive away. The entire time people were staring at us as if we were starring in a silent comedy film.

Another unforgettable incident with Cyrano occurred when Vili and I borrowed the car and I was driving without a license, of course. We came to a fork on the highway near a tollbooth where orange-colored cones were set up in a V shape to divert traffic to the left and right. Vili and I weren't sure which direction to choose, and as we were debating left or right, I ended up going straight to the front cone and managed to stop the car about three inches from it.

Since Cyrano didn't have a reverse gear, we got out of the car and started to push it, when suddenly a policeman showed up. He asked what we were doing, and as I explained to him that we didn't want to crash into the concrete cones, he nonchalantly walked over to the orange cones in front of Cyrano and picked up the first three to make room for us to turn around. Our jaws dropped; we thought those cones were made up of concrete. We were embarrassed yet also relieved that he didn't ask for my driver's license.

I couldn't persuade Vili to come back to Montréal in the fall of 1957 to start college with me. He came to visit Montréal from time to time, but he wasn't yet ready to move. He was making good money, bought himself a 1956 Chevrolet, and enjoying life, in spite of carrying one hundred pounds of dynamite up and down mineshafts.

It turned out that it was his fear of passing calculus and some of the other courses that kept him from returning to Montréal until 1959, when he finally decided with much encouragement and the promise of help from me to come back and start college at Sir George Williams. Looking back at this time in our lives, I have to give Vili a lot of credit for pursuing a university degree after many interruptions and failed courses in English and calculus. It took him nine years, but he managed to graduate with decent grades in 1968.

By this time Sir George extended evening engineering to eight years, and you could earn a bachelor of science degree. A year later, in 1969, he immigrated to the US when I was able to arrange for a job for him. Bill, as his name was changed to officially in 1974 when he became an American citizen, retired in 2006 after a long career as a mechanical engineer. It gives me a great sense of satisfaction that I might have had some influence on his successful professional career by encouraging him to get a college education.

My life became fairly routine in Montréal after I started my job at Northern Electric. I worked during the day and went to evening school at least three times a week for four hours. Nonschool evenings, after-school nights, and weekends were spent translating textbooks and school notes and preparing for exams. The first two years were the toughest, while I was learning English and engineering simultaneously. Fortunately, I met another Hungarian immigrant at school, and we helped each other out a great deal.

I still remember the very first evening class I had in September 1957. The professor called out the names of about thirty engineering students to see who was present. He came to a name at the beginning of his alphabetical list and seemed to pause as if he didn't know how to pronounce it. He finally blurted out an Italian-sounding name, "Zakani." I looked at the fellow who put his arm up to indicate he was present and knew immediately that he was Hungarian. I even guessed that his name was probably "Csákány," a safe bet, having gotten used to how my name was mispronounced.

After class, I went over to him and introduced myself, which is how Péter Csákány and I met and went on to become lifelong friends. We had much in common; Péter was also Jewish, and he, too, had lost his father during the Holocaust. He left Hungary with his uncle after the 1956 Revolution and was trying to bring his mother and grandmother out to join them at that time. He also needed to work and decided to start evening engineering classes, as I did.

Having another Hungarian in class with me had many advantages. We were both struggling with English and helped each other out. We both took the same courses during the first two years and could share our workload. Typically, we took the textbook assignments and divided the work of translating it into Hungarian so that we could fully understand it. Naturally, we collaborated on all homework assignments. Many nights were spent at Péter's place, working until dawn to finish our homework.

In addition to our poor English, we were also culturally disadvantaged, as illustrated by an incident during a test we had to take in one of our engineering courses. One of the questions on the written final exam asked how far a golf ball would travel when hit by a golf club with a certain force and at a certain angle. Some additional specifications may also have been given.

I stared at the question and had no clue as to what it meant. What is "golf" and what is a "golf club"? These words didn't exist in my vocabulary. The word *club* does exist in Hungarian as "klub," but with a single meaning: that of a social, literary, athletic, political, or other organization. "Golf club" didn't make any sense to me within the context of the question.

Professor Jack Bordan, the instructor, noticed my puzzled expression and came over and asked what the problem was. When I told him that I didn't understand the question, he immediately understood and told me to forget about that one. He went over to Péter Csákány and told him the same thing. That was my introduction to golf, a hobby I didn't take up until four decades later. Golf didn't exist in communist Hungary. First, nobody could afford it; and second, communist ideology considered golf to be the pastime of the bourgeois class of the imperialist West.

As I mentioned earlier, I didn't have much of a social life. I had no discretionary money to spend and had very little spare time, especially during the first two years of my academic life. However, I managed to get to know some Hungarian immigrants in Montréal. Most of them didn't pursue a college education and chose to become salesmen, taxi drivers, or other skilled workers.

I socialized some weekends and during holidays with these fellow Hungarian émigrés. We had parties to celebrate birthdays and New Year's, and it was through one of these Hungarian friends, Tibi Krausz, that I met my future wife, Éva Verő,[1] in the spring of 1959. It wasn't love at first sight, but the blind double date that Tibi Krausz begged me to go on with him—a nonnegotiable condition laid down

---

[1] Her family name, Weisz, was changed to Verő in Hungary after the war. The umlaut on top of the letter o was dropped when they arrived in Canada.

by his girlfriend Judy Klauber—did ultimately lead to my marrying Éva four years later in 1963.

When I met Éva, she wasn't even sixteen—a minor detail Tibi forgot to mention when he talked me into the blind date. Éva's friends decided to throw a sixteenth birthday party for her, where I presented her with sixteen red roses, a memorable event that will go down in the annals of our family history as one of my most romantic gestures.

We attended some very memorable and fun New Year's Eve parties that lasted until dawn. In the morning, after a night of celebration, we went ice skating and bowling, making it an all-out exhausting event.

Occasionally, Péter Csákány and I would skip our evening classes and go see the "bloody" movies on St. Laurent Boulevard. Back in those days, we could watch three consecutive movies for fifty cents, one of which was always a Western. Ever since then, Westerns have been my genre of choice.

A few times in late 1957, I reconnected with my old boyhood friend Gabi Erőd, whom I last saw in Budapest and whose decision to leave Hungary had in turn influenced my decision to leave. Gabi had become a life insurance salesman for Norwich Union Life Insurance Society. He struggled to establish himself and practically starved during the first couple of years he was in Montréal.

Gabi's financial struggles and to feed himself properly became obvious. Many evenings, Gabi would casually drop by around dinnertime for a friendly visit. In our shared kitchen, Jocó and I often cooked a basic Hungarian dish, *paprikás krumpli*—roughly translated as "paprika potatoes." It was made up of many potatoes and some sausage cooked with seasoning, including red paprika. When Gabi showed up, we always asked him if he wanted to join us for dinner, his answer always being a predictable yes. We then poured another glass of water into the pot, making it a meal for three instead of two.

I took pity on Gabi one day and bought a $10,000 life insurance policy from him just to put some money in his pocket. I wasn't even twenty years old, barely scraping by with my low-paying jobs, so the last thing I needed was a life insurance policy. As it turned out, this was the first and last life insurance policy I ever bought, and policy number 1446424 was still active until 2009[1] when we decided to surrender it for its cash value. In fact, Gabi managed to become a largely successful insurance agent and financial adviser. He married an English lady, had two children, and is now semiretired and living in Ottawa.

If Jocó and I had depended on our cooking skills to have a balanced diet, we would have been in deep trouble. Equally troublesome from a financial perspective, it would have been irresponsible to eat out all the time. Fortunately, family connections I didn't even know about before I ended up in Montréal saved us.

It turned out that my mother's Cousin Imre Sárosi[2] owned a café/restaurant called Mokka in downtown Montréal, just a few blocks from where we lived. Imre is the younger brother of Laci Sárosi, who literally saved my life during the terrible times in late 1944 in Budapest. Imre offered Jocó and me a deal that we could eat lunch and dinner at his place and pay a minimal amount significantly below the menu price. From then on, I ate at Mokka frequently.

I never doubted that sacrificing two years of my life to rejoin my mother was a worthwhile decision, and I was eagerly waiting for her move to Canada. But fate had intervened. She met a widowed man and remarried in 1960. I tried not to be selfish, and I don't recall showing her my disappointment. I rationalized that she was forty-five years old and deserved a happy marriage. Fortunately, this marriage turned out to be wonderful for her.

She married Rudolf Politzer, a widowed tailor and shop owner, who adored my mother and provided her with a lifestyle she could never have dreamed of on her own. Rudi had a ten-year-old son, Tamás, who became a substitute son for my mother. Luckily, an excellent relationship between my mother and Tamás evolved, and he took care of my mother long after his father died until the very end of my mother's life.

---

[1] The company's name has changed since 1958 and is now called AIG Assurance Canada.

[2] Spitzer before he changed his name in Hungary after the war. His father, Samuel Spitzer, and my grandfather, Vilmos Spitzer, were brothers. All of Samuel's sons, Imre, Pali, and Laci, changed their names to Sárosi.

I thought it was rather endearing that my mother, or perhaps it was my new stepfather, thought of inserting my high school graduation picture into their family photograph. I am sure that it was their way of showing me that I didn't lose a mother but gained a new family.

Many years later, I concluded that deep down in her heart, perhaps subconsciously, my mother never really wanted to leave Hungary. I think she felt insecure and unprepared for starting a new life in a strange country at her age. Also, her brother, my Uncle Laci, who became the de facto head of the Spitzer family, strongly opposed the idea of my mother joining me. He was convinced that I would be better off in the New World without her. In retrospect, he was probably right. As a single guy with no one depending on me, I had a much easier time making decisions in pursuing my career goals.

37. I was photoshopped into my new family picture next to my stepbrother Tamás, 1961.

After the first year, I was performing well academically and was on the dean's honor list for my "excellent scholarship record during the 1958–59 academic year." The only difficulty was passing a rigorous English course that all immigrant, non-English-speaking students were required to take. The emphasis was on composition and grammar. I first failed it in the summer of 1958 and then again in the summer of 1959.

I only had one more chance to pass this course during the summer of 1960, when my future wife, Éva, came to my rescue. She was still in high school and already had three years of English, significantly more than what I had. With her coaching, I somehow managed to squeeze out a D and put this nerve-racking situation behind me.

In my defense, besides never having had any formal English education prior to college, everybody flunked this course the first time while 60 percent flunked it the second time. The English teacher, whom I erased from my memory long ago, must have been one hell of a sadist.

It was in 1959 while studying at Sir George at night that I had my first capitalist experience in profiting from a new business venture. There was one course, which I believe was a history class that was mandatory for all students in every discipline of study. Péter and I discovered that the professor followed the same course outline year after year, but one had to take copious notes at every lecture in order to prepare for the final exam.

It was a very large class with probably over a hundred students. Attendance was not a requirement, but without the notes taken during class, there was no way to prepare for the final exam. Somehow we found out that a handwritten copy of the class notes was available. This gave us the idea of making copies of the notes, after having typed them up, and selling them in front of the classroom as the students were arriving for the class.

Since I was working as a diazo machine operator at the time and had access to a reproduction machine, I made a deal with my supervisor to let me copy the notes for free as long as I brought my own paper. We determined that the total cost, not including labor of course, was about thirty cents per note. Péter and I would station ourselves at the entrance to this class before the bell rang and would sell the notes for three dollars apiece. This was an outright bargain; if you bought the notes, you didn't have to attend any classes at all but just show up for the final exam.

Everything went smoothly at first, and I was elated at the ease with which we could make $100 a night. Unfortunately, after a few weeks of our "operation," one night we were approached by a school official and told that we couldn't engage in this private enterprise on school property. They didn't object to our selling the notes but told us that we had to do it outside the school building. This meant an end to selling to a "captive" audience; thus, we terminated our venture.

My future plans were fairly settled by the end of 1960. My mother was happily married in Hungary, and I was looking forward to finishing up at Sir George and starting day classes at McGill in the fall of 1961. By then, I was again living in the Montréal suburbs, on Victoria Avenue with a Hungarian family, Mrs. Braun and her son, Péter, who was about my age. I had room and board and got along really well with Péter and his mother. I tried to talk Péter into going to college, but he claimed that he had no head for calculus and "stuff like that." Instead, he became a salesman for a light fixture manufacturing company.

Jocó Mezőfényi, my old roommate on Drummond Street, continued to work for Bell Canada, where he rose to become a manager of the Outside Plant Engineering team, which designed and maintained cable networks. Jocó married his girlfriend, Connie, a French-Canadian girl, in 1961. They had two daughters, but the marriage didn't last, and they got divorced in 1981. He eventually retired in 1992 and lived in Ottawa, Canada, until he died about ten years ago.

Éva and I were still seeing each other, although we did have some breaks in our relationship from time to time. During our on-and-off courtship, I got to know Éva's parents really well. They too had escaped from Hungary in 1956 and were living in Montréal with their two daughters, Éva and her younger sister, Zsuzsi.

I liked and respected Éva's parents from the beginning. They were a typical immigrant family, who gave up a fairly luxurious life in communist Hungary to try their luck in a free society. At the time I met Éva, her mother, Ibi, was a pretty young woman. She was an excellent cook, which I can attest to, having eaten many meals at their home. Éva's father, Bandi Verő, was a precision tool and die maker. He decided that his family's fortunes would be better served in the United States.

With the help of relatives in New York City, the Verő family immigrated to the US in 1960. Éva was left behind in Montréal and lived with her aunt in order to finish high school in the spring of 1961. She then followed her parents to New York City to attend Hunter College.

The only luxury I allowed myself was the purchase of a pair of new skis and ski boots in 1959. I loved skiing, but back in Hungary, I had to contend with hand-me-down boots and skis from my Cousin Péter Oszman. I skied at Mount Tremblant up in the Laurentions and suffered from many falls on the icy, steep slopes. Of course, staying at a hotel was out of the question. We drove two to three hours each way, took our lunch with us, and made the ski trip into one very long but happy day.

My budget allowed me to join my Hungarian friends in renting a summerhouse in the Laurentions at Trout Lake. It was an old house and not very well kept, but it had enough bedrooms to accommodate many people. By splitting the rental six ways, we could all afford it. We would spend our vacations and many of the short Canadian summer weekends there.

Typically, the girls often joined us, and we had a great time. Éva, Judy Klauber, and some of the other girls cooked fried chicken or some other Hungarian dishes, which they brought with them. Seldom did we have to go to a restaurant to eat. Everyone was welcome to visit and stay with us. Every one of my Hungarian friends I already mentioned—Péter Csákány, Jocó Mezőfényi, Gabi Erőd, Péter Braun—and many others stayed at this house at one time or another.

And so, by early 1961, another chapter in my life was coming to an end. Now that I had finally passed my English course, I had nothing to worry about as far as graduating from Sir George. My mother was happily married in Hungary, so I no longer had to worry about her. Éva was to graduate from Northmount High School, and then she was going to live with her parents in New York City. How or whether our relationship would survive this separation, we didn't know.

I was looking forward to a peaceful summer when I no longer had to take any courses and could just relax in anticipation of entering McGill in September. I had almost $1,000 saved, which would be enough to see me through the next two years at McGill in addition to some student loans and scholarships.

Culture Shock

Although I had a small taste of living conditions in the West, having lived in Vienna for about three months, I had not truly experienced the tremendous changes in lifestyle and culture that a free society offers compared to my life back in Hungary. Montréal was the introduction to many new experiences, almost all very positive, and to a whole new way of life.

The first and most obvious changes I experienced were the product of what we now call the "consumer society." Never in my earlier life had I ever seen such an enormous quantity as well as variety of consumer goods as I did in Montréal. The variety of goods and services available was staggering compared to what was available to ordinary citizens in Hungary.

Steinberg's[1] supermarket, where my uncle and aunt used to shop, was a huge store with an unbelievable variety of goods to choose from. The selection of meats, cheeses, fruits, vegetables, and other goods was almost endless. The stores were large and clean, and the shelves always well stocked, incomparable to the typical Hungarian neighborhood stores. And on top of all that, Steinberg's delivered what you bought right to your doorstep.

The department stores were the same. A joke in Hungary was that you could buy any color shoes you wanted as long as they were black. In Montréal, I discovered a bonanza of goods of all varieties, sizes, shapes, and price ranges that blew my mind. It didn't matter that I couldn't afford anything; it seemed as if everything was available, and I knew that one day I would be able to enjoy most of the plenty I saw.

Neighborhoods, especially downtown Montréal, were full of a variety of stores all owned by private individuals and not by the government. The role of the government was invisible in everyday life. I

---

[1] Steinberg's Supermarket began as a grocery store founded in 1913 in Montréal by a Jewish-Hungarian immigrant, Ida Steinberg. Her five sons, led by Sam Steinberg, grew the company into the most popular and largest supermarket chain in Québec. After Sam's death in 1978, the company's fortunes declined, and by 1990, it was gone.

know that in order to appreciate this subtlety, it is necessary to have lived in a closed, government-controlled society.

Another obvious difference was the customer service that one experienced in day-to-day life. Whether it was the milkman delivering milk to my uncle's apartment, the saleslady in a department store, the bus driver, or the waiter in a restaurant, people were generally civil, courteous, and willing to go out of their way to please you. This attitude was in stark contrast to the dour "I don't give a damn" approach typical of a service employee in Hungary.

Salespeople, or government employees, in Hungary treated their customers as nuisances. Since performance was never related to pay, promotion, or job security, the customer experience was of no importance. No surprise there since everyone in Hungary worked for the state.

In Canada, the customer was always king. The motivation to work hard is an integral part of the capitalist system since you could be rewarded for hard work or initiative. In contrast, the employee attitude in Hungary could be summed up by the familiar slogan: "The government pretends to pay us and we pretend to work." Slowly, I had begun to understand that the profit motive of private enterprise and the ability to hire and fire anyone at will within reason, conditions that didn't exist in communism, were at least partially responsible for the differences.

It also struck me how easy it was to rent an apartment at reasonable prices in Montréal. Decent housing was impossible to get in Budapest. Many homes were destroyed during World War II, and the government didn't have the money to build new homes or even repair many of the old ones. It was common for two or three generations of a family to live in the same apartment.

In Montréal, Jocó and I could afford to rent a decent room in one of the most desirable downtown locations. As a taxi driver, my uncle could support his family of five and rent a three-bedroom apartment in a nice Montréal neighborhood.

In Canada, I could go and live anywhere, try any job I could qualify for, and spend my money on anything I could afford. I felt a sense of openness in Canada that was refreshing. People publicly expressed their opinions on anything, including their elected politicians, which would have had severe repercussions in Hungary. In general, there was much more openness and trust in interactions with organizations, as well as at a personal level. The typical cynical and pessimistic attitudes of the Hungarians steeped in communist dogma, and pretend happiness was nonexistent.

As a Jew, I particularly felt a certain liberation from sensitivity to anti-Semitic attitudes. Montréal had a large and very active Jewish population, and our holidays and customs were well respected. Éva's high school, run by the Protestant school district, was virtually empty during the Jewish High Holidays. I lived near the Jewish Y, where we used to go play tennis or swim. I had no fear of discrimination, being a non-English-speaking immigrant or as a Jew. The only incident I recall happened in 1957 when I was working as a busboy at Miss Montréal.

One day, I was in the kitchen preparing the coffee machine, a huge container that had to be filled from the top with boiling water. I was standing on a stool with a steaming pot of water when one of the waiters, a young Swiss man, came into the kitchen and made some disparaging remarks about some Jewish customers he was serving. I lost control and flung the steaming pot of water toward him. I missed, and he came after me.

We wrestled on the floor until the cook separated us. I was then told to go home and come back the next morning. When I showed up the next day, I was asked to go and see Mr. Novak, the general manager. He asked me what happened, and I told him. He listened and told me to go back to work. Later that day, I found out that the Swiss waiter was dismissed.

When it came to my social circle, I knew hardly anyone outside my little Hungarian immigrant community. I had no native Canadian friends at all. At Northern Electric, where I spent most of my time, I worked mostly with French Canadians, but I didn't socialize with them. Most of my nighttime schoolmates were immigrants from different parts of the world, as well as a few French Canadians who were trying to get an English language education. I didn't get to know anybody at school other than Péter Csákány. I had my circle of Hungarian friends outside school and work, and that was it.

My early experiences in Montréal proved what I always suspected back in Hungary. It didn't take long to realize that the relentless daily bombardment of propaganda in Hungary about the ruthless exploitation of workers in the "imperialistic West" was nothing but lies. Certainly, there was some exploitation and discrimination, but I could see that people had choices as to where to live, where to work, to study or not, and in general, could take responsibility for their own lives.

As young non-English-speaking immigrants fresh out of a totalitarian system, it wasn't easy to cope with all the freedoms and individual responsibilities the free society imposed on us. In fact, I knew a couple of Hungarians my age that couldn't adapt and decided to go back to Hungary. They were either scared to make decisions for themselves or too lazy to make the effort to start a new life. They needed the "system," or the "state," to tell them what to do; and in exchange for a guaranteed job, free health care, and education, they gave up all the autonomy they could have enjoyed in a free society.

I, on the other hand, loved what I saw in Canada. Perhaps this was not quite the America I wished for back in Vienna in 1957, but it was promising to be a wonderful opportunity for me. I was eager to move on to the next phase of my life.

By 1961, I had lived in Montréal, Canada, for four years in a free, democratic society, with a capitalist economic system. This was a significant change from living in communist Hungary behind the Iron Curtain. By necessity, my focus of attention was very narrow during those years, and I learned nothing about the political system—the importance of the citizens of a free country to exercise their rights and to protect their privileges and to hold their elected representatives responsible. And I was certainly ignorant about the theoretical foundations of the economic system. It took many more years while in America to understand the full measure of benefits and the commensurate responsibilities of living in a free capitalistic society.

In retrospect, the culture shock I experienced during those four years wasn't a shock at all. Somehow, all the changes in my everyday life seemed natural, as if this was how life was meant to be.

Once Upon a Train

I dedicate this story to the memory of my late father-in-law, Andrew Vero, whose inspiration and encouragement has changed my life.

For most people, train rides are merely a mode of transportation to get from one place to another. For me, they tend to be journeys leading to unknown destinations full of dangers, surprises, and opportunities. I am referring to my train ride out of war-torn Budapest in 1945 when I was seven, as well as my train ride to the border to escape Hungary in 1956 when I was eighteen.

I embarked on another memorable train ride in the summer of 1961 heading home to Montréal from Boston, following a visit to the Massachusetts Institute of Technology (MIT) admissions office in Cambridge. The visit to MIT and the events leading up to my visit were totally unanticipated and had the potential to turn my whole life topsy-turvy again, just as I was to see the light at the end of the tunnel after four hard years of work and study. So how did I get to be on this train, contemplating a change of direction in my life?

This and similar questions raced through my mind as the train began its long ride to Montréal. Sitting across from me on the train was Péter Csákány. I was glad that I wasn't alone facing another major life decision. During the past four years, Péter had become a close friend, and our friendship lasted until he died in 2014.

As I have mentioned already, Péter and I shared much in our backgrounds. Most importantly, we shared a very strong commitment to getting a decent higher education. We attended many of the same classes at night, and we studied together during the weekends, in the evenings, and many times through the night until dawn. While our goals were the same, our personalities were quite different.

Péter was more serious and more mature than I was. He knew things I never even thought of and had an explanation for things I never bothered to question. He was deliberate; I could never envision Péter as a happy-go-lucky guy. He was frugal, a natural condition in our circumstances, and counted his pennies. This too was good for me, because while I was never frivolous, I tended to be a lot freer with my hard-earned money.

He was very particular about neatness and paid attention to details—not exactly a strength of mine. Although he was serious, he had an excellent sense of humor, and we had some great fun together. But most importantly, he was dependable. I could fully trust him, and he provided solid emotional support for me to stay the course during those difficult four years while we studied together.

We settled into our seats for the duration of a ten-to-twelve-hour train ride to Montréal. We sat opposite each other, with Péter facing in the direction the train was heading. There was a small table that folded up between the seats where we put all the materials we had collected while at MIT.

I was still in shock and somewhat confused about what had happened in the admissions office. Up until then, I had never seriously considered going to MIT. How could I? A few months earlier, I had never even heard of it, and the financial obstacle of attending there seemed insurmountable. In addition, both Péter and I had the potential of full scholarships waiting for us at McGill University in the fall. However, here we were, facing the complications of being accepted to MIT as transfer students.

Just a few hours before we boarded the train home, Péter and I had walked into the MIT admissions office and been greeted by the admissions officer. We told him that we appreciated being admitted to MIT, but we had a problem with our finances. We explained that when we added up all our expenses—tuition of $750, expenses for books and other school materials, and room and board—the total amount needed for just one semester would likely exceed the $1,000 we each had as our total life savings. Therefore, we would run out of money just as we were to complete our first and probably last semester at MIT some time in December of 1961.

Surprisingly, our financial dilemma didn't disturb the admissions officer at all. He kindly informed us, "No one ever left MIT because they couldn't afford it." I remember it clearly, and I still choke up when I think about the impact these few kind words had on me. It was then that it dawned on me that what had started as a nice little travel adventure was beginning to turn into something much more serious and daunting.

To support his claim, the admissions officer explained that if we worked hard and got good grades during our first semester, MIT would make student loans and scholarships available to us. However, there were no guarantees, of course. I have no memory of walking out of the admissions office, and the rest of the day was a blur up until we sat facing each other on the train.

As our emotional high began to wear off, we wrote down a list of all the pros and cons. Clearly, we thought that if we were to stay calm and rational about this decision, it would take no time at all to see the absurdity of the whole idea, and we could enjoy our train ride home.

Under "Risks," we had:

> Losing our $1,000 life savings and starting all over again when we return to Montréal after a disastrous failure at MIT.

> Losing the scholarship we were offered at McGill University with no assurance whatsoever that we would be offered one again.

> Much tougher competition at MIT than at McGill, since MIT attracted the very brightest and best of American and foreign students. And grades at MIT were on the curve, meaning that our performance on tests would be graded relative to everyone else.

Under "Benefits," we had:

> Getting an education and a degree from MIT would give us important benefits down the road, such as better jobs and better pay.

We were stuck; we couldn't think of any additional benefits. We repeatedly went over these points and stared at the sheet of paper on the table between us. We tried to quantify the benefits, but no matter how we looked at this balance sheet, the idea of going to MIT just didn't make any sense. The risks were clear, and the benefits were elusive.

The train kept moving north through the New England and New York countryside, and my initial sense of euphoria had turned into a sense of dread and disappointment. I was on an emotional roller coaster.

It was only a few months earlier when Péter and I had the idea of finding out which technical universities in the US were the best. We talked to our professor, Jack Bordan, who attended MIT in 1951 to take some graduate courses. He told us that MIT and the California Institute of Technology were two of the best technical schools in the world.

To find out if we were good enough for the crème de la crème of engineering higher education, we marched into the administrative office at Sir George Williams University and filled out all the proper forms, paid for the transcripts, and fired off our applications. Then we promptly forgot about the whole affair. It wasn't until a few months later that we discovered that our actions, which were mostly bravado and a waste of our precious money, led directly to unexpected events with the potential for irrevocably changing our lives.

In June, we each received a letter from MIT advising us that we had been accepted as transfer students, starting in the fall of 1961. As soon as I read the letter, my jaw dropped, and I felt that my heretofore-unrecognized inherent intelligence and genius were finally acknowledged. As far as I was concerned, that was the end of it. It was a good dare; I had proven something to myself, so it was time to forget about it and enjoy the remaining days of the summer of 1961 before entering McGill in the fall.

The idea of actually accepting MIT's invitation to visit the admissions office in preparation for entering this sanctum of higher learning had never occurred to me. Apparently, Péter felt the same way. Had fate not intervened again, the affair would have ended.

However, destiny proved a worthy opponent, so there I was, sitting on the train, heading home to Montréal with mixed emotions about what to do.

My future father-in-law, Bandi Verő, happened to be in Montréal when I received my acceptance letter from MIT. In fact, he was visiting me at our summer rental house in Rawdon, where we spent the weekend. To my surprise, when he found out about my acceptance to MIT, he was more excited than I was, and he objected to my quick dismissal of the opportunity.

I tried to explain to him that we had never intended to go to MIT for obvious reasons. He dismissed all my objections. He wanted me to pursue the invitation, and as an incentive, he offered Péter and me a ride to Boston on his way back to New York, where he lived. He insisted that the very least we could do is visit MIT and meet with the admission officers.

38. My father-in-law,
Bandi Verő, 1978.

Not being familiar with the New York and New England geography at the time, I didn't appreciate the fact that the detour to Boston on the way to New York was at least two hundred miles of extra travel. I am sure he knew, but didn't seem to care, so he insisted that we go with him. Not until I learned a lot more during the ensuing years about my future father-in-law's past did I understand his feelings.

Interestingly enough, it didn't take long to convince Péter to join me on the trip to MIT. His quick agreement should have set off alarm bells in my head. Unlike me, who tends to jump out of an airplane and then check for a parachute, Péter was less likely to embark on such an adventure without having thought through the consequences.

We agreed with Bandi to get started very early one morning, drive all the way to Cambridge, a 350-mile trip, where he would drop us off near the MIT campus in the afternoon. We planned to put in a brief appearance at the admissions office and catch the next available train home to Montréal.

We found out the price of a one-way ticket from Boston to Montréal and planned to take a few extra dollars with us in case of an emergency. A few days later, we were on our way in Bandi's new red two-door Corvair. That is how we ended up on the train going home, trying to rationalize a dilemma, which didn't lend itself to analysis.

The train kept moving us closer to home, but we weren't closer to a decision. Neither of us had the emotional strength nor the self-confidence to decisively say yes or no to the opportunity. There were psychological dynamics at play between us that neither of us could see. Only now, decades later, can I understand the interplay.

Our debate of pros and cons focused solely on the obvious material circumstances of money, time, and academic standards. We took it for granted that we would either both decline the invitation, or we would both accept it. The idea of considering this major detour in my carefully planned academic career on my own—and without Péter—had never occurred to me. Our debate of what to do was always in the context of "we."

Neither Péter nor I had the guts to say that it was a crazy idea, with the risks far outweighing the potential benefits. Nor did we offer the other to go ahead by himself and take up the challenge. I am certain that had Péter said something like this, it would have been the end of it for me too. We needed a joint decision, which might not have been the most mature route, but for emotional and psychological reasons, that was the only option available to us.

I depended on Péter, and I think he depended on me. Honestly, I was probably sold on the idea of going to MIT as soon as we walked out of the admissions office. To me, the risks were acceptable, and the challenges would have to be dealt with as they arose. All I needed was Péter's agreement to join me. Péter, on the other hand, was likely more troubled by the very real and more immediate risks of our situation than he was attracted by the distant, potential benefits of an MIT education.

We continued our debate but still couldn't reach a decision. The hours went by as the train slowly wound its way north through the small towns and the countryside, and we were a hung jury. We decided to take a break at some point and eat the can of peas we had bought at the supermarket before boarding the train.

We had some loose change in our pockets, so Péter had suggested that we buy something for the road. We had just enough money for one can of cooked peas. I have not the slightest idea now why we had bought a can of peas instead of something more pleasant like a chocolate bar, but all decisions concerning food and nutrition were in Péter's domain. So, we set our papers aside and decided to take a pea break. The only problem was that we didn't have a can opener.

This minor technical challenge was quickly overcome with Péter's house key. We divided the peas into two paper cups, and that was our first and last meal on the road. I am sure that Péter missed having the plates, utensils, and the folded napkin all properly laid out in front of us as he was accustomed to having in order to savor our meager but highly nutritious meal.

It was now dark outside, except for the flickering lights of distant towns. We got used to the monotony of the noise created by the train. Sleeping was out of the question, so we revisited our problem while slowly realizing that we had reached an impasse. Finally, after exhausting ourselves with the repetition of the same old arguments, we looked at each other and both knew we had the answer.

I don't recall which one of us actually said it, but the words came out and hung in the air, "The hell with it. This makes no sense at all. Let's do it!"—and the rest is history. We had transformed a simple train ride with a known destination into a journey with many risks and an unpredictable outcome.

Many years later, I realized that there was one more benefit to add to the ledger that Péter and I were constructing on the train. I failed to appreciate the psychological impact that being an MIT graduate would have on me. To this day, I have a sense of pride of being able to compete with the very best and smartest. I am certain that I gained a sense of confidence at MIT that helped me down the road in my ability to solve complex problems and to compete in the business world.

Bandi, my father-in-law, died in 1978. I now know that my acceptance to MIT, together with his personal influence, gave him tremendous vicarious satisfaction. I was able to accomplish much of what he was denied in his youth back in Hungary during the gathering storm of the Holocaust. I never thought of him as a father-in-law; he was more like a friend to me. My admiration for this man and his gutsy personality, cynical outlook on life as shaped by a lifetime of disappointments, his intrinsic intelligence, and his resolute curiosity about everything grew deeply over the years. I miss him greatly.

MIT

Péter and I collected all the information we could about financial aid, the cost of books, fees, and room and board during our first visit to MIT in the summer of 1961. We also learned that fraternities played an important role in providing off-campus housing for undergraduate students, since there were not enough dormitory units to accommodate the entire student body.

I don't have the statistics for the year 1961, but today MIT has twenty-five nationally affiliated fraternities and six sororities, which didn't exist then. Most fraternities occupy houses owned by their national chapter's corporation in the Boston, Cambridge, and Brookline suburbs and are managed completely by the students themselves. MIT's admissions office told us that living at a fraternity might actually cost less than living in a dormitory on the MIT campus.

The concept of a fraternity was new to us at that time. There were no fraternities or sororities at the Technical University where I was a freshman in communist Hungary or at Sir George Williams University in Montréal. However, the idea of joining a fraternity intrigued both of us, from both financial and social perspectives.

In late August 1961, we packed up all our belongings and took either a train or a bus (neither of us can remember which) from Montréal to Boston to attend "rush week." a week before classes started. I was twenty-three years old, and everything I owned fit into one suitcase and a handbag. The only thing I couldn't fit into my suitcase was the new pair of skis I bought, one of those very few luxuries I allowed myself. I felt a bit self-conscious carrying a pair of skis during a hot autumn day.

Rush week is the beginning of the "pledging" process designed to encourage students, primarily the freshman class, to join a fraternity.[1] This is when all the fraternities open their houses and invite incoming freshmen to see which one they might fit in with. A series of "meet and greet" events and parties make up the whole week. The upperclassmen organize and run these events with plenty of female companions from the local colleges and girls-only schools. The goal of these events is for the fraternity brothers to get to know potential new members, and vice versa.

There are subtle ways to discover one's social, economic, and religious backgrounds during rush week's plethora of activities. It works both ways. No group wants to invite a student who would fail to fit into the particular social and cultural mold of a fraternity. Likewise, no student wants to join a fraternity where he wouldn't feel totally at ease. The process of pledge selection is simple. At the conclusion of rush week, the fraternity brothers select those they want to invite and extend a bid to join their fraternity as a pledge.

39. Main entrance to MIT from Massachusetts Avenue.

---

[1] MIT no longer allows freshmen to live in fraternities. All unmarried first-year students must live in one of the institute's residency halls—except those who commute from home. All upperclassmen may live at a fraternity house off campus or may elect to remain on campus.

Péter and I eagerly participated in rush week for the class of '65 and hoped that we could join one of the fraternities, even though we were technically class of '63, having transferred as juniors and not freshman. We participated in many events at several fraternities and learned that our age difference didn't seem to be a problem, although it was a bit strange for us to be several years older than even the seniors were.

For me, and I suppose Péter felt the same way, my Jewish background wasn't a consideration in selecting a fraternity until I discovered that in fact it was—and quite an important factor in the case of some fraternities. I suppose that had we been born and raised in America, we would have known that this kind of discrimination existed.

The truth is that we were quite ignorant of the segregation that existed in America, whether in country clubs, fraternities, and other areas of life. Due to our ignorance, and due to the fact that our names didn't suggest a Jewish background, we attended events and were welcomed at fraternities that clearly didn't wish to recruit Jewish students.

It's important to note that Péter and I were not paranoid when we discovered some faith-based discrimination at MIT. This was 1961, just one year before James Meredith, a black student, won a famous lawsuit that allowed him admission to the University of Mississippi in September 1962. He was escorted by US marshals to enter the university and enroll. That night, students and other whites began a riot that resulted in two people being killed and 160 injured.

John F. Kennedy[1] was sworn in as president of the United States only nine months before we started at MIT. Although he proposed sweeping civil rights legislation, it fell to his successor, Lyndon B. Johnson,[2] to get a bill through Congress in July 1964 after Kennedy's

---

[1] John F. Kennedy (May 29, 1917–November 22, 1963), often referred to as JFK, was the thirty-fifth president of the United States, serving since 1961 until his assassination in 1963.

[2] Lyndon B. Johnson (August 27, 1908–January 22, 1973), served as the thirty-sixth president of the United States. He was primarily responsible for designing the "Great Society" legislation, the Civil Rights Act of 1964.

assassination. The famous Civil Rights Act banned discrimination based on "race, color, religion, or national origin" in employment and public places.

By the end of rush week, we managed to connect with a couple of Jewish fraternities, one of which was Sigma Alpha Mu. As I mentioned earlier, although we didn't set out to find a Jewish fraternity, we were delighted at the prospects of joining a group where we felt accepted. By the way, I'm not implying that a Jew could only join a Jewish fraternity at MIT. There were probably many fraternities then, and probably more now, where religious affiliation in pledge selection was not a factor.

When a couple of brothers from Sigma Alpha Mu asked me if I would like to join their fraternity, I gladly accepted and asked if they were going to invite my friend Péter as well. I could tell that my question was a bit embarrassing to them, and the answer was that they didn't plan to invite him. I explained that we were very close friends, and if Péter couldn't join, then I wouldn't join either.

I must admit that my courageous and principled position was a difficult one to take, and I have no idea what would have happened if they didn't invite him. Would I have deserted him and joined anyway, or would I have refused? I would like to think I would have stuck with my friend, but the real test of my courage did not materialize. The impasse was quickly resolved when they assured me that they liked Péter very much and that they would extend an invitation to him.

Looking back, I think I know why they invited only one of us. First, I don't think they appreciated our close friendship. Second, they probably figured that one twenty-three-year-old Hungarian was enough to introduce both age and cultural diversity into the fraternity. In the end, everything worked out, and I still remember the two upperclassmen, Ed Linde and Joe Perkell, both class of '62, who came in their cars to pick us up at the dormitory and take us to the fraternity house.

The Sammie house[1] was located at 34 Fenway Drive in Boston, about a twenty-to-thirty-minute walk across the Harvard Bridge to the main campus. Its proximity to campus was an important benefit for us because we could save the expense of public transportation.

Rush week ended on Friday, and classes started on Monday. A traditional "welcome" beer party was held on Saturday at the Sammie house, where all the new pledges, the fraternity brothers, including seniors who no longer lived at the house, and those in graduate school attended. I had a great time and drank an inordinate amount of beer along with everyone else. Obviously, my judgment was somewhat impaired because at some point in the evening, I found myself arm wrestling with John Rothchild, class of '62, at the table.

John's nickname was Bear—a suitable name considering his six-foot and several inches height and massive body. In the basement, the noise level was several decibels above normal hearing range where we were sitting at the corner of a table and were trying, with much perspiration and groaning, to win. I was actually in good physical shape at the time, and I was not surprised that I was able to overcome the Bear's strength. However, before I could fully enjoy my victory and the respect I gained from my future brothers, the Bear announced that he was left-handed, and that for the sake of fairness, we should go at it again.

I agreed, but once we started, I immediately knew I was in trouble. I was weaker with my left arm, while the Bear was much stronger. I resorted to trickery, one that worked for me before, and relaxed my arm for a second and then put all my strength to try to push him down. Feeling like I was pushing against a solid wall, I then remember hearing a very sharp, cracking noise as I was looking at my arm, completely limp, hanging down at my side off the table. I grabbed my arm and pulled it back to its normal position, despite the fact that it was entirely numb.

---

[1] To my great regret, Sigma Alpha Mu no longer has a chapter at MIT, but the house, now called the Fenway House, is still standing and serves as an independent housing unit.

No sooner had everyone in the room heard the loud noise than it was silent as everybody gathered around us trying to see what happened. I felt no pain at all, and my first thought was that I had suffered a dislocated elbow. Clearly, I needed medical attention, and Bob Morse, class of '63, volunteered to take me to the campus infirmary in his two-seater convertible sports car. I apologized for interrupting the party, and off we went.

The nurse at the infirmary immediately called the doctor on call for the weekend, and she offered me some painkillers in case I needed it, but I declined since I still felt no pain. I was still in good spirits when the doctor showed up. He asked me what happened and didn't say much when I told him about my arm-wrestling match. He had my arm x-rayed and came back to inform me that my upper arm, or the humerus, was broken and that he had "never seen this before." I presumed that he meant that he had never seen an arm-wrestling match result in a broken bone.

He showed me the x-ray, where I could see the break line across my upper arm at a forty-five-degree angle. Fortunately, he told me that it was a clean break, and the bones were set perfectly without any bone spurs present. Therefore, instead of putting my arm in a cast, he could simply tape it to my chest and, in about six weeks, my arm would be good as new.

He said that I could spend the weekend at the infirmary and attend classes on Monday morning if I felt up to it. In fact, I learned later in one of my engineering materials courses that my fracture was a "shear stress break." My arm broke as if someone had twisted both ends in the opposite direction (as it so happens in arm wrestling), with the fracture occurring along an exact forty-five-degree line.

I think it was about this time that the effect of the alcohol started to fade. The physical pain I was beginning to feel was nothing compared to the psychological pain. It suddenly dawned on me that I would start classes on Monday with a broken arm taped to my chest, making my left arm useless to hold a book, turn a page, eat with a fork and a knife, get dressed, or carry anything.

I literally felt that I was at the starting line of the race of my life with the world's best students with "one hand tied behind my back," except in my case it was taped to my front. That is how I started my MIT career in the fall of 1961. The moral of this story is that winning isn't everything, and I shouldn't have pushed so hard that I essentially broke my own arm trying to win a frivolous arm-wrestling match.

Due to my injury, I was excused from the traditional pledge duties assigned at the fraternity house during the first semester. Nevertheless, even if I didn't have a broken arm, my tasks would have been undemanding regardless. In deference to our age, Péter and I had a very light version of house chores that were assigned to the pledges.

I didn't sleep much during the first semester, but this was only partially due to my broken arm. The bigger obstacle to sleep was one of my three young roommates, Joel Kalman from Cheyenne, Wyoming. Joel was a tall, lanky fellow with slumped shoulders and thick glasses. He was one of the very few people who had a car, an old clunker, and would gladly give a ride to anybody to the campus or anywhere else if it fit his schedule.

Joel's parents owned a dry-cleaning business in Cheyenne and saved enough money to send their son to MIT. He was a nice person, but he had a habit of starting to study around midnight while listening to music on his radio until he finally went to sleep around three in the morning. It was too bad that iPods[1] weren't invented until four decades later. The four of us shared a room on the basement level, and no matter how low he set the dial on his radio, I couldn't sleep while he was up. Luckily, after the first semester, I ended up in another room with different roommates, so I could finally get some sleep.

The routine at the fraternity house was very simple. There were no parties or social activities Monday through Friday or on Sunday. Studying was the order of the day, and no loud activities were toler-

---

[1] On October 23, 2001, Apple introduced the iPod digital music player. The iPod is the market leader in portable music players by a significant margin, with more than 220 million units shipped as of September 9, 2009.

ated. One of my younger fraternity brothers used to practice his flute in the coat closet in the foyer so that he would not bother us.

Our cook prepared dinner for us every night during the week, and we were on our own for the weekend. It was during the next year and a half while I lived at the fraternity that I developed a real taste for peanut butter and jelly sandwiches. To this day, I can't eat white "cotton" bread unless it is served as toast or with peanut butter and jelly. The refrigerator, located in the basement kitchen, was always loaded with these ingredients, and there was plenty of milk to go with it. As far as keeping the house in good order, everybody was responsible for their own rooms, and the common areas were kept clean by the pledges.

To my amazement, I quickly discovered that most of the students at MIT actually wanted to learn something and not just pass their tests. I was rather impressed by how seriously and diligently my fraternity brothers studied all week. I should have anticipated this, because one of the selling points emphasized by the fraternities we visited during rush week was how well their brothers were doing academically. This was a warning I had to heed if I wanted to succeed.

Indeed, this turned out to be the perfect environment for me, and for the first time since I left Hungary in 1956 when I was freshman at the Technical University, I had nothing else to do but study. Unlike in Montréal, I didn't have to go to work during the day and study at night. I am certain that living at the fraternity house helped me achieve better grades.

Life in the fraternity also provided my brothers and me the experience in self-governance and management. The prior (president) and officers for key positions, such as finance, operations, planning, social activities, and others, were elected by a majority vote. Periodic meetings were held, and Robert's Rules of Order[1] were used

---

[1] The genesis of the Rules goes back to English parliamentary law. It provides common rules and procedures for deliberation and debate in order to provide equal opportunity for everyone to express an opinion and participate in decision-making.

to conduct the meetings and to arrive at decisions. This marked my very first participation in a democratic form of governance.

Péter and I knew that MIT charged a flat tuition[1] per semester and that students could take as many credits as they wished. If they failed a course, it was their problem. Graduation was subject to completing the required number of credits and not how long one stayed at MIT. We both decided to take a calculated risk and take more than the normal workload in order to graduate earlier and save the tuition.

This seems like a reckless decision in retrospect, since our ability to get financial aid, scholarships, and loans depended on our grades. In order to qualify for student loans, we needed to have a grade point average of 3.0, and to qualify for scholarships, we needed a 3.5.[2]

Getting good grades was quite challenging since most professors graded tests "on a curve." The only thing that mattered on a test was the number of correct answers relative to everyone else's correct answers. It was a little bit intimidating to know that we were competing against the very best students in America and perhaps in the world.[3]

I completed the fall semester in 1961 with a grade point average of 3.2, thus qualifying for a student loan. I completed the spring term in 1962 with a 3.8 and qualified for both a student loan and a scholarship. I finished my final semester in the fall of 1962 with a 4.3 and received my bachelor of science degree in mechanical engineering in January 1963, one full semester ahead of schedule. However, I am getting a little ahead of myself. As time went on, I gained more and more confidence in my ability to compete and get decent grades. I was driven to do well and put all my energy into studying.

My life at MIT and the fraternity house fell into a monotonous routine: 90 percent work along with maybe 10 percent recreation and social activities. Occasionally, we had parties at our house, and

---

[1] MIT operates on a two-semester academic year. One semester tuition in 1961 was $750. It was $18,755 for the 2009–2010 academic year, and it is $26,725 for the 2019–2020 year.

[2] Grade points were given as follows: A = 5; B = 4; C = 3; D = 2.

[3] For the class of 2019-2020 international students represent 10% and 42% of the undergraduate, and graduate classes respectively.

we were periodically invited to parties at other fraternities. Dates were easy to get, but I never developed a serious relationship while at MIT.

My former girlfriend, Éva, left Montréal in the summer of 1961 after finishing high school and joined her parents in New York, where she started her higher education at Hunter College in the fall. Looking back, I now realize that I never really emotionally parted with Éva when we said goodbye to each other in Montréal. She was still very young, eighteen years old at the time, and I had no clue what I was going to do or what she might do while I was at MIT. Furthermore, I had not given any thought to what might happen when I returned to Canada after graduation.

Having known Éva since just before her sixteenth birthday, we had a very close and loving relationship. While it was not love at first sight, as I got to know her, I loved her more and more. I saw her as a shy, self-conscious, somewhat introverted person—quite the opposite of me. Behind the glasses she hated to wear and the skin with pimples that were difficult to conceal, there was a person with tremendous intellectual integrity and curiosity.

She lacked self-confidence in most social situations, which I had in abundance, but she felt comfortable with my circle of friends in Montréal. She was more mature than her teenage friends and demonstrated a sense of grown-up responsibility when it came to helping her immigrant parents and other family members.

Last but not least, she was very smart. She was fourteen years old when she arrived in Montréal with her parents in 1957 and started high school without knowing any English. She graduated in 1961 with good enough grades to get accepted to McGill University on a scholarship. It was always a regret of hers that her parents were not willing to let her stay in Montréal and go to McGill.

Éva was not just a girlfriend but also a friend with whom I could share all my dreams and ambitions. We had so much in common—our Jewishness, the horrors of the Holocaust, our escape from Hungary, and our immigrant status in Canada. And she was there for me whenever I needed her, whether it was for sympathy when I got sick or when I desperately needed her help to pass my English course at Sir George Williams University.

We made no promises to each other when we parted, and I tried to put our past relationship behind me during the first year at MIT—an effort at which I obviously did not succeed. We might have spoken on the phone a few times, but our relationship remained dormant for a while.

Fraternity house rules required that when a brother became a senior, he had to move out. This rule was waived for me when I became a senior in the fall of 1962, a year after I joined the fraternity. I was elected prior (president) and was allowed to live at the house until I graduated in January of 1963.

In addition to the prestige of being the prior, one of the most important benefits I had was the choice of the best room in the house on the upper floor with only one roommate. Péter was asked to move out of the house, something he was not happy about. He asked me if I could use my position as prior and arrange for him to stay at the house for the fall term of 1962. I did, so Péter was allowed to live at the house for one more term just as I was.

It is true that our actions often have unintended consequences. In late 1962, in anticipation of moving out of the fraternity house in January 1963, Péter started looking for a place to rent around the Fenway. I will never forget the day when he came into my room and told me about the results of his search. It was not clear to me if he had found a place to rent, but he was excited to tell me that he met a very lovely young woman, Marlene, at a nearby apartment building. What surprised me was not this news but the expression on his face. He had a grin and the self-satisfied look of a cat that ate the canary. All I know is that ever since that encounter, Péter rarely slept at the fraternity house.

It became clear that whatever sleeping arrangement Péter found, it came with some fringe benefits he had never anticipated. Péter's marriage to Marlene, a divorcée with a young child, took place in December 1964. They lived in Montréal, Canada, where Péter returned in 1966 after spending a few years in graduate school at

MIT. They have a daughter and a son, both born in Montréal. Sadly, Péter died a few years ago.

While finishing my third semester in the fall of 1962, I was emboldened by my good grades and the prospects of continued financial help from MIT and decided to continue with my engineering studies to get a master's degree as well. I was influenced by the observation that many of my fraternity brothers, including my friend Péter, planned to continue their higher education beyond a bachelor's degree.[1] Most importantly, I sensed that a postgraduate degree would help me a great deal with getting a better job.

In retrospect, this might have been a poor decision. I should have been driven by only the love of engineering and/or the prospects of going all the way to get a PhD. I received my bachelor's degree in January 1963, and I was accepted to graduate school in the spring term in 1963. My application to graduate school was contingent on two aspects: securing a part-time position as a research assistant, and additional financial aid, conditions that were both met.

A strange thing happened to me in 1962. I was surrounded by friends and my fraternity brothers, but I felt lonely. My mother remarried in 1961, and whatever emotional ties I had with her, some of it based on a sense of responsibility for her, had faded away. While I had much family all around the world, the ones on this continent all lived in Canada. Unlike my fraternity brothers who called their parents on the weekends and went home during vacation time, I had nobody to call and nobody to go home to. Even Péter had his mother in Montréal to connect with.

During the summer break in 1962, Péter got a job in Wilmington, Delaware, and managed to visit his mother in Montréal a couple of times, whereas I didn't return once to Montréal. I had no place to stay there, and I got a summer job with Metals & Controls Inc.—a small engineering firm in Attleboro, Massachusetts, a small town about a fifty-minute drive south of Boston. I carpooled back

---

[1] A 2005 survey shows that 48 percent of MIT graduates with a bachelor's degree continue their education for a master's or PhD degree.

and forth and paid extra to stay in the Sammie house during the summer.

As I think about it now, it was strange that instead of being exceedingly happy with my life and my future prospects with no attachments and obligations to anybody other than my financial obligations, I felt unhappy and lonely. It was then that I realized that my feelings for Éva, the young girl I surprised with sixteen roses on her sixteenth birthday, meant more to me than just a fading memory from the past.

I realized that I missed the person who probably knew more about me—who I was as a young adult, my likes and dislikes, my ambitions and goals—than anybody else in the world, including my mother. I then realized that I loved her more than I thought before we parted. It is clear that some of these feelings contributed to my decision to reconnect with Éva.

I don't remember the sequence of events that led to our renewed relationship, but my feelings toward her are illustrated by the words I wrote inside the cover of a little book titled *Love Is a Special Way of Feeling* by Joan Walsh Anglund that I gave her as a present:

> Love is a happy feeling
> that stays inside your heart
> for the rest of your life.
>
> Shall these words be remembered in all our life,
> and shall these words be a symbol of our feelings
> towards each other.
>
> 12/7/62
> Robi

Right around this time, I visited her at their apartment at 2050 Valentine Avenue in the Bronx, New York. Even though I don't remember how I got to New York City that day, I do remember taking the elevated "L" train on Jerome Avenue. I was supposed to get off at Burnside Avenue and head directly toward the Grand Concourse, cross it, and continue to Valentine Avenue, a few blocks away.

That evening, I got off the "L" one stop earlier by mistake and had to walk along Jerome Avenue until I got to Burnside. I was slightly apprehensive about walking in the dark in this neighborhood, but I figured that the streetlights and the open shop windows on both sides of the street provided sufficient illumination to ward off any dangers.

I was about halfway to the corner when I spotted three black men on the other side of the street coming toward me. As they got closer, two of them crossed the wide avenue, approached me, and stood in front of me, blocking my way. Both of them were at least six feet tall, but my eyes were drawn to their hands, which held a razor blade with a handle, like the one used for opening cardboard boxes.

I instantly recognized the situation I was in, but before I had a chance to think of what to do, I heard one of them mumbling something unintelligible. He must have recognized the puzzled look on my face and repeated his original message. Again, I couldn't understand what he said except the words "Two dollars." Now I understood that I was being held up for two bucks. I had maybe twenty dollars on me, but instead of giving them two dollars, my reflexes took over, and I said that I was a student and had no money except the fifty cents in my pocket.

As I was speaking, I started to move away from them in the direction I was going. They seemed to be puzzled and hesitated for a second, but I decided not to stick around to find out if their puzzlement was due to their inability to understand my English, or if they were shocked at my obvious defiance of them. I sensed some hesitation on their part as if they were silently debating whether to let me go or take a more aggressive or even violent action against me.

I continued on my way at a rapid walking pace, thinking that if they came after me, I might have to dash into one of the open stores on my right. I didn't dare to look back. Just as I got to the corner of Burnside Avenue, a police car pulled up at the corner with their front windows down. I ran over to the driver, and with my heart still pounding in my chest, I yelled, "Those two guys just tried to rob me!" I turned and pointed in the direction I came from. I was surprised to see the two men still standing there, but I didn't wait for an acknowledgment of my complaint. I turned the corner and took off hurriedly on Burnside Avenue. That evening I had some exciting news to tell Éva and her parents.

It was during my first or second visit in her parents' Bronx apartment when I proposed to Éva. However, I didn't want to get married until I had a job and could afford to support a family. Nonetheless, either I was too stupid and in a weak emotional state of mind to make a hasty decision, or I was extremely wise and foresighted and concluded that I couldn't let someone as precious as her get away from me.

I let the facts answer these questions. Since we got married in 1963, Éva has been a wife to me, a mother to our children, and equally importantly, she has been a true friend and partner in life.

Unfortunately, I didn't prepare well for my proposal. I took my fraternity pin with me on my visit to New York, and according to her, I sort of tossed it to her across the kitchen table and said, "I always knew that you wanted to have this." I was so nervous and flabbergasted that it is possible that these were my less than romantic utterances. It is never too late to apologize, so now she can have my apology in writing.

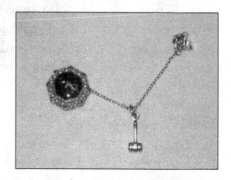

40. My fraternity pin with the gavel attesting to my status as prior in 1962.

I don't remember Éva's immediate reaction, but since she neither slapped my face nor showed me the door, my unorthodox proposal was accepted. Éva's mother rejoiced and showered me with kisses and hugs as if I proposed to marry her. Her father found a bottle of lukewarm sparkling wine, and we drank a toast to our future happiness.

I would be remiss if I didn't mention the sole opinion I got on marrying Éva before I proposed to her. The only person in Boston who actually knew her was Péter. One day, I told Péter that I was thinking of proposing to Éva. I don't even remember if this was a statement of fact, or if I asked for his thoughts on the idea. All I remember is that Péter said something like, "She is a very smart girl"—something I already knew. Péter doesn't have any recollection of this conversation, but I am certain that it took place. I just hope that my wife forgives Péter for making an encouraging remark about my marrying her.

I don't remember what happened after proposing to Éva, nor do I recall deciding when and where we would get married. We were both in school; Éva was in her second year at Hunter College, and I was in graduate school at MIT. Perhaps we left things up in the air and made the decisions later.

I had to move out of the Sammie house before the start of the spring term in January 1963, so I ended up moving into the MIT graduate house that was located across the street from the main campus on Massachusetts Avenue. I was pretty much by myself, and I missed having my fraternity brothers around. This was actually the very first time that I lived by myself since I had left Hungary.

I never made any friends at the graduate house, since I was too busy studying and working as a research assistant. The only person I remember meeting is the grandson of the famous Mahatma Gandhi.[1] As I walked

41. Entrance to 34 Fenway, Éva wearing sweatshirt that says, "Property of Sigma Alpha Mu," spring 1963.

through the lobby of the building, a young man, obviously from India, approached me and asked me if I had any aspirin for a bad

---

[1] Mohandas Karamchand Gandhi (1869–1948) was the preeminent political and spiritual leader of India during the Indian independence movement. He was the pioneer of resistance to tyranny through mass civil disobedience, a philosophy firmly founded upon total nonviolence, which led India to independence and inspired movements for civil rights and freedom across the world.

headache. I said yes, so he followed me up the stairs to my room, where I gave him a couple of aspirin. We introduced each other, and I caught the name Gandhi. I asked him, half-jokingly, if by any chance he would be related to the famous Gandhi, and he said that he was his grandson. I was impressed, so we chatted for a while, and he gave me his room number. We agreed to meet again, but I never saw him again while I lived there.

Our plans for a wedding must have fallen in place quickly because we planned the wedding for the summer of 1963. I made a budget and figured out how the two of us could survive on my monthly research assistant salary of $375 per month, plus whatever financial aid I thought I could get from MIT. The only budget item I remember was our weekly food and household allowance of $15 per week.

After the wedding, Éva would transfer to Boston University[1] and continue her education there while I would finish mine at MIT. Éva's parents agreed to have the wedding in Montréal as a major concession to me. In retrospect, I am absolutely certain that if they had known how many of my close and not-so-close relatives would come out of the woodwork to attend the wedding in Montréal, they would have insisted on having it in New York.

I recall Éva visiting me in Boston once or twice after our engagement, and it was during one of those visits that there was a romantic pinning party held at the fraternity house. She officially became a "Sweetheart of Sigma Alpha Mu," only the second such distinction in our class of 1963. A year before, Sally, Howie Leibowitz's future wife, was also honored with that title.

What happened before the summer of 1963 is a bit blurry now. I was in graduate school, and the courses were tougher than in undergraduate school. The only research assistantship available was in the

---

[1] Boston University (BU) founded in 1839 is a private, nonsectarian research university located in Boston, Massachusetts. With more than four thousand faculty members and more than thirty-one thousand students, Boston University is one of the largest private universities in the United States.

fluid mechanics department run by the famous Dr. Shapiro,[1] whose *The Dynamics and Thermodynamics of Compressible Fluid Flow* is considered a classic, an expensive book I had to buy. It was in his department that a research assistantship was available, and by default, I was to major in fluid dynamics and pursue a research project that would be the topic of my thesis, a requirement for graduation.

Planning a wedding in absentia is not easy, but thanks to my in-laws, somehow it was done. Éva came back to Montréal that summer and stayed with one of my uncles.[2] My primary responsibility was to arrange for my mother's Canadian tourist visa and to arrange a place for us to stay in Montréal. I signed all the papers required to assume financial responsibility for her and rented an apartment for three months.

Not only did Éva meet my mother for the first time, but it was also the first time that I had the two most important women in my life in the same place. I got a summer job with Sperry Gyroscope in Montréal, where I made about one thousand Canadian dollars as an engineer.

Our wedding date was set for August 18, 1963, which allowed us to have a one-week honeymoon and wrap up our affairs in Montréal before returning to Cambridge as husband and wife.

I had not seen my mother since I left Hungary on December 6, 1956, so meeting in Montréal that summer of 1963 was an emotional reunion. I quickly noticed something strange in our relationship. In my head and in my heart, I still had the same emotional ties with her that I had when I was eighteen years old. The many letters and phone calls we exchanged over the years did not suggest a shift of feelings. Yet something had changed.

Was it the fact that I was now a grown-up? Or was it that she got married? Or that now there was another woman in my life, her

---

[1]   Ascher H. Shapiro (1916–2004) was professor of mechanical engineering at MIT for over fifty years. He was a pioneer in the field of biomedical engineering and a leader in fluid mechanics research and education.

[2]   My father's older brother Sanyi Reichmann and his wife, Ella, lived in Montréal at that time. Their stay there was short-lived, and they soon returned to Israel where they lived ever since they left Hungary in 1945.

place in my heart would be taken? Of course, I still loved my mother and always felt responsible for her well-being even after her marriage, but things had changed. I couldn't be fully open and honest with her about my intimate feelings. After a few days of living with her, I realized that there were certain things I would never be able to discuss with her. The truth is that we became emotionally estranged.

Plans for our wedding went ahead, invitations were mailed, and I had my very first fight with my future wife. She was upset because the list of "relatives" on my side who asked to attend our wedding was growing like kudzu. The problem was that I wanted to be nice to everyone instead of putting my foot down and saying no. I was clearly not sensitive to Éva's parents' financial condition and failed to limit the attendance to those of my closer family members only.

This was the first time since I had known Éva that she lost her cool and screamed at me. Of course, she was right, but what shocked me more than my own stupidity was her temper and willingness to pick a fight with me days before our wedding. Nobody, friend or family, had ever talked to me like that. Since then I have gotten used to her temper, but at that time, it was a shock to me; it was a revelation that marriage may not be all wine and roses.

The sad reality is that out of the thirty-two people in the family picture, only sixteen are our relatives, and that is being generous. Of those, only four were from Éva's side.

42. My beautiful bride; Montréal, Canada, August 18, 1963.

For whatever reason, her closest relatives that attended our wedding, her only aunt and her husband, as well as my Uncle Elek are not in the picture.

The wedding was held at a conservative synagogue, and neither Éva nor I remember much about the ceremony and the reception that followed. Only the pictures remain to remind us of what we missed. One memory stands out, and that is the sheer beauty of my bride. Moreover, a couple of my fraternity brothers actually drove up to Montréal to attend our wedding, and all our Hungarian friends from Montréal were there.

We spent the night in a hotel room, and the next day, we were off to our honeymoon at the Grey Rocks Inn resort in the Laurentions. However, before turning in for the night at the hotel, we conducted a highly nonromantic event of counting all the money we received from our wedding guests. We knew that every penny was needed for us to survive in the months ahead, and I think all our guests knew that money was the best gift they could give us.

My father-in-law was quite generous. In addition to paying for a wonderful wedding, he surprised us with a three-year-old white Plymouth as a wedding present. This was our and my first car ever, and we both loved it.

My mother went back to Hungary after our honeymoon while we went back to Cambridge to move into our brand-new married-student, high-rise building called Westgate. Our apartment, number 609, faced south toward Boston over the Charles River. It was a tiny efficiency apartment with a kitchenette, but it was enough for us. There wasn't much room for furniture, and whatever we had, we bought used at the Salvation Army store, except for our sofa bed and a rug. Éva refused to sleep on a used mattress.

Looking back, it amazes me how happy we were without owning anything. What was even worse was the reality that I owed thousands of dollars. During the ensuing decades, having accumulated real wealth compared to where we started, I cannot claim that our future happiness had much to do with that. A lesson here for my progeny is that it is important to work hard and reap the financial rewards of your work, but don't count on wealth to be the source of your happiness. Happiness more likely lies in the intangible and in the subjective spheres of our world, such as positive relationships with friends and family, a sense of accomplishment of challenging tasks, overcoming life's unavoidable hurdles, helping others, and being unselfish.

This last one reminds me of the only handwritten words I have left from my father. I discovered it on one of my many visits to Hungary to see my mother after I got my American citizenship. My father wrote on the inside cover of Victor Hugo's Hungarian translation of his book *The Man Who Laughs*,[1] "I wonder if selfish people are happy?"[2] Perhaps the question is a transcendental message to me to not be selfish.

I must be honest and admit that when I saw this question my father posed, I was proud of him. He was an uneducated man with about eight total years of schooling, who earned a living through physical labor. Yet he read Victor Hugo and, more importantly, was able to formulate a deep, philosophical question. Intelligence and wisdom about human nature aren't something one learns in school, and my father was proof of that.

In 1963, I had two more semesters to go at MIT and figured I would soon be making a lot of money.

The next unexpected surprise came in the fall of 1963 when Éva discovered that she was pregnant. As she is still fond of saying, "This pregnancy happened before we knew what caused it." Sure enough, a little over nine months from the date of our wedding, our son David was born on May 30, 1964.

Truthfully, we were a bit shocked about the pregnancy, not because we didn't want to have children, but because of the timing. We just didn't know how this would affect our short-term plans with both of us in college and without a full-time job. Until this time, I

---

[1] Victor-Marie Hugo (1802–1885) is a famous French poet, playwright, novelist, human rights activist, and exponent of the Romantic era in France. *L'Homme Qui Rit* (*The Man Who Laughs*) was published in 1869 in which he painted a critical picture of the aristocracy and showed sympathy for the working class.

[2] The writing is in pencil, and it has faded a lot. I decided to include the original Hungarian words he wrote, "Vajon boldogok e az önző emberek," in order to preserve it for posterity.

had never given much thought to fatherhood. I didn't have a father growing up, so I lacked a role model in that regard. This isn't an excuse for whatever mistakes I made as a father, but it would have been nice to have had this experience.

My isolated world of school and work was brutally intruded upon on November 22, 1963, when John F. Kennedy was assassinated. Péter broke the news to me when he came to the MIT lab where I was working. He had this strange expression on his face and plainly announced, "John Kennedy was assassinated." My involuntary reaction was a nervous laugh and I replied, "You got to be kidding"—fully anticipating that what he said was a sick joke.

Of course, it was not. This was shocking news to me, even though I was not an American, didn't much follow politics, and never voted in any election. However, since the Cuban Missile Crisis in 1962, the most dangerous nuclear threat the US ever experienced, I was aware of the fact that we lived in a very dangerous world. But the assassination made me sensitive to the ever-present violence in American society. I was still a political novice in 1963, but both of us liked and admired the charismatic John Kennedy, and that is why we chose "John" as our son's middle name in honor of him.

Near the end of 1963, it was time for me to think about a job after graduating in June 1964. I contacted Jack Borden, my old professor at Sir George Williams University in Montréal, about a job. He promptly offered me an associate professorship at the school at an annual salary of six thousand Canadian dollars. In a follow-up letter dated January 7, 1964, he further pointed out that my summers would be "completely free" for private, outside work, that I would have to teach four courses, some maybe in the evenings, and that McGill University, where I previously gave up my full scholarship, offered "some PhD work."

Éva and I discussed this offer, which would have meant a return to Canada, and decided against it. Money was an important part of the reason, because I knew I could get a much higher starting salary in the US, but I saw a much wider career opportunity for myself in this country. It wasn't an easy decision, but we finally decided that I should apply to immigrate to the US, which I was now eligible for as the husband of an American immigrant. I received the much-coveted "green card" in early 1964.

However, as I mentioned before, there are always unintended consequences of our actions. I don't believe that Éva or I ever thought of the draft and its potential impact when I applied for my green card. I soon got an invitation to visit the Selective Service Local Board No. 17 in Cambridge, Massachusetts, where a board clerk named Gladys Allen assigned me my Selective Service No. 12-17-38-644. She informed me that I would be asked shortly to present myself at the local draft board for an interview, where they would decide on my draft classification. Sure enough, on April 17, 1964, I was called in.

The interviewer was a nice middle-aged lady, and before she could say much, I opened with a rehearsed argument that since I had already gone through one world war and a revolution, seen my share of maimed and dead bodies, and my wife was eight months pregnant, I should get a deferment. She listened politely and informed me that I was classified as "5-A," the classification for those over twenty-five years of age. I had turned twenty-six on January 11, 1964.

Maybe it was something in the air in our Westgate apartment building, because by January 1964, it seemed like all the wives were pregnant. The married MIT students who lived there were unquestionably a very smart group, but "birth control technology" was obviously one of the undergraduate courses we all missed.

I worked very hard to eke out a grade point average of 3.3 and a 3.6 during my first two semesters in graduate school. In January 1964, I started my third and last semester before graduation. I was also working on my research project, which would become the topic of my thesis for graduation. The work, financially supported by a US government agency,[1] involved both theoretical and experimental research.

---

[1] My research was sponsored by the Advanced Research Project Agency (ARPA) of the Ballistic Missile Defense Office and technically administered by the Fluid Dynamics Branch of the Naval Research under contract no. 1841 (93).

I had to do a great deal of research; my bibliography lists sixteen published works on my topic. Just reading one of the titles gives me a headache today: "A Comparative Study of Accommodation Coefficients by the Temperature Jump and Low-Pressure Methods," *Journal of Chemistry and Physics*, 22, 300 (February 1954) by L. B. Thomas and R. C. Golike. If I read this today, I am certain I wouldn't understand a word of it.

Much of my work at MIT involved the use of the school's mainframe computer. Back then, in the stone age of computers, we all had to learn how to program one, and if my memory is correct, we all used FORTRAN[1], which was designed for scientific work. The demand for the single mainframe available to students at MIT was so high that I used to get up at two o'clock in the morning and go to the computer room to generate my punched cards that we used for input and to run my programs.

By the end of May, I managed to complete all my requirements for graduation, my thesis and my courses—just about the same time when David was born. A couple of weeks later, I said goodbye to MIT and took off to start my first engineering job. Éva also miraculously managed to complete all her junior year courses at BU, and she and our son followed me a few weeks later after David was old enough to fly on an airplane.

Finding the right job turned out to be a frustrating experience. The job interview process in the spring of 1964 was simple. Corporations who wanted to hire MIT graduates registered with the MIT Career Office, and their on-campus interview schedule was posted, together with the academic requirements. I was excited about talking to company representatives, and I was confident in being able to line up a good job. To my surprise and disappointment, I soon learned that I was disqualified for the most interesting and better-paying jobs in the defense industry.

My initial job interviews were very short. After I said a few words during the introduction, my interviewer would ask me what

---

[1] An acronym derived from Formula Translation, is a programming language especially suited for numeric computation and scientific computing.

country I was from or where my accent came from. When I told them that I was from Hungary, the next thing they wanted to know was if I had any relatives living there. After I confessed that my mother lived there, they politely thanked me for my time and asked the next job applicant to come into the room.

It wasn't necessary to spell out the issue for me because I quickly caught on. The concern was that if a company hired me and assigned me to classified and sensitive defense-oriented work, I would pose a security risk because of my mother, who lived in a country behind the Iron Curtain. In plain language, the threat was that the communist regime in Hungary could pressure me to reveal sensitive technical information by threatening to punish my mother.

As farfetched as it may seem today, I knew that this was the real world due to the height of the Cold War we were living in. Once more, geopolitics had interfered with my life. The irony of which did not elude me. Two different defense agencies of the US government sponsored the work I did at MIT for my master's degree, but I couldn't get a job in the defense industry because of the risk I posed as a Hungarian immigrant.

I was frustrated because I had to compromise on both the type of job I was looking for and the salary I could get in the commercial world. The Vietnam War was heating up, so there was plenty of money pouring into the defense industry in the '60s. The federal government spending on defense increased 78 percent between 1960 and 1970,[1] and that is where the most interesting and best-paid jobs were for engineers and scientists.

Having no choice, I accepted a position as a design engineer for General Electric's Switchgear Division in South Philadelphia, starting in June 1964. My starting salary was $9,100 a year, about 50 percent more than I would have made teaching in Canada. I didn't know anything about General Electric, except that they made washing machines and refrigerators. Nor did I know anything about switchgear, which is just a fancy name for a large circuit breaker used in the

---

[1]   Federal expenditure for 1960 and 1970 were based on federal data published in the president's Budget of the United States government.

high-voltage electric networks of the nation. Absolutely nothing that I learned in graduate school in fluid dynamics and heat transfer in rarified gases would apply to my new job.

My years at MIT were certainly transformative. The future seemed well defined when I made the decision to attend MIT in the fall of 1961. My long-range plan was based on a gutsy assumption that I would meet the academic requirements to survive, that I would get my bachelor's degree in engineering in June 1963, that I would return to Canada to start my professional career, and that I would apply for my Canadian citizenship after fulfilling my five-year residency requirement. I planned to get married and start a family after I had my college education behind me, but I had no specific plans when to marry and to whom, although my old sweetheart from Montréal was always on my mind.

However, the reality turned out to be far different. I received my bachelor's degree in January of 1963, a semester earlier than planned. Instead of returning to Canada, I stayed at MIT for another year and a half to get my master's in engineering in June 1964. By June 1964, instead of being back in Canada as a single man, I was married to Éva, and we had a one-month-old baby.

Instead of pursuing job opportunities in Canada and waiting to become a Canadian, I stayed in the United States and applied for my American citizenship as the husband of an American immigrant. Professionally, I had a job, not necessarily the one I wanted, at one of America's largest corporations, General Electric. My wife and I were ready to start living the "American Dream," with a total college debt of about $6,000, which would be around $60,000 today.

Epilogue

I set out to write my stories in order to leave something behind for my progeny. Unless I wrote them down, my grandchildren and future generations of my family would not understand either the events or the times in my early life. Anyone can research the Holocaust, life under communism in Hungary, the 1956 Hungarian Revolution, or life as an immigrant in America in the mid-twentieth century. It is my hope that giving these events a voice through my personal experience and perspective will be not only entertaining but also informative and educational.

My last story takes me through 1964, when I finally embarked on fulfilling my "American Dream." I was twenty-six years old, married, and the father of a baby boy. All the hard work and sacrifices I made to prepare myself for a successful career were behind me.

Of course, there were further sacrifices to be made in the decades to follow by my wife, my children, and myself as my professional life and our family life continued to evolve. There were plenty of rough times, sleepless nights, and worries about money, children, and other typical familial trepidations. There just wasn't anything exceptional or unusual that arose during those decades to compete with the interest in the stories I wrote about in this book.

I was only one of many immigrants who came to this country with nothing and accomplished great success. These émigrés have invented new technologies, built large and successful businesses that employed thousands of workers, developed new medicines, or became famous artists or economists. The only amazing aspect of my professional career is that it can still happen in this country. We are still a country of immigrants, and anyone can accomplish their dream through hard work and some occasional good luck.

I have always believed that there are some risks in one's life that are worth taking. I certainly have never regretted mine. I never lamented escaping from Hungary in 1956 when I was eighteen years old or taking a chance on going to MIT with no money and less than adequate academic preparation. Having invested years of hard work and a great deal of money to get two advanced degrees in engineering, I restarted my career in the business world and never looked back.

The idea of being comfortable in a job never occurred to me. Every time I changed jobs and assumed new and greater responsibilities, I had great anxiety about my ability to perform. There were many sleepless nights, sometimes for weeks and months, after starting a job at a new company before feeling secure about my performance.

The epitome of risk-taking was starting my own business at the age of forty-eight. I soon learned that the fundamental difference between working for a corporation and for myself was the change from a false sense of security to a real sense of insecurity.

Taking risks and working hard is not enough. We all need some luck in our lives, and fortunately, I did have my share of it. The relationship between risk and luck is a matter of statistics. The more often you take a chance, the more likely you will succeed at least some of the time. Failure along the way just increases the chances of eventual success.

If I had to start all over again, I would definitely balance my family life and professional life differently. I would devote more time to my children in order to have developed a stronger emotional bond with them. Now I regret that I fell short in that regard. Ultimately, the choice is a matter of selfishness. How much and at what price are we willing to satisfy our own desire for success?

It is a delicate balance because I do believe that we all owe it to ourselves to become the most we can be and achieve as much as we can. Denying those aspirations will ultimately lead to sorrow and regret, which I never wanted to have. Perhaps none of us can make the wisest decisions, and we will not realize it until we look at our life in a rearview mirror.

I discovered that being Jewish could be a disadvantage, even in America. Prejudice does exist and always will as long as there are human beings in this world. In fact, being Jewish probably cost me one of my early corporate jobs. Even in the world's most tolerant society, there is intolerance against minorities—whether they are black, Muslim, Jewish, or members of any ethnic minority. The problem with prejudice and intolerance in the business world is that they are obscure. They can exist in your boss, your colleagues, your subordinates, or the customers you serve, and you will never find out until it is too late.

Besides my professional experiences, I've delved into a slow but steady self-education about contemporary political and economic systems during these past decades. This is an ongoing process that started in communist Hungary and still continues to this day. I have learned about the foundations of our unique form of government, our democracy, and our capitalist system by a combined process of osmosis and reading.

From the people I met in my professional and social life who hail from different parts of the world, I have gotten a real sense of one of the unique aspects of our society. We are a nation of immigrants, and all those who come here are accepted and treated as equals as long as they are willing to assimilate.

The truth is that from the moment I immigrated to the United States, I felt more at home in America than in Hungary, where I was born and raised. I came to appreciate the significance and value of two important documents that shaped and continue to shape the lives of all Americans: The Declaration of Independence and the Constitution of the United States. A small 2005 publication of these documents by the Cato Institute[1] is never far from my reach in my home. The tenets in these documents are what make us unique and

---

[1]   The Cato Institute is located at 1000 Massachusetts Avenue, NW Washington, DC, 20001.

exceptional. Of course, we are not perfect, and I also discovered the darker side of our history.

It was fifty-nine years ago when I arrived in the US as a student. Significant positive changes took place during those years. There has been an unparalleled economic boom, primarily driven by productivity improvements, which I was lucky to participate in. Improvements in technology have brought unimaginable goods and services that are affordable to ordinary people. We now have laws to provide protection and equal opportunity to many segments of our society that were previously discriminated against in terms of age, sex, ethnicity, or race. The foundation of our political system, almost 250 years old, is still solid, although some argue that there are serious cracks in that foundation. All in all, it has been a terrific fifty years for my generation.

However, there are some worrisome signs as I look ahead to the future of my grandchildren and succeeding generations of Americans. I am no longer certain that we are leaving this country in better shape than it was a few decades ago. The quality of our K–12 education compared to other developed countries is poor, denying our future generations' ability to increase productivity and improve their standard of living.

The changing ethos of the American people from self-reliance, individualism, rewarding hard work, and risk-taking (often referred to as the Protestant work ethic) to the "entitlement society"—emphasizing fairness and redistribution of wealth in the name of social justice—will irreversibly tilt our "democratic welfare state" to be less "democratic" and more "welfare." My generation is guilty of allowing an enormous and untenable debt burden relative to our GNP that will have major economic and national security consequences.

I have always been an optimist and will not change. However, I think that our future generations have a major task ahead to reverse some of the current trends in this country in order for it to remain what Ronald Reagan[1] liked to refer to as "the shining city upon a hill" or, going even further back in American history and quoting Abraham Lincoln,[2] as "the last best hope" on earth.

---

[1] Ronald Wilson Reagan (1911–2004) was the fortieth president of the United States from 1981 through 1989. The original quotation of "City upon a hill..." comes from a sermon made by one of the pilgrims, John Winthrop, on board of the *Arbella* en route to Massachusetts in 1630.

[2] Abraham Lincoln (1809–1865) was the sixteenth president of the United States from March 1861 until his assassination in April 1865.

Acknowledgments

I have to thank the many people who contributed to writing my stories. These include childhood friends Vili Fodor and Gabi Erőd, from the Budapest neighborhood where we grew up. I want to thank one of my closest cousins, Péter Oszmann, who made a profound impression on me when I was a teenager in Hungary and who encouraged me to write my stories and contributed some important details.

I have to thank two other Hungarian immigrants I became friends with in Montréal: Péter Csákány and Jocó Mezöfényi. A significant contribution came from my Cousin Miklós Grossman, who was with me during the horrible times of the Holocaust. All these people helped fill gaps and correct errors in my memory of the events that took place decades ago.

I want to thank my friend Jim Montgomery, a retired veteran reporter-writer for the *Wall Street Journal* and for other newspapers for thirty years. I owe Jim many thanks for his tireless efforts reading my first drafts and suggesting changes. He also encouraged me to continue to write down my stories after I completed two stories and thought I had nothing else interesting to say.

I want to give special thanks to my high school friend Sándor Méry (Kis-Méry) for his efforts to put me in touch with the appropriate Hungarian authorities to get permission to include copyrighted pictures in my stories and to provide pictures from his own collections.

I have to thank my wife, Éva, for the care and perseverance with which she read, typically more than once, all my stories and the many editorial changes she suggested. There is no doubt that her contribution made these stories more readable and more enjoyable.

Appendices

A. Holocaust Statistics
B. Important Hungarian Holocaust and Related Events in the Twentieth Century
C. Guide to Hungarian First Names

Appendix A: *Holocaust Statistics*

	Year	Jewish Population During 1933–1944 Population	Number of Jews killed in Holocaust	% of Jews killed in Holocaust	Jewish population 1950	Jewish population 2012	Total popu- lation 2012	Jewish Population % 2012
Eastern Europe								
Poland	1939	3,350,000	3,001,000	89.6%	45,000	3,500	38,626,349	0.01%
European part of USSR[1]	1941	3,500,000	1,500,000	42.9%	2,000,000	410,000	201,824,937	0.20%
Romania	1939	980,000	271,000	27.7%	280,000	11,000	22,355,551	0.05%
Baltic States[2]	1939	255,000	224,000	87.8%	43,500	15,000	7,255,869	0.21%
Subtotal		8,085,000	4,996,000	61.8%	2,368,500	439,500	270,062,706	0.16%
Central Europe								
Germany	1933	566,000	160,000	28.3%	37,000	95,000	82,424,609	0.12%
Hungary[3]	1944	725,000	540,554	74.6%	180,000	100,000	10,032,375	1.00%
Czechoslovakia[4]	1939	350,000	146,000	41.7%	17,000	6,100	15,669,745	0.04%
Austria	1938	250,000	65,000	26.0%	18,000	9,000	8,174,762	0.11%
Subtotal		1,891,000	911,554	48.2%	252,000	210,100	116,301,491	0.18%
Western Europe								
Denmark	1940	7,500	77	1.0%	7,500	6,400	5,413,392	0.12%
Norway	1940	1,700	728	42.8%	1,000	1,200	4,574,560	0.03%
Luxemburg	1940	3,500	700	20.0%	1,500	600	462,690	0.13%
France	1940	350,000	83,000	23.7%	235,000	520,000	60,424,213	0.86%
Belgium	1940	65,000	24,387	37.5%	35,000	31,500	10,348,276	0.30%
Netherlands	1940	140,000	106000	75.7%	30,000	26,500	16,318,199	0.16%
Subtotal		567,700	214,892	37.9%	310,000	586,200	97,541,330	0.60%
Southern Europe								
Greece	1941	77,000	71,301	92.6%	17,000	4,500	10,647,529	0.04%
Yugoslavia[5]	1941	75,000	56,200	74.9%	3,500	3,500	23,413,060	0.01%
Italy	1943	48,000	8,000	16.7%	35,000	29,500	58,057,477	0.05%
Subtotal		200,000	135,501	67.8%	55,500	37,500	92,118,066	0.04%
Total		10,743,700	6,257,947	58.2%	2,986,000	1,273,300	576,023,593	0.22%

[1] Russia, Ukraine, Belarus.
[2] Latvia, Lithuania, Estonia.
[3] Includes territories annexed from Czechoslovakia, Romania, and Slovenia.
[4] Became Czech Republic and Slovakia on January 1, 1993.
[5] Bosnia-Herzegovia, Croatia, Macedonia, Serbia and Montenegro, Slovenia

The statistics shown on page 316 are a composite from many sources. Unfortunately, I was not able to find one or two sources that could provide the full picture of what I wished to represent. I also discovered that the statistics available from different sources are inconsistent with each other in many instances. The circumstances of the Jewish communities prior to, during, and following the Holocaust were such that accurate population information is almost impossible to determine. The sources of conflict and inconsistencies are a lack of reliable data, the different years when various population data was recorded, and in the case of Hungary, the changing boundaries of the country during the years 1938–1942. Since I did not intend to provide scholarly research on this topic, I decided that the data are good enough to provide a "big picture" of the Holocaust in reasonably realistic statistical terms. The sources I used for the statistics and for my story include the books listed in the references and the following internet websites:

http://www.historyplace.com/worldwar2/holocaust/timeline.html
http://www.historyplace.com/worldhistory/genocide/holocaust.htm
http://www.historyplace.com/worldwar2/holocaust/h-statistics.htm
http://www.ushmm.org/wlc/en/
http://www.holocaustcenter.org/
http://www.bh.org.il/communities/jewpopworld.aspx
http://www.makkabi.hu/english/history/
http://zsido.hu/english/history/
http://www.jewishvirtuallibrary.org/
http://www.cia.gov/library/publications/resources/the-world-factbook/index.html

Appendix B: *Important Hungarian Holocaust and Related Events in the Twentieth Century*

1920	
September 20	Official discrimination of the Jews begins with the Numerus Clausus law, limiting the number of Jewish students in universities to 6 percent.
1938	
March 13	Germany annexes Austria into the Third Reich (Anschluss).
May 28	The First Anti-Jewish Act is ratified by the Hungarian Parliament, restricting the number of Jews in liberal professions, administration, and commercial and industrial enterprises (lawyers, doctors, engineers, journalists, actors, etc.) to 20 percent. Definition of "Jew" includes all those who had been born to Jewish parents after 1919 regardless of their later conversion to a Christian faith.
November 8–9	Germany and Austria: During the infamous *Kristallnacht*, on November 8 and 9, 1938, the Nazis terrorize their Jewish neighbors. *Kristallnacht* may be considered as the actual beginning of the Holocaust. The news reaches Hungary within days, if not hours.
1939	
March	The Arrow Cross Party, made up of the population's most virulent anti-Semitic and pro-Nazi segment, is established.
May 5	The Second Anti-Jewish Act is passed by Parliament. It excludes Jews from public life (from Parliament and other representative bodies) and prohibits Jews from working for public corporations and from holding office in professional organizations. It limits their participation in economic life and their right to purchase and hold property. Furthermore, it reduces their numbers, in mostly white-collar professions, to 6 percent. It extends the application of the term "Jew" on a racial basis and includes some 100,000 Christians (apostates and their children).

September 1	Germany invades Poland, and World War II begins.
1940	
April 27	Germany: Heinrich Himmler, the head of the SS, orders creation of the Auschwitz (Poland) extermination camp, where most of the Hungarian Jews ended up in 1944.
May	Special forced labor units are set up for enlisting Jews. These units are sent to the eastern front along with the Hungarian Army to fight against the Soviet Union.
October 14	From a letter of the Regent Miklós Horthy to the prime minister, Count Pál Teleki: "I have been an anti-Semite all my life. I find it unendurable that here in Hungary virtually all the factories, banks, properties, shops, heathers, newspapers and the entire economy should be in Jewish hands. Nevertheless, since I am convinced that the most important task of the Government is to improve the standard of living and become prosperous, it is impossible [...] to eliminate Jews, and replace them with incompetent, mostly worthless and bigmouth individuals. Otherwise we will go bankrupt... We cannot tolerate cruelty against Jews or their pointless humiliation in a sadistic manner since we shall need them later."
December 2	Jews serving in the army are expelled from their units and stationed in "labor battalions," exposing them to arbitrary, cruel treatment by their commanders.
1941	
May	The total number of persons liable to racial discrimination reaches close to 800,000 ethnic Hungarian Jews. In post-WWI Hungary: 445,000 (1930); Converted Jews: 100,000. From territories added under German occupation: Slovakia, 78,000 (November 2, 1938); Czechoslovak province, 72,000 (March 15, 1939); Transylvania, 149,000 (August 30, 1940).
June 27	Hungary enters the war as an ally of Germany.

August 8	The Third Anti-Jewish Act is published, prohibiting marriage and sexual relations between Jews and non-Jews under the penalty of imprisonment and other types of punishments.
December 11	Germany: Hitler declares war on the United States. On the same day, Roosevelt declares war on Germany, saying, "Never before has there been a greater challenge to life, liberty, and civilization." The USA entered the war in Europe and concentrated nearly 90 percent of its military resources to defeat Hitler. As a German ally, Hungary is drawn into the war.
1942	
January 20	The Wannsee Conference is held, officially approving the execution of the "Final Solution to the Jewish Question" (the official German name for the project to eliminate 11 million European Jews). All 11 million Jews are listed by country, with Hungary having 742,800 Jews.
April	The Hungarian government pledges the "resettlement" of 800,000 Jews—as the "final solution of the Jewish question"—pointing out, however, that this could be done only after the war, presuming they would win.
July 29	A bill known as "Determining the Status of the Israelite Religious Community" is passed, removing the Jewish religion as an "accepted" religion in Hungary, therefore denying any support or protection normally given to Hungary's "accepted" Christians.
July 31	The (Jewish) Labor Battalion Act is officially adopted by Parliament, even though the Battalions had existed for over a year (see December 2, 1940).
September 6	The Fourth Anti-Jewish Law is adopted, banning Jews from owning or purchasing land. Jews are deprived of properties they have accumulated in the course of the past one hundred years. Four hundred thousand acres had been expropriated from fourteen thousand Jewish small landholders.

1943	
June 25	Poland: Newly built gas chamber/crematory III opens at Auschwitz. With its completion, the four new crematories at Auschwitz had a daily capacity of 4,756 bodies to "process."
November	The US Congress holds hearings regarding the US State Department's inaction regarding European Jews, despite mounting reports of mass extermination. There is still time to save 600,000 Hungarian Jews, but no decisive action is taken.
1944	
March 12	Adolf Eichmann, head of the SS, begins preparations in Mauthausen, Austria, for setting up the Sondereisatzkommando (Special Task Force) destined to direct the liquidation of Hungarian Jewry, the last remaining large Jewish population in Europe.
March 19	Germany invades Hungary. Eichmann comes to Hungary and sets up headquarters to oversee the execution of the "Final Solution" of Hungary's Jewry.
March 22	A new Hungarian government is set up, consisting of extreme pro-Nazi elements who are willing to collaborate with Germany in the accomplishment of the "Final Solution."
March 31	An order is issued for Jews to wear a bright canary-yellow six-pointed star of 10 × 10 cm (4 × 4 inches) on the top left of their clothing in public. Effective date of wearing the yellow star for everyone over six years old is April 5, 1944.
April 2	The American Air Force starts bombing Budapest. The British follow at nighttime.
April 7	The Ministry of Interior issues an order stating, "The Royal Government of Hungary will soon cleanse the country of Jews. This cleansing will be carried out by region." It also forbids Jews to travel anywhere without a travel permit. Furthermore, the decree imposes a curfew on Jews from 8:00 p.m. to 8:00 a.m. and announces plans to "concentrate" the Jews in ghettos and deport them afterward.

April 7	Alfred Wetzler and Rudolf Vrba, two Slovak inmates, escape from Auschwitz. Their description of Auschwitz, including the preparations for "processing" close to a million Hungarian Jews, reaches the world and becomes known as the "Auschwitz Protocols." In subsequent weeks, translated copies are sent to Christian church leaders in Hungary, to the Allies, to international Zionist organizations, and even to the Vatican. No international outcry or reaction is observed.
April 15	An agreement is reached between the Hungarian government and the Germans, stipulating the delivery of 100,000 able-bodied Jews to German factories.
April 30	A government decree is issued "concerning the protection of Hungarian intellectual life against literary works written by Jewish authors." Subsequently, half a million books written by Jewish authors are actually pulped on June 15, 1944.
April 30	Hitler confers with Horthy, Hungary's regent, and condemns Hungary's handling of the "Jewish question" as irresolute and ineffective.
May 10	The ghettoization of Hungary's Jews, except in Budapest, is completed in the rest of the country.
May 15 through July 9	Deportations from Hungary: • 290,000 Jews from Sub-Carpathian Ruthenia and northern Transylvania • 50,000 Jews from northwestern Hungary and north of Budapest • 41,000 Jews from southern Hungary, east of the Danube • 55,000 Jews from Transdanubia and outskirts of Budapest A total of 500,000 Jews are transported, 450,000 of them to Auschwitz via central Slovakia by freight train. Each freight car carries about 45 persons, but in most cases 80–100 persons are packed in for the five-day journey. Hungarian state institutions, administration, police, and gendarmerie carry out 147 transports of more than 30 freight cars each. The SS reports collecting 88 pounds of gold and white metal from the teeth of those gassed. Only 10 percent of, or about 44,000, Jews survive.

June 15	The Ministry of Interior orders the concentration of 220,000 Budapest Jews living in 21,259 apartments into 2,681 designated apartments. These apartments are located in houses that had to be marked with the yellow star, 12 inches in diameter on a black background. Deadline to implement the move is set for June 24, 1944. Apartments vacated by Jewish families are assigned to Christians.
June 22	The Chief Mufti of Jerusalem sends a letter to the Hungarian Ministry of Foreign Affairs in Budapest requesting that the government prevent by all means the emigration of Hungarian Jews, legally or otherwise, to Palestine.
June 26	Responding to the request of the Apostolic Nuncio Angelo Rotta, the representative of the Vatican in Budapest who was familiar with the Auschwitz Protocols, and of the American Congress, Pope Pius XII (1939–1958) appeals to the regent of Hungary in an open telegram to spare the lives of Hungarian Jewry, who had already suffered much.
June 26–28	In a message sent through the Swiss Embassy, Franklin D. Roosevelt, the president of the United States, reminds the regent that Hungary would be held responsible for all the atrocities committed against Jews. The Foreign Department of the US Congress issues an appeal to the countries allied with Germany, especially to Hungary, to stop torturing the masses of innocent Jews. By this time, most of the 437,000 Jews deported were dead.
June 30	Sweden's King Gustav V appeals to the regent, asking that Hungary treat the Jews according to its chivalrous tradition.
June 30	The "Blood for Goods" (*Blut fuer Ware*) transactions begin to save Jews by paying $1,000 per head to the Germans. A total of 1,658 Hungarian Jews are sent to Switzerland. It is financed by the American Jewish Joint Distribution Committee, the Jewish Agency, and the War Refugee Board. These and subsequent transactions save the lives of the very rich, those with good political connections, and the Budapest Jewish Council leadership members.

July–August	This is a hopeful period for the remaining Budapest Jews. The regent, Horthy, and his supporters are trying to negotiate an armistice with the Allies.
July 2	The Allies deliver the greatest air raid against Budapest, this time including residential areas of the city.
July 9	Raoul Wallenberg, the Swedish diplomat who is tasked with saving as many of the Budapest Jews as he can, arrives in Budapest.
August 18	Another "Blood for Goods" deal is concluded; 318 Jews are rescued.
August 23	Romania joins the Allies in the war against Hitler.
September 4	Hungary declares war against Romania. With this, all hopes for saving the Budapest Jews through an armistice deal with the Allies has faded.
October 15	The regent, Miklós Horthy, declares Hungarian neutrality, but it is too late. The same day, backed by the Germans, the fascist Nazi-sympathizing Arrow Cross Party takes control, and the fate of the Budapest Jews takes a dramatic turn for the worse, and the deportation of Jews, which had temporarily ceased due to international political pressure, resumes.
October 17	Eichmann returns to Budapest and immediately begins organizing the deportation of the remaining Jews of Budapest.
October 21	Directed by Eichmann, the Hungarian Royal Minister of Defense orders every Jewish male between the ages of 16 and 60 and every Jewish female between the ages of 18 and 40 to participate in "forced labor for the defense of the country."
October 29	A report of the International Red Cross from Budapest indicates that 50,000 Jews were taken to forced labor service in Germany, another 50,000 were performing forced labor in the territory of Hungary, and about 30,000 were working in Austria.

November 8	The first of the "death marches" along a 120-mile route from Budapest to the Austrian border begins with 25,000 Jews. A second group of 50,000 shortly follows. The conditions of these marches, supervised by Hungarian gendarmes and Arrow Cross units, are so dreadful that even some hardened Nazis protest. A high percentage of persons on these "death marches" perished on the way. (My mother was probably part of this event.)
November 23 through November 27	Based on on-site inspections, the International Red Cross reports that the *Fussmarsch*, or foot-march, of Jews being herded towards Austria turned into a *Todesmarsch*, or death march. Confidential reports say that 10,000 Jews died along the western roads of Hungary.
December 3	The "gold train," containing the stolen valuables, arts, jewelry, gold, money, and other treasures of the Budapest Jews, leaves the capital with Austria as its destination.
December 6	Another "Blood for Goods" deal concluded; 1,368 Jews are rescued.
December 10	The gates of the Budapest General Ghetto are closed and guarded by Arrow Cross men and SS soldiers on the outside.
December 15	The government flees and the capital becomes the free prey of the Arrow Cross bands. They start a systematic murder of Jews all across the city. All activities of the Red Cross are banned.
December 22	Eichmann personally visits the General Ghetto and orders the Jewish Council members to meet him the next morning at 9:00 a.m. His plan is to personally supervise the execution of the Jewish Council and then order the massacre of the entire Jewish population of the ghetto in one fell swoop.
December 23	At dawn, Eichmann decides to leave Budapest, as the news of the latest Soviet Army thrust on the northwestern outskirts of the city becomes known. However, Eichmann's plan did not die with his departure (see January 15, 1945).

December 24	On Christmas Eve, the Arrow Cross launches a great number of raids on all places of refuge for Jews outside the ghetto, including the Jewish children's homes. Hundreds are killed and their bodies are dumped into the Danube.
1945	
January 15	Following Eichmann's plan, the Arrow Cross and SS plan the invasion of the General Ghetto to slaughter everyone. General Schmidhuber, overall commander of the SS troops and one of his detachments, are to spearhead the massacre. The secret plans, developed by the now absentee Eichmann, leak out, and Raoul Wallenberg convinces Schmidhuber to intervene by telling him that he will see to it that the general is held responsible and hanged as a war criminal after the war. The plan is not carried out.
January 17	Wallenberg leaves Budapest to meet Marshal Malinovsky, the Soviet commander, in Debrecen, where the Hungarian provisional government had been established under the auspices of the Russians. He wants to appeal to the marshal for emergency food and medical supplies for the two ghettos. This is the last that anyone has ever seen of Raoul Wallenberg as a free man.
October 15, 1944–January 18, 1945	About 98,000 Jews lose their lives in marches and in train transport, through Arrow Cross extermination squads, starvation, disease, and cases of suicide. Some of the victims are shot and thrown into the Danube.
January 18	The Big Ghetto of Budapest is liberated around 9:00 a.m. by Soviet forces.
January 21	The Budapest National Committee, the highest authority following the liberation, rescinds all the Jewish Laws.
January 27	Soviet troops liberate Auschwitz.
March 17	The temporary government of Hungary, still located in Debrecen, repeals all the previously passed Jewish Laws.

April 4	The Soviet Army liberates Hungary.
Mid-April	The Allies liberate the camps in southern Austria.
April 30	Hitler commits suicide in his Berlin bunker.
November 20	The Nuremberg International Military Tribunal opens.
1946	
March 11	The British arrest former Auschwitz Kommandant Höss, posing as a farm worker. He testifies at Nuremberg and then was tried in Warsaw, found guilty, and hanged at Auschwitz on April 16, 1947.
October 16	Göring commits suicide two hours before the scheduled execution of the first group of major Nazi war criminals at Nuremberg.
December 9	Twenty-three former SS doctors and scientists go on trial before a US military tribunal at Nuremberg. Sixteen were found guilty, and seven were hanged.
1947	
September 15	Twenty-one former SS Einsatz leaders go on trial before a US military tribunal in Nuremberg. Fourteen are sentenced to death with only four (the group commanders) actually executed. The other death sentences are commuted.
1960	
May 23	Adolf Eichmann is captured in Argentina by Israeli Secret Service.
1962	
May 31	Following the trial held in Jerusalem in 1961, Eichmann is convicted of crimes against the Jewish people, crimes against humanity, and war crimes. He was found guilty and hanged in Israel (the last capital punishment in Israel).

Appendix C: *Guide to Hungarian First Names*

Hungarian nickname	Formal Hungarian first name	English equivalent
Artúr	Artúr	Arthur
Bandi	András	Andrew
Béla	Béla	Bela
Caga	Elek	Elek
Erzsi or Bözske	Erzsébet	Elizabeth
Éva	Éva	Eve or Eva
Feri	Ferenc	Francis
Gyuri	György	George
Imre	Imre	Emery
Iván	Iván	Ivan
Jancsi	János	John
Jenő	Jenő	Eugene
Jóska, Jocó	József	Joseph
Juci	Júlia	Julia
Jutka	Judit	Judith
Kati	Kata	Kate
Klári	Klára	Clara
Laci	László	Laszlo
Lena	Lena	Lenora
Lili	Lili	Lillian
Magda	Magda	Magda
Manci	Mária	Maria
Miki	Miklós	Nicholas or Michael
Pali	Pál	Paul
Piri	Piroska (little red)	Piroska
Pista	István	Stephen
Robi	Róbert	Robert
Rutka	Rutka	Ruth

Samu	*Sámuel*	*Samuel*
Szidi	*Szidóra*	*Sidonia*
Tibi	*Tibor*	*Tibor*
Tomi	*Tamás*	*Thomas*
Vili	*Vilmos*	*William*
Zoli	*Zoltán*	*Zoltan*
Zsuzsi	*Zsuzsanna*	*Susan or Susanna*

Bibliography

A Holocaust Childhood

Bierman, John. *Righteous Gentile: The Story of Raoul Wallenberg, Missing Hero of the Holocaust.* New York: The Viking Press, 1981.

Braham, Randolph L., and Scott Miller, eds. *The Nazis' Last Victims: The Holocaust in Hungary.* Wayne State University Press, 1999.

Frojimovics, Kinga, Géza Komoróczy, Victória Pusztai, and Andrea Strbik. *Jewish Budapest: Monuments, Rites, History.* English ed. Budapest: Central European University Press, 1999.

Goldhagen, Daniel Jonah. *A Moral Reckoning: The Role of the Catholic Church in the Holocaust and Its Unfulfilled Duty of Repair.* New York: Alfred A. Knopf, 2002.

Goldhagen, Daniel Jonah. *Hitler's Willing Executioners: Ordinary Germans and the Holocaust.* New York: Alfred A. Knopf, 1998.

Goldhagen, Daniel Jonah. *Worse than War; Genocide, Eliminationism, and the Ongoing Assault on Humanity.* New York: Public Affairs, 2009.

Herczl, Moshe Y. *Christianity and the Holocaust of Hungarian Jewry.* New York and London: New York University Press, 1993. (Translated from Hebrew by Joel Lerner.)

History Place. "Holocaust Timeline." http://www.historyplace.com/worldwar2/holocaust/timeline.html.

Makkabi Ltd. "A Brief History of Jews in Hungary" (in Hungarian). http://www.makkabi.hu/. Owned and maintained by Makkabi Ltd., Budapest.

Marton, Kati. *The Great Escape: Nine Jews Who Fled Hitler and Changed the World*. New York: Simon & Schuster, 2006.

Pelle, János. *Sowing the Seeds of Hatred: Anti-Jewish Laws and Hungarian Public Opinion*. East European Monographs, 2004.

Pinker, Steven. *Enlightenment Now: A Case for Reason, Science, Humanism, and Progress*. Viking, an imprint of Penguin Random House, 2019, 202.

Verkhovskaya, Anya. *Jewish History of Hungary*. Founder and president of Heritage Films. www.heritagefilms.com/Hungary.

Zweig, Ronald W. *The Gold Train: The Destruction of the Jews and the Looting of Hungary*. New York: HarperCollins, 2002.

The Hungarian Uprising of 1956

Barber, Noel. *Seven Days of Freedom: The Hungarian Uprising, 1956*. New York: Stein and Day, 1974.

Grant, Julianna. "Hungary 1956." *Socialist Appeal*. Article first published on the fortieth anniversary of the Hungarian Uprising. London: Socialist Appeal, issue 45, October 1996.

Kopácsi, Sándor. *In the Name of the Working Class*. Translated into English from French original. New York: Grove Press Inc., 1986.

Lipták, Béla. *A Testament of Revolution*. College Station: Texas A&M University Press, 2001.

Lomax, Bill, ed. *Eyewitness in Hungary: The Soviet Invasion of 1956*. Nottingham, England: Bertrand Russell House, 1980.

Lutton, Charles. *Book Review of Uprising! One Nation's Nightmare: Hungary 1956*. By David Irving. London, Sydney, Auckland, Toronto: Hodder and Stoughton, 1981.

Pamlényi, Ervin, ed. *A History of Hungary*. Budapest: Corvina Press, 1973.

BIBLIOGRAPHY

Pryce-Jones, David. *The Hungarian Revolution*. New York: Horizon Press, 1970.

Author unknown. *"Armed Revolt in Hungary 1956."* Paper written for a politics class about communist and post-communist societies, University of California at Santa Cruz.

Illustrations

Permission for the use of illustrations in the book are obtained from the following organizations. Numbers refer to the numbered illustrations in the book. The numbers in parenthesis are the archive numbers of the respective organizations listed below.

Photo archives courtesy of the United States Holocaust Memorial Museum (USHMM): 1 (77221, 77241, 77231, 77236, 77349, 19444), 3 (45662), 10 (02433),

Hungarian Ministry of Defense, Military History Institute and Museum (MoD MHIM): 24 (90205), 25 (6437), 26 (5485), 27 (57954), 29 (Itsz. 241.14), 30 (G8-53), 32 (90159), 33 (4189)

Fortepan.hu website: 22 (Faragó György 128725), 23 (Faragó György 128750), 28 (Balla Demeter / Hagyi Zsolt 148102), 31 (Nagy Gyula 40195)

Henry Holt and Company: 7

Author's private collection: 2, 5, 6, 9, 11, 12, 13, 14, 15, 16, 18, 19, 20, 35, 36, 37, 38, 40, 41, 42

Public domain: 4, 8, 21, 34, 39